EICHMANN
INTERROGATED

EICHMANN INTERROGATED

Transcripts from the Archives
of the Israeli Police

Edited by Jochen von Lang
in collaboration with Claus Sibyll

Translated from the German by
Ralph Manheim

Introduction by Avner W. Less

Farrar, Straus & Giroux

NEW YORK

INTRODUCTION

I saw Adolf Eichmann for the first time at about 4:45 p.m. on May 29, 1960. Colonel Hofstaetter (my immediate superior) and I had sent for him to be brought to the room where the hearings were to take place. We waited in a state of acute tension; even the colonel, ordinarily a model of self-restraint, was unable to conceal his nervousness. My first reaction when the prisoner finally stood facing us in khaki shirt and trousers and open sandals was one of disappointment. I no longer know what I had expected—probably the sort of Nazi you see in the movies: tall, blond, with piercing blue eyes and brutal features expressive of domineering arrogance. Whereas this rather thin, balding man not much taller than myself looked utterly ordinary. The very normality of his appearance gave his dispassionate testimony an even more depressing impact than I had expected after examining the documents.

Eichmann began our dialogue with a request. He had worn glasses in Argentina; they had been taken away from him and he needed them now. I sent for them. Later on, plastic lenses were substituted for the glass ones, and since he wanted to prepare himself between sessions by jotting down notes, I obtained permission for him to wear his eyeglasses in his cell during the day.

Because he was a heavy smoker, I arranged for his cigarette ration to be increased; and whenever I lit up a cigarette for myself, I would offer him one. Not that I had any personal reason to extend such generosity: I did it because it made him more talkative and improved his powers of concentration.

(v)

When Eichmann sat facing me for the first time, he was a bundle of nerves. The left half of his face twitched. He hid his trembling hands under the table. I could feel his fear, and it would have been easy to make short work of him. He only knew his own methods of interrogation and those of his former colleagues in the Gestapo. It must have seemed less than likely to him that the Israeli police would treat him with extreme fairness.

As I watched Eichmann sitting there in this condition, I suddenly had the feeling I was holding a bird in my hand, a creature who felt completely at my mercy. But that impression soon passed. His statements and the documents we examined together revealed the cold sophistication and cunning with which he had planned and carried out the extermination of the Jews. Occasionally, this filled me with such loathing that I couldn't bear to be near him and would cast about for excuses to postpone the next hearing to another day, just to avoid having to follow his horrible descriptions or listen to his brazen lies.

Nevertheless, from the very beginning the hearings were conducted in a conversational manner. During the first days, in the heat of argument, we would occasionally speak at the same time or interrupt each other. When the secretaries who transcribed the tapes complained of the confusion, Eichmann and I agreed that he would stop talking in response to a pre-arranged signal from me.

His German was hideous. At first I had a very difficult time understanding him at all—the jargon of the Nazi bureaucracy pronounced in a mixture of Berlin and Austrian accents and further garbled by his liking for endlessly complicated sentences which he himself would occasionally get lost in. After the first visit of his lawyer, Dr. Servatius, Eichmann asked me: "Herr Hauptmann,* do you know what Dr. Servatius said? He objected to my German. He said: 'You'll have to relearn your

* See footnote on page 5.

language. Even the best translator won't be able to find his way through those convoluted sentences of yours.' Is my German actually that bad, Herr Hauptmann?" I had to agree that it was. Eichmann seemed almost offended.

I was especially struck by his complete lack of humor. On the few occasions when his razor-thin lips smiled, his eyes remained mirthless; each time, the look on his face was sardonic, even aggressive.

His defense strategy was set from the start. I was already acquainted with it from my study of the Nuremberg trials. Knowing that his life was at stake, he clung from the beginning to the tactics of the major defendants at Nuremberg. He would lie until defeated by documentary proof, just as Kaltenbrunner, his former chief, had done. When that didn't help, he would present himself as a little cog in the machine and put all the blame on others, subordinates as well as superiors. And most frequently he would plead Befehlsnotstand, "orders from above."

He used all three methods by turns in the course of the interrogation and later at the trial in Jerusalem. Convinced that he could save his neck by demonstrating his own unimportance, he spoke at length and in detail about mass executions he had witnessed but in which his own role had been purely passive. In return for these volunteered accounts of crimes committed by others, he evidently expected me to give credence to whatever lies he produced to conceal his own crimes.

And yet, in the course of the hearings, I became something of a personal confidant for him. I was the one person to whom he could tell everything, lies as well as truths. Occasionally, he was so shaken by a damaging piece of evidence that he would unexpectedly confess everything. But then the extent of his admission would dawn on him, and at the next session he would ask for permission to add to his most recent testimony. Then he would deny everything he had previously admitted.

Once Eichmann actually paid me a compliment. We had

been discussing the draft of a letter from the Reich Minister for Occupied Eastern Territories; it dealt with gassing equipment and contained the following sentence: "Permit me to state that this procedure meets with the approval of Sturmbannführer Eichmann, the specialist for Jewish questions at Reich Security Headquarters." This document was gravely damaging to Eichmann, but he spontaneously admitted that he had conferred with the writer of the letter along these lines. The next day, as we were checking the transcript, Eichmann said that he would like to say something more about the letter at our next meeting. I remarked that he was perfectly free to say whatever he wished. Eichmann replied that he was well aware that throughout the hearings I had not once attempted to obtain confessions by promises or threats. For this reason— and he said this quite formally—he felt the need to tell me that he was grateful for the fair hearing. These words were underscored with a ceremonious bow.

He was, as I said, extremely nervous at the beginning; but after about a week he recovered his composure. Evidently the tenor of the hearings had calmed him. There was one moment of panic, however—it must have been during the first half of June 1960—when he believed his last hour had struck. The officer of the guard stepped into the room and informed Eichmann that he had come to escort him to the judge. Badly frightened, Eichmann rose to his feet. One of the guards blindfolded him, and his knees buckled. "But, Herr Hauptmann," he cried in a pleading voice, "I haven't told you everything yet!" I reassured him: "You're only being taken to the justice of the peace so he can renew the order for your detention. Then we will continue with our hearings." Whereupon Eichmann recovered his soldierly posture and marched out of the room, flanked by the two guards. The blindfold, incidentally, was intended to prevent him from getting an overall view of the prison compound.

I was particularly irritated by Eichmann's attempts to ingratiate himself with me. One day he pointed to the insignia of the Israeli police and said: "Herr Hauptmann, when I see this badge, I realize that you and I are colleagues. I was once a policeman myself." I replied: "You were never a policeman. You were in the SS and the SD." He gave me a baffled look. "Is that so?" After a brief pause he continued: "But I'm not afraid of the police. I know them. The court is something else again; the fact is, I've never been on trial."

I am recounting these particular scenes to give an idea of the sort of man who sat opposite me during the interrogations and during the sessions when we checked the transcripts for errors. What elicited my sense of outrage more than anything else was that Eichmann quite obviously had no feeling for the monstrousness of his crimes, and that he did not show the slightest twinge of remorse. When on January 1, 1961, I mentioned the fact that a new year had begun, Eichmann replied: "Herr Hauptmann, may I take the liberty of wishing you a happy New Year?" And he performed a sort of seated bow and clicked his heels under the table. All I could say was that it was impossible for me to wish him the same. His reply: "Yes, Herr Hauptmann, I understand very well that you are not allowed to do so." It never occurred to him that I simply wasn't able to do so.

This insensitivity became even more evident the day he asked me whether I had any brothers and sisters, and whether my parents were still alive. I told him that my father had been deported to the East by his organization in January 1943, in one of the last transports from Berlin. Eichmann opened his eyes wide and cried out: "But that's horrible, Herr Hauptmann! That's horrible!"

I did not feel capable of telling him more about the fate of my family, but an account of my own fate might be a relevant addition to the transcripts of the hearings.

I was born in 1916 in Berlin, on Prager Strasse. My father's family came from East Prussia; my mother's had lived in Berlin for several generations. My parents were good Jews and equally good Germans. My father worked hard and conscientiously in Germany, for as long as he was permitted to do so. In 1914, when the First World War broke out, he volunteered. He survived the war; he was always very proud of his Iron Cross. My mother—almost fortunately, I might say—died of cancer at the age of forty-five, very soon after Hitler came to power.

I owe the happiest years of my youth to the Höhere Waldschule, a high school in the Grunewald district of Berlin. This was the first coeducational school in Germany. We spent the whole day at school, were served lunch there, did our homework after an hour's nap, and devoted a good part of our time to sports. The spirit of the Waldschule was so indelible that its former students still hold reunions each year in Berlin.

I was barely sixteen when Hitler seized power. Just a few days later, the SA and the Gestapo searched our apartment. Even on the day when my mother was taken to the hospital from which she never returned, heavily armed storm troopers came and accused us of having smuggled out seditious material on my mother's stretcher. During the summer months of that year, my father became convinced that the storm troopers had it in for me in particular, and I was sent to France.

On September 5, 1933, I arrived in Paris, a refugee, without a work permit. Once, I was thrown out of a hotel because I couldn't pay my bill. The owner kept all my belongings, except for the clothes I was wearing. I was wearing sneakers —not the most adequate footwear for winter in Paris. But when you are young, you know how to bend under pressure and somehow you manage to get by. Thus, Paris became my new home. But at the same time it became clear to me that as a Jew I could not remain in the new Europe that was taking shape.

For this reason I joined He-Halutz, a Zionist youth movement which trained young people to become farmers in Israel, or rather Palestine, as it was then called. Early in 1935, the writer Alfred Döblin gave a lecture in Paris. I went with some of my friends, and one of them mentioned that a new girl from Germany was there, a very beautiful girl. I resolved to have a look at this marvel. I went up to where she was sitting, had a look, and fell in love. I informed my friends tersely: "I'm going to marry her."

The girl came from Hamburg, and when she told her family there of our marriage plans, it seemed as though the world had come to an end. I was less than a have-not, I wasn't even twenty yet, and I had no trade. The family shipped Vera off to Stockholm to put some distance between her and me. She held out for three months and then came back to Paris. Her family in Hamburg admitted defeat and set only one condition: I would have to learn a trade. I signed up for a course in ladies' hairdressing and graduated with an impressive diploma; now at least I could give Vera beautiful hairdos. On November 7, 1936, we were married in the Mairie of the 5th arrondissement of Paris.

He-Halutz first sent us for farm training to one of its kibbutzim in southern France. At the end of August 1938 we obtained an immigration permit for Palestine and on September 5 we disembarked in Tel Aviv. We found work in the orange groves of Hadera. Vera was used only for picking and pruning, which was seasonal, but I was given a steady job. It was backbreaking work and the boss wasn't always able to pay us on time, but at least we had some security.

In October 1939, in her sixth month of pregnancy, Vera came down with spinal polio. At first she was paralyzed from head to foot and suffered from severe neuralgia, so that the merest touch was torture. No hospital would take her. There were no trained personnel, nor could the necessary equipment be found—an iron lung, for example, or a water bed. In

Hadera we had a room with a small kitchen; the "toilet" was about thirty meters away, in the garden. We had no electricity, only petroleum lamps and a petroleum cooker. I had to give up my job to take care of Vera. The doctors tried very hard to help her, but they knew relatively little about polio. They speculated whether it might not be best to terminate her pregnancy. Luckily, they decided against it in the end. Our daughter, born in February 1940 with great difficulty, is now the mother of two delightful girls.

My sister, who lived in Tel Aviv, quit her job and took over the care of the baby. I learned to massage Vera; for twenty-two months I was exclusively occupied with her care. The unemployment benefits and welfare money we received were just enough to keep us alive, not enough to live on. Some minor benefit accrued to us from the misfortune that had befallen Vera's mother. She had succeeded in leaving Germany shortly before the Second World War broke out, but on the way to us she got stuck in Belgrade, and the Nazis caught up with her. She was murdered there, along with many others, on March 30, 1942. Her household effects did eventually reach us, though, after a long and confused voyage; she happened to have sent them off in time. I sold every single object for a pittance.

Vera had an iron will; she wanted to conquer her illness. She learned to move about at home and was able to do some of the work. Even during the greatest heat, she had to wear a high orthopedic corset all day long. Out of doors she could only move about with a cane and my arm for support. The first time I took Vera out in the street in a wheelchair, she burst into tears; it was only then that she realized she would never again be able to walk about like healthy people. Nine years later we had another child, a son. During the delivery, Vera's life hung in the balance; but then she was very proud of being able to diaper our baby herself.

When Vera was well enough to be left on her own during

the day, I went to look for a job. The British Mandatory government was recruiting auxiliary policemen. I signed up, was given four weeks of military training, and was sent to Haifa to work as a guard at the airport there. I did night duty because that enabled me to take care of Vera and the household during the day. I kept that job for four and a half years.

Then I was given a chance to transfer to the price-control section of the Mandatory government's Ministry of the Economy. I accepted at once. The pay was much better, and for the first time we were able to live without worrying about money. In 1946, with the help of a bank loan, we were even able to buy an apartment of our own. It was very small, but now we were no longer living to pay the rent, so those tiny rooms seemed almost a paradise on earth. When the State of Israel was proclaimed, I was immediately recruited into the economic-control apparatus, and when the police were entrusted with the campaign against economic crimes, I was given an officer's rank.

In 1954 I was sent to the United States for three and a half years, in the line of duty, and Vera and the children went with me. I arranged for Vera to be examined by specialists there. They said: "Mrs. Less, you are a medical miracle. You should not be able to make the movements you do. Somehow your body has learned to adjust to the loss of certain functions. All we can do for you is advise you not to overexert yourself." As it turned out, they were right: starting in 1968, Vera's general condition began to deteriorate; from 1974 on, she needed the wheelchair more and more often; and in 1980 she died of a brain hemorrhage.

Twenty years before, on May 23, 1960, when she was still in relatively good health, the evening papers carried a sensational report under banner headlines: Adolf Eichmann had been arrested and Prime Minister Ben-Gurion had announced in the Knesset that Eichmann would stand trial in Israel for his crimes against the Jewish people. No Israeli citizen, no Jew anywhere in the world could remain indifferent to this event. Was there a home anywhere in Israel that had no victims to mourn?

The news filled me with satisfaction, but also with dread at the thought of reopening wounds that had scarcely begun to heal. How much agony and grief would be stirred up by these memories? Thoughts and feelings that had been hard to suppress and forget would be reawakened. But then, did we have the right to forget? Wouldn't we be endangering our children's future if we turned our backs on the past? I discussed these questions until late into the night with Vera and several friends. The following day my friend and colleague Yehuda Kaufmann told me he would like to become involved in the Eichmann case. The thought of such a task horrified me; and besides, it wouldn't bring a single one of the murdered millions back to life.

But the next day, May 25, Colonel Shmul Roth called me and said General Selinger wished to see me at once. Selinger at that time was chief of police for Haifa and the whole northern district. With him in his office was Colonel Efraim Hofstaetter-Elrom, head of the criminal investigation department of the Tel Aviv district. I had always regarded General Selinger as the prototype of the Israeli police officer, and Colonel Hofstaetter was considered one of the most capable criminal investigators.

Selinger said: "Less, the government has entrusted the police with the Eichmann investigation. I am putting together a group of officers to prepare the case against Eichmann. I have chosen you to be his interrogator. It won't be an easy task, and in all probability it will take a good deal longer than three months. Are you willing?"

My first impulse was to decline. I dreaded the thought of

our tracking down the evidence of so much horror. When Selinger noticed my hesitation, he said: "Less, I am convinced you are the right man for the interrogation." When Colonel Hofstaetter joined in urging me to accept, I overcame my revulsion; after all, somebody had to do it.

Selinger and Hofstaetter agreed that the incriminating evidence should be organized along geographical lines, and that for every country where Eichmann and his machine had been active, an officer conversant with that country's language should be appointed. It was then decided that since Eichmann was being transferred to a prison near Haifa, our staff headquarters would have to be in that city as well. In conclusion, General Selinger impressed on us the need for total secrecy; we were not to discuss any details, not even at home.

As I was leaving police headquarters that evening, a journalist accosted me on the street: "Captain, I hear you're a member of the group entrusted with the Eichmann hearings. I'd like to ask you a few questions." I was flabbergasted, for I was convinced that only a handful of people were informed. So I merely said: "The only thing I'd be willing to discuss with you is the weather." At that moment a major came out of the building, a man who happened to be the official spokesman for the police force. The reporter complained to him that I had been unwilling to tell him anything about myself. The major said: "Less, you're quite free to tell him about yourself." This I did, although very sparingly. When I got home, our daughter exclaimed with great excitement that she had heard on the radio that I was part of the police team that would be investigating Eichmann. So it took just a few hours for the cat to get out of the bag. Some time later, Eichmann's place of detention became the best-kept "secret" in Israel; everyone knew where he was, but no one talked about it.

The following is a brief summary of the guidelines I was given for my work.

OBJECT: To obtain a complete statement from the defendant concerning his goals and activities during the Nazi regime.

PREPARATIONS: All the materials assembled under the deputy director of Bureau 06 (that was our team's official name) were placed at my disposal. The research staff had instructions to direct my attention to every document, every piece of testimony or bit of information that could be of use in the hearings or that could be authenticated or verified by the defendant. For my part, I had to prepare in writing all questions I planned to ask the defendant.

THE HEARINGS: They would be recorded on tape. I was to mark each tape with an identifying label immediately after the end of each hearing. If I considered it desirable that Eichmann amplify his voluntary testimony with written notes, and if Eichmann agreed to this, I could supply him with paper and writing implements. Whenever I handed him a document, I was to solicit his commentary. He was free to refuse such comment.

THE TAPES: After each hearing, I was to hand over the tapes of our conversation to the director of the 06 archives. He would have them transcribed and stored in a safe, but first Eichmann and I had to make a word-for-word comparison of each transcript and tape. If any changes were made, Eichmann was to make them by hand; furthermore, he had to confirm in writing that he had approved the correction and that the text of the final transcript was identical to that of the tape recording. The transcript would then be read aloud to the research staff for the purpose of analysis and discussion. The entire body of evidence (the transcripts of the hearings, the documents, the testimony of witnesses) would have to be translated into Hebrew.

No one on our team had detailed knowledge of the Holocaust. We immediately attacked the many books General Selinger supplied us with, plowed through the forty-two volumes of the Nuremberg trials of the major war criminals, as well as the many thousands of pages of the subsidiary Nuremberg trials. Yad Vashem, the Holocaust memorial center in Jerusalem, opened its archives to us, and its research staff helped us in every way possible. Reitlinger's *The Final Solution* became almost a bible for us; Poliakov's works and Adler's *Theresienstadt* proved equally indispensable. We sat reading day and night, reading, reading . . . None of us slept more than three or four hours at a time. We were exhausted, nervous, sometimes irritable. It was a most stressful and trying time.

We obtained our first important documents from Tuvia Friedman, a journalist who on his own initiative had set up a documentation center in Haifa. (He had been a victim of the Nazis himself, in Poland.) An especially important adviser was Robert Kempner, the American prosecutor at the Nuremberg trials. He became our "gray eminence" and gave active assistance to the prosecution authorities later on at the trial. Mountains of documents poured in from all the countries that had received appeals for help from Bureau 06—all except the Soviet Union.

As a result of this strenuous and sometimes hectic work under the leadership of Selinger and Hofstaetter, we became a homogeneous unit with an esprit de corps that has kept us together until this day. If Eichmann amazed us at first with his knowledge of the material, the day soon came when we knew a lot more about his actions than he could have liked. The evidence grew, and with it the files of the prosecution. I myself contributed a good part of this material, having questioned Eichmann for 275 hours, which came to 3,564 pages of transcript. But this would have been impossible without my colleagues' painstaking research.

The reader of the transcripts of the hearings should know that criminal investigations in Israel are conducted along English rather than Continental European lines. The police, who are not under the authority of the Attorney General, conduct the investigation from beginning to end, independently and in the framework of their own guidelines. The police officer conducting an investigation does not have the function or powers of an examining magistrate. After the police investigation has been completed, the whole dossier goes to the Attorney General's office, which examines it for errors and inconsistencies, and then presents the court with a written indictment.

Contrary to Continental procedure, the official in charge of the interrogation is not permitted to subject the accused to cross-examination. Before the hearings begin, he must inform the accused of his rights and make it clear to him that he is free to speak or not, as he chooses, but that everything he says will be taken down and may be used in evidence. The interrogator is not even permitted to say that any statement made by the accused "may be used against him," since the word "against" implies a threat that could intimidate the accused. Under such conditions, the questioning of a suspect is somewhat difficult. The interrogator can base his questions only on statements the accused himself has made. If, as was the case with Eichmann, the accused asks the interrogator to refresh his memory with questions, he is free to do so.

Throughout the police investigation of Eichmann, we worked in close association with Attorney General Gideon Hausner and Gavriel Bach, currently a judge on the Supreme Court in Jerusalem. They had to familiarize themselves with the complex material very quickly; the government insisted on holding the trial in the near future, and so the indictment had to be drawn up in a hurry. The volume and content of the documents would have required another year's work for a complete police investigation. We of Bureau 06 were quite unhappy about having to break off our research prematurely. On the other hand, the state had already incurred considerable expense on account of Eichmann. He was the only inmate of a large prison complex, all the other inmates having been transferred for security reasons. In addition to the members of Bureau 06—there must have been well over thirty police officers in the group—a detachment of border police was put in charge of security. This detachment also supplied the guard personnel. None of the guards spoke either of Eichmann's two languages, German and Spanish. Their officers, however, had to speak at least one of those languages. To prevent any acts of private revenge, no one who had lost family members in the Holocaust was chosen for the guard unit. For fear of attempts to free Eichmann, the entire area was kept under strict surveillance day and night.

Eichmann's cell, measuring roughly ten by thirteen feet, contained only a cot, a table, and a chair. The electric light was left on all night. Every day he cleaned his cell and the adjoining toilet and shower room unaided. He did these chores with thoroughness and dedication. A guard sat in the room with him day and night, and outside the cell door sat a second guard, who watched the one in the cell through a peephole, to make sure there was no contact between him and Eichmann. The second guard was in a kind of vestibule, outside the door of which a third guard kept constant watch on him.

These security measures were not designed to prevent Eichmann from attacking the guard in his cell so much as to prevent him from committing suicide. That was our greatest fear; if he had succeeded in committing suicide, no one anywhere in the world would have believed it. That is why we guarded him like the apple of our eye. During the first weeks, when the electric light disturbed his sleep, he would pull his woolen blanket over his head, whereupon the guard would pull it back to make sure Eichmann was not trying to kill himself under the blanket. Twice a day he was examined from head to toe by our police physician.

The room where the hearings took place was considerably larger than Eichmann's cell, but also very simply furnished. A large military-style desk was placed close to the center of the room, with a chair on either side. I sat facing the door, and Eichmann sat across from me. To my right, on a stand beside the wall, was a large tape recorder, which I operated. On the desk, two microphones, one in front of me, the other in front of Eichmann. On a small table beside me, a telephone.

I was never alone with Eichmann. Each hearing proceeded according to a fixed ritual. I would leave the headquarters building and go to the gate leading into the main prison block. The sentry, who had been notified of my approach, would examine my papers and let me pass. I would cross the large inner court, surrounded by an outer wall and a one-story cell complex, and arrive in the interrogation room. There I would arrange my papers and documents, put a tape on the tape recorder, and phone the officer of the guard to bring the prisoner in.

The officer responsible for Eichmann's transfer from his cell to the interrogation room would come in first, followed by two guards with Eichmann between them. Eichmann would stand at attention behind his chair until I said he could be seated. Though I told him there was no need to stand at attention, he went on doing so until the end. Maybe it was a habit he couldn't shake off, or maybe he wished to show that fifteen years after the war he still wanted to be treated like a soldier.

By this time, the guard officer would have told the two guards to sit down, one by the window, the other in the open doorway. The guard in front of the window was supposed to keep his eyes fixed on us at the table; the guard in the doorway had to watch his comrade. Neither of them understood a word of what Eichmann and I were saying. Our conversation would not begin until after the officer of the guard had left us, and he would return only when the guards were relieved (every two hours) or whenever I notified him by phone that the hearing or the session of correcting transcripts was at an end.

As time went on, I noticed that each time Eichmann said "Never! Never! Never, Herr Hauptmann!" or "At no time! At no time!" he was lying. That was always a cue for me to ask my colleagues to search for additional material with which to probe the sensitive spot. They often located just what was needed, and thanks to their stubborn determination I would be able to present Eichmann with additional damaging documents at a later hearing. When I read to him from the book *Commandant of Auschwitz* by the notorious concentration-camp commander Höss, Eichmann became increasingly nervous. He denied every accusation with the argument that he hadn't had the slightest influence on the way the camps were run; intermittently, he would try to belittle Höss's statements with sarcastic laughter, but his quivering hands betrayed his fear.

On October 9, 1960, Colonel Offer, commander of the prison, came into the room and informed Eichmann that his defense lawyer, Dr. Servatius of Cologne, was expected that day. Two days later, as we were going over some tapes, Eichmann told me in a buoyant, almost peppy manner about his first meeting with his attorney. Servatius looked exactly the way he had imagined him. He made a very competent impression. No doubt he had gathered some important and highly relevant insights at the Nuremberg trials. He, Eichmann, would need that kind of experience; he understood the gravity of his situation very well, he said; he was not harboring any illusions. One thing was definite, though: his trial would be a historic event of the first order; he as a person was less important than the "historical factors." After all, he had just been "a little cog" in Hitler's gigantic machine.

I replied that this might very well turn out to be the central issue of the trial—whether he wasn't in fact the flywheel of that merciless extermination machine. In any case, this was an issue which neither he nor I had to decide; it was the court's task to arrive at a judgment.

About four weeks later, I presented Eichmann with a document dated September 21, 1939, when there was still fighting in Poland. It dealt with a meeting in which he had participated and where, among other items on the agenda, the "ghettoization" of all Polish Jews as a step toward the final solution was decided. It was precisely this that Eichmann had categorically denied just a short while before. It was a noticeable shock for him to have to admit that he had been aware of the plan to exterminate the Jews as early as September 1939. This document completely robbed Eichmann of his appetite; he sent his meal back without touching it. Ordinarily, he ate heartily.

In February 1961, as we were correcting one of the last transcripts, the officer on duty led our photographer, Gerber, into the interrogation room. As Gerber set up his equipment, Eichmann looked at me with large, questioning eyes. I said: "I believe we're going to have our picture taken." Eichmann buttoned the collar of his shirt, said "Ah, good," sat up straight as a stick, and put on a serious and thoughtful expression. He was vain enough to want to be remembered as an important historical personage. (I never saw this photo, incidentally. It seems to have been lost.)

Two months after the last hearing, Eichmann stood trial before his judges in Jerusalem. The State of Israel paid his defense costs. His trial was of exemplary fairness. Not one of his victims received comparable treatment.

AVNER W. LESS

Translated by Joel Agee

EICHMANN
INTERROGATED

Sturmbannführer Adolf Eichmann

Eichmann at the time of the
pretrial interrogation

The only extant photograph of Adolf Eichmann (*left foreground*) and Captain Avner Less (*third from the left*). The order for Eichmann's detention is being renewed by a justice of the peace. *Right foreground:* Colonel Efraim Hofstaetter-Elrom

More than once in his public speeches, Hitler announced his intention of exterminating the Jews. On October 8, 1942, addressing the "old warriors" of the National Socialist Party at the Munich Löwenbräukeller, he said: "People have laughed at my prophesies. Countless numbers of those who laughed are no longer laughing today. And those who are still laughing may not be laughing for long." The chimneys of the crematoriums in the death camps were already smoking, day and night. That speech was broadcast by every radio station in Germany and was printed, word for word, in the newspapers. Yet most Germans regarded those words as rhetorical threats designed to frighten Hitler's enemies.

Reichsführer-SS Heinrich Himmler spoke much more concretely of the "extermination of the Jewish people." On October 4, 1943, addressing the highest-ranking leaders of the SS in Posen [Poznan], he said: "Most of you probably know what it is to see a hundred corpses lying together in one place, or to see five hundred or a thousand. To have gone through that and yet, aside from exceptions due to human weakness, to have preserved our decency—this is what has made us hard."

Since neither the Führer nor the Reichsführer wanted to bloody their hands, they needed tools; in other words, an apparatus of commanders and followers, organizers and thugs, murderers and whitewashers. Most of these were provided by the SS; they were the most disciplined and the most unscrupulous. They regarded themselves as the elite of the National

Socialists. One of this breed was Adolf Eichmann, head of the Bureau for Jewish Affairs at the Reich Security Headquarters [Reichssicherheitshauptamt, RSHA].

In the Third Reich, Adolf Eichmann was as unknown to the general public as were ten thousand other high-level bureaucrats. At the end of the war, his name came to be identified, all over. the world, with genocide and murder. What sort of man was he? How could he bring himself to do the work he did? What sort of times and circumstances molded him? He himself provided answers to these questions.

Avner Less, a captain in the Israeli police, has been appointed to interrogate Eichmann in preparation for his trial. Beginning today, May 29, 1960, Captain Less will spend nearly three hundred hours face to face with the man who sent millions of Jews to their death, including the captain's father and a dozen close relatives. In January 1943, Avner Less's father, a Berlin manufacturer and veteran of the First World War, was sent first to the Theresienstadt concentration camp and then to the gas chambers of Auschwitz. As his son has observed with bitter irony, his father's Iron Cross won him "the privilege of being one of the last to be deported from Berlin, and thus one of the last to be liquidated."

HOFSTAETTER: You recognize me, I presume. I am Colonel Hofstaetter of the Israeli police.

EICHMANN *(clipped, military manner)*: Jawohl!

HOFSTAETTER: Herr Eichmann, I am told that you are willing, eager in fact, to give us your version of your role in the so-called Third Reich? Is that right?

EICHMANN: Yes, that is right.

HOFSTAETTER: You are fully aware that you are not being coerced in any way?

EICHMANN: Jawohl!

HOFSTAETTER: Then Captain Less will stay here with you and

start taking your statement. I realize that you will need certain documents. In the course of your statement, Captain Less will draw up a list of the documents you need, and as far as possible we shall procure these documents. That is all, I believe.

LESS: I believe we should begin with your curriculum vitae.

EICHMANN: I was born on March 19, 1906, at Solingen in the Rhineland. My father was a bookkeeper at the Solingen Light and Power Company. That was the name more or less. In 1913 my father was transferred to the Linz Light and Power Company in Linz on the Danube, probably in connection with a loan which the AEG [Allgemeine Elektrizitätsgesellschaft, or General Electric] gave that Austrian company, in which he served as commercial director until 1924. In 1914 my father moved his family to Austria. So, from 1914 on, I lived in Linz on the Danube in Upper Austria with my parents and my brothers and sisters.

LESS: Suppose we go back a little. What was your father's name?

EICHMANN: My father's name was Adolf Karl Eichmann. My mother's name was Maria Eichmann, née Schefferling.

LESS: What other children were there?

EICHMANN: My father married twice. My first mother died in 1916. She bore him five children. The next after me was Emil, two years younger than me.

LESS: He was born in 1908?

EICHMANN: I believe so, Herr Hauptmann,* because the next one, Helmuth, was three years younger than me. He was killed in Stalingrad during the war. The next was a sister, Irmgard. She is four or five years younger than me, I believe.

* Eichmann attaches great importance to Captain Less's rank and invariably addresses him as Herr Hauptmann, Mr. Captain. In a similar situation, an English-speaking defendant would address an interrogating officer, regardless of rank, simply as "sir," which struck me as all wrong for Eichmann. I have therefore, in most instances, left "Herr Hauptmann" in German.—*Trans.*

LESS: Do you remember the exact date of your sister's birth?

EICHMANN: I haven't seen any of my brothers and sisters for eighteen years. The next brother from that marriage was Otto, our youngest. The quick succession of births was responsible for the early death of my first mother. In 1916 my father remarried; his second wife was a very strict, religious Protestant.

LESS: Are you affiliated with any religious denomination?

EICHMANN: I belonged to the Evangelical Church until 1937. Then I left. After that, in the course of the fifteen years since 1945, during which I acquired new insights—after those times—I have gone back to it inwardly, but I did not join officially, because I felt uncomfortable. Mainly because of my father, who was a very religious man; for a good many years he was an honorary elder of the Evangelical congregation in Linz. He died on February 5 of this year.

LESS: You also belonged to the Young Men's Christian Association for a time?

EICHMANN: I joined when I was very young. The whole family was taken to church at nine o'clock Sunday morning, and either after church or on Sunday afternoon we went to the YMCA. It was only when they put in a new young people's training director, with whom we did not see eye to eye, that I went over to the Wandervögel [Scouts], to be exact, the Greif [Griffon] group, which belonged to the Federated Youth Organizations. I was still a member at the age of eighteen when I was at vocational school.

LESS: What school did you attend in Linz?

EICHMANN: In Linz I attended elementary school up to the fourth grade, and then Realschule [scientific secondary school], also up to the fourth year.

LESS: What Realschule?

EICHMANN: The Kaiser Franz Staatsoberrealschule. Later it was renamed Bundesoberrealschule, because that was the time of the Anschluss.

At an earlier date, Eichmann would undoubtedly have pointed out that Adolf Hitler had gone to that same school a few years earlier.

LESS: How long did you attend this secondary school? Four years? What year did you leave?

EICHMANN: I must have finished elementary school in 1916–1917. During the revolution I was at secondary school. I can still remember that there was rioting during classes.

LESS: What street did you live on in Linz?

EICHMANN: 3 Bischofstrasse.

LESS: Was that an apartment house?

EICHMANN: It was. Right in the middle of town.

LESS: When you finished school in 1921, at the age of fifteen, did you enlist for one year?

EICHMANN: No, one-year enlistment had been discontinued. I went on to vocational school—Höhere Bundeslehranstalt für Elektrotechnik, Maschinenbau und Hochbau [School for Electrical, Mechanical, and Structural Engineering]. Still in Linz. I was there for four terms.

LESS: Were you employed at that time?

EICHMANN: Yes. My father took an early retirement about then and went into business for himself. First in Salzburg, where he founded the Untersberg Mining Company, in which he held fifty-one percent of the stock. The mines were between Salzburg and the German border. But the company never really got off the ground. Next he acquired an interest in a mill-construction enterprise in the Innviertel region of Upper Austria. My father often regretted this later, because it was just at the time of the economic crisis that he went into business in Austria. He not only failed to make money, but his savings and my second mother's, too, were put into the businesses and evaporated. I forgot to mention that my father also had an interest in a machine shop in Salzburg, where they made locomobiles. The original owner hanged himself after spending the money that his partner, that is, my father, had put into the business. Then one day my father shut down the Untersberg Mining Company, but for years after that he went on paying so-called prospection fees to the Mining Authority.

LESS: In which of your father's firms did you work?

EICHMANN: When I—well, you see, my father took me out of school, because, I may as well admit it, I hadn't been exactly the most conscientious of students. He put me into the Untersberg Mining Company. I had to work both below and above ground. It was a small mine. The main tunnels were no more than three hundred meters long. There were a few side tunnels and some small shafts. The purpose was to extract oil from oil shale, shale oil for medicinal purposes, residues, asphalt, etc., etc. A foreman kept after me, and I had to work my shifts just like the rest of them.

LESS: How many workers were there?

EICHMANN: Ten in all, I believe.

LESS: How long did you work there?

EICHMANN: It must have been about three months. It couldn't have been any longer. Then I was sent to Austrian Electro-tech [Elektrobau] as a volunteer, as they called it at the time. I had been to secondary school, and I had my one-year voluntary enlistment, as they used to say; of course, it wasn't valid. All parents in those days liked their children to get at least their one-year voluntary enlistment behind them. Then, instead of calling it apprenticeship, they called it the volunteer period, and I stayed with Austrian Electro-tech for two and a half years.

LESS: All this in Linz?

EICHMANN: Yes. Austrian Electrotech and the Austrian Water Power Company were subsidiaries of the Light and Power Company. Electrotech manufactured and sold electrical appliances. The Linz Light and Power Company was the sole producer of electrical current. The current was produced by Austrian Water Power in their plant in the Mühlviertel region.

LESS: In what department were you apprenticed? Did you go through all the departments?

EICHMANN: No. I was sent to Electrotech. My father wanted me to become a salesman. Radio was just coming in. I concentrated on this new item because of the novelty. After two and a half years, my father said I wasn't getting anywhere and decided I should become a "traveling agent," as they called it then, meaning a traveling salesman, for the Vacuum Oil Company in Upper Austria. It seems my parents had just seen an ad in the daily paper. My mother, who usually took the initiative in such matters, had got in touch with a cousin of hers, who was president of the Austrian Automobile Club. He lived in Vienna and was a close friend of the head of the Vacuum Oil Company for Austria. A Herr Weiss.

LESS: Did you meet this Herr Weiss personally and speak to him?

EICHMANN: No. I had to report to the provincial director in Linz, who told me there were plenty of openings but that he'd have to send me to Vienna to introduce myself.

LESS: How old were you at the time?

EICHMANN: I was very young. I beg your pardon. I'll have to think a minute.

LESS: That's quite all right, Herr Eichmann. Would you care for a cigarette?

EICHMANN: If you don't mind.

In 1928 I was twenty-two. I went to Vienna, reported to the main office of Vacuum Oil, and was taken to a Herr Popper, who told me I was too young but I had been hired at the request of Herr Weiss, the president. Evidently, the man had received instructions from his top boss. I reported back to the Linz office and spent the next few days learning about Sphinx gasoline, kerosene, and the various grades of Gargoyl-Mobiloil. Then I was let loose in the city of Linz, and after a week or two of preparatory work, I was assigned a district of Upper Austria as my exclusive territory.

LESS: Was it a large district?

EICHMANN: Oh, yes, it was half of Upper Austria.

LESS: Were you living with your parents at the time? With your father and stepmother?

EICHMANN: Yes, I lived with them, but I only came home on Saturdays and Sundays, or once in a while in midweek when my route was changed. That year, most of my work consisted of setting up gas stations in my territory. At the same time I arranged for the kerosene deliveries in most of the Mühlviertel, because electrification hadn't gone very far in that district. I was especially interested in supplying kerosene, because it took me into territory where modern life and high speed hadn't yet penetrated. The Mühl-viertel is a dreamy little district, the people were still living as they had been fifty or even a hundred years before. That appealed to me. And then there was the natural beauty of the place. Mixed forests, partly deciduous, partly evergreen. And then the romantic feel of the place. It's amazingly rich in old castles, or it might be more accurate to speak of the ruins of many generations of nobility; some are very old, real ruins, you could say. On all my trips I visited those ruins. I stayed there until 1933, and then I was transferred from Upper Austria to Salzburg. That transfer went against my grain. They gave me no advance notice. The greater part of the Salzburg district was assigned to me. At first I was happy, because it was winter and the high mountains were all covered with snow. Then came the spring season, the tourists crowded into Kitzbühel, Hofgastein, Dorf Gastein, Bad Gastein, and all that bustle repelled me. I didn't enjoy my work anymore, I lost interest in selling, in calling on customers. I went on doing my daily work, but after the Whitsun holidays of 1933, Director Blum said to me: "We've got to cut down on personnel." He said I was the only unmarried salesman, and that's why he had hit on me. So they gave me notice.

LESS: That was in 1933? After the Whitsun holidays?

EICHMANN: Personally, I was glad to be dismissed. But my parents weren't happy about it. I was given five months' pay, one for each year I had been with the firm.

LESS: And what did you do after returning to Linz?

EICHMANN: I stayed with my parents and tried to figure out what to do next. My father's industrial ventures had all failed. He had lost everything and was looking for work as district sales manager for Upper and Lower Austria. He still had the connections built up in twenty-four years with electrical concerns. His first sales managership was with Philips Radio Tubes, then with Varta Storage Batteries. He started again at the bottom and had already built up a good business. But I had no desire to sell radio tubes and storage batteries. I thought of starting a business of my own, selling lubricants. As agent for some unknown brand, not for any cartel member. I knew plenty of prospective customers, especially in Upper Austria. While I was making preparations, I ran into some sort of difficulties, I don't remember what, maybe something financial, or maybe something was wrong with the proposition. Anyway, I remember that I was on my way to Eferding to see my first customer and I suddenly decided to turn back. I said to myself: After all, I'm a German citizen. Why not go to Germany and try my luck with Vacuum Oil?

LESS: What prompted that decision?

EICHMANN: I was a relatively young man and used to being led, in business and in everything else. Maybe I just lost my nerve, I really don't remember. I probably had other difficulties of some kind; anyway, I broke off my trip and

told my parents I was going to Germany. Germany was a
big country, I said, and there was sure to be work there,
probably even in the oil business. Because at that time there
was a lot of unemployment in Austria.

LESS: All that was in 1933?

EICHMANN: Yes, sir. To make this part of my story perfectly
clear, I have to switch from business matters to the so-called
political sphere.

*It should be pointed out that the employment situation in
Austria was scarcely worse than in Germany at the time. True,
Hitler kept trumpeting his promise that the six million
German unemployed would be back at work within four
years, but in view of the world crisis, that was hardly credible.*

EICHMANN: Quite aside from economic considerations, I had
other reasons for wanting to get away. To leave Austria
and go to Germany. Even in my school days, we had
political groups, all perfectly harmless, of course: nationalists, socialists, monarchists. The kind of thing youngsters go
in for, revolutionary and so on. Without thinking about it
very much. For instance, you'd join the monarchists or the
nationalists just because you had a good friend in one of
these groups. That was the first political talk I had heard.
At home the subject was never mentioned. My father
wasn't interested in politics. I had an old friend in Linz, his
name was Friedrich von Schmidt, his father was Field
Marshal Lieutenant von Schmidt, whom I never met because he died before I made friends with his son. The family
was enormously proud of the father, because he'd risen
from private to field marshal lieutenant in the days of the
Emperor Franz Joseph; so he must have been very brave,
a fine, upstanding soldier and a fine, upstanding man. Anyway, it was a distinguished family. My friend's mother had
been a Countess So-and-So. Their world had collapsed in

1919, but they were still living with the old ideas. They kept up the old forms as if nothing had happened. But sometimes my friend Friedrich von Schmidt would forget his fine manners and then he was just a good fellow. He had connections with First World War veterans organizations, since he associated mostly with military men. One day he persuaded me to join the Young Veterans Association; that was the youth section of the German-Austrian Veterans Association. Its slogan was: "Public Need Before Public Greed." Except for the Social Democratic Schutzbund [Defense League], it was the only organization that dared to march through the streets, and not very often at that. It evidently had the support of the government. Most of the members held monarchist opinions. Some were Christian-oriented, and only a vanishing minority were nationalists. National Socialism was still unheard of.

LESS: So most of you were loyal to Austria?

EICHMANN: We young men sometimes took the streetcar to Klein-München, a suburb of Linz. A marksmen's organization had a rifle range there. A rifle was put into my hands for the first time and I was taught marksmanship. That I remember well. Those early days in the Veterans Association must have been in 1928–29. Around 1931, there was friction between nationalists and monarchists. By that time, the SA [Nazi storm troopers] were also marching through the streets. The SS tried to recruit members of the Veterans Association in Linz, because we were tolerated by the government and allowed to practice marksmanship, and at that time the SS had no objection. One day the NSDAP [Nationalsozialistische deutsche Arbeiterpartei, or National Socialist German Workers Party; in other words, the National Socialists], as they called themselves, staged a mass meeting in the Märzenkeller, a big Bavarian-style beer hall. Gauleiter Bollek made a speech. And then a certain Ernst Kaltenbrunner came up to me. We'd seen each other around. His father was a lawyer in Linz, and his father and my father had had business connections for twenty years. Ernst Kaltenbrunner put it to me straight from the shoulder: "You're going to join us!" That's how it was done in those days, all very free and easy, no fuss. I said: "All right." So I joined the SS.

LESS: That was in . . .

EICHMANN: It was either late 1931 or early 1932. It must show up in my papers. I don't remember exactly.

Eichmann's personnel records have been collected and preserved. They include a curriculum vitae written in 1937 by Eichmann himself. It gives April 1, 1932, as the date when he joined the party and the SS. Party serial number 889,895. SS number 45326. That date and those numbers mean that even in Austria he was not regarded as exactly an "old warrior."

EICHMANN: In Salzburg I attended to my regular work at Vacuum Oil. I returned to Linz every Friday. That's where I did my SS duty, because during the week I was never available. Every Friday I was on duty at the so-called Brown House in Linz, which the party had bought. I slept on a straw pallet and did night guard duty. Since I was one of the few who was working and making good money, they were always glad to see me, because next door to this Brown House there was a restaurant, and I regularly treated the boys to beer or cider and cigarettes. On Saturday mornings I went home, washed, and finished up my work for Vacuum Oil; that is, I wrote reports and cleared up certain questions. That was when the uniform with the beret came in. I had one of those uniforms made. One day we went to Freilassing.

That was near Salzburg, just over the German border. Parades of uniformed National Socialists were then forbidden in

Austria. The old uniform consisted of a brown shirt and black woolen trousers. To these was now added a black woolen jacket with insignia of rank on the turnover collar. The tall black kepi, shaped like that of the French Foreign Legion, was now replaced by a black woolen beret.

EICHMANN: An SS auxiliary police unit was stationed in Freilassing. The members of SS-Standarte 37 from Salzburg and Linz [an SS regiment] went there every Sunday to be whipped into shape. In the evening we'd be driven back to Salzburg, and the next morning I went back to my work. I happened to be in Pinzgau when I heard that the party had been suppressed in Austria.

LESS: What year was that?

EICHMANN: That was in 19 . . . 33, just before Whitsun.

In the middle of May 1933, three German party bigwigs —the lawyer Dr. Hans Frank, later Governor General of Poland; Dr. Hans Kerrl, the future Church Minister; and Dr. Roland Freisler, the future president of the notorious People's Court—tried to organize National Socialist demonstrations in Austria. No sooner had they landed at the Vienna airport than Engelbert Dollfuss, the Christian Socialist Chancellor of Austria, shipped them back to the Reich. On June 19, 1933, as a result of the ensuing diplomatic incident between Berlin and Vienna, the NSDAP and all its subsidiaries were prohibited in Austria.

EICHMANN: My uniform was at the tailor's, bought and paid for, but I never called for it, because the party was suppressed. Besides, as I've told you, I had been fired from my job. On the way to Eferding to close my first personal business deal, I said to myself: There's no point in this. I'm going to Germany. So one fine morning I set out from

Linz with my parents' blessing, a German passport, and a letter from the German consul stating that I came from one of the most respected families of the Linz German colony, and requesting the assistance of the German authorities. The usual sort of recommendation.

LESS: Before leaving, you had to give your SS-Standarte notice, didn't you?

EICHMANN: Yes, that came next. I went to see Dr. Kaltenbrunner, you know, my friend Ernst, who then held the rank of Truppführer, which later became Oberscharführer. But his duties were much more important than the rank indicates. You see, he was also a lawyer, and he had gone into his father's firm. He said: "Come back tomorrow. I'll give you some letters. You'll put them in your suitcase. Hide them. Take them across with you and report to Gauleiter Bollek in Passau." That was the Gauleiter in exile. I picked up the letters . . .

LESS: From Kaltenbrunner junior?

EICHMANN: Yes, junior. His old man was dead by then. At the border I didn't have to open anything. The headquarters of the Upper Austria Gauleiter were right there on Bahnhofstrasse. I sent the letters in and then I had a long wait in the waiting room. Finally I was taken to Gauleiter Bollek. I told him why I'd come and asked him if he knew how I could get into Vacuum Oil, the Bavarian branch of the Vacuum Oil Company. He said it would be better if I played soldier for a while. It was high time I learned how to walk. I said to myself: All right, I'll be a soldier. I had no one to provide for. So then they sent me to Kloster Lechfeld.

LESS: Was that a school or an army post?

EICHMANN: It was a big training station from First World War days, set up by the old army. There were barracks, lots of them, and nearby there was a monastery [Kloster] and a brewery. Those barracks weren't new, and there had also been a big canteen there. Bavarian state police were in charge of our training. We were all known as the Austrian Legion.

LESS: Lechfeld was both an SA and an SS camp?

EICHMANN: Right! There was a complete Sturmbann [battalion] of SS, three Stürme [companies], but probably more than five hundred men. And probably quite a lot more SA men. Training was given. To all intents and purposes, there were only two branches of service, infantry and engineers. The engineers were given shock-troop training. The doctor did all the selecting; the huskiest went to the shock troop, the rest to the infantry. I went to the shock troop, because I was stronger than I am now. We were trained mostly in street fighting. Since my handwriting was fairly decent, they made me a topkick right away, you know, company first sergeant, and I had to keep the marksmanship records. In addition to our military training, we marched for hours every day on the drill ground, in preparation for the Party Congress. Later, it must have been in October 1933, I received orders to report to a Sturmbannführer Pichl in Passau. He was head of the Reichsführer-SS's liaison team in Passau. The work of his liaison staff, consisting of eight, maybe ten men, was to patrol the border between Austria and Bavaria regularly, in collaboration with the border police. Because at that time fugitives were crossing over from Austria to Germany both by day and by night, and they had to be taken care of. The ones who were members of the SA or SS were sent to the Austrian Legion. At the same time, propaganda material was being smuggled from Bavaria to Austria. The duty was monotonous, but I enjoyed it, because it took me through the Bavarian Forest, which is pretty much like the forests in the Mühlviertel, my second home. I don't remember my first home at all; in my heart, I suppose it's Austria. I felt very happy there. We ate in a butcher shop, where they also sold hot sausages and potato salad. Sturmbannführer Pichl made me his assistant. I was allowed to handle minor matters on my own responsibility. He gave me a small sum of money, fifty marks at a time I think it was, with which I bought lunch for all the men involved, and soap and things like that, and we'd settle up afterwards. I was also used for writing letters and reports to SS headquarters in Munich. It was a dead, lazy sort of existence, and I was pretty sure Herr von Pichl had private interests in Passau; he was a man who liked to live well, he had fine manners, and it seemed to me that some of the ladies in Passau took up a lot of his time. Strictly speaking, the work of the liaison staff was worthless. This evidently dawned on the higher-ups after a while, because after Christmas 1934 the staff was dissolved and we were all sent to Dachau. By that time, I had one star on my collar patch. In other words, I was an Unterscharführer, or sergeant.

LESS: And what happened in Dachau?

EICHMANN: There they went in for strict military discipline; up until then, I hadn't seen anything like it. We were a battalion of the Deutschland Regiment, which consisted entirely of Austrians. Our quarters were outside the concentration camp, in an enormous iron and concrete hangar formerly used for storing munitions. We slept in triple-decker bunks.

In 1933 this area, near the small town of Dachau, north of Munich—used as an ammunition dump in the First World War—was converted into a concentration camp for Jews and political oppositionists. The buildings and terrain were also used by party organizations for paramilitary training. The treatment of the concentration-camp inmates was so notorious that the mere place name Dachau came to be used as a threat and a warning to enemies of the regime.

EICHMANN: The concentration camp was guarded by Bavarian SS men. They wore the death's-head on their collar patches. We Austrians called them Death's-headers. Our collar patch had the runic SS symbol with the figure 1.

LESS: Who were your commanding officers there?

EICHMANN: Our commanding officer was a Prussian police major, converted into an SS officer. The company commanders were Hauptsturmführers, previously Prussian police captains. On parade, the commanders would lead their units on horseback. We were all foot troops. They gave us regular military training, the same as in the Reichswehr. None of the shock-troop nonsense we'd had in Lechfeld. Strict military discipline was the rule. I stayed there until September 1934.

A short time before, I had heard that the Reichsführer's SD [Sicherheitsdienst, or Security Service] was recruiting men with army experience. The men couldn't talk of anything else, because a lot of them were dissatisfied with the hard military life. I didn't mind that, what bothered me was the monotony. Let me tell you a story to show how little I minded the tough training: I used to tell it later on to the officers and noncoms under me. —This was still in Lechfeld. A common punishment—later it was forbidden—was to make us crawl through rushes and over gravel. The first time it happened, some of the men went on sick call and got themselves declared unfit for duty. Because I thought we were being treated unfairly, I gritted my teeth and stuck it out. The skin had been scraped off my elbows, but I didn't have them bandaged. After lunch we had to start in again, the bits of plaster I'd stuck on my wounds were scraped off in a minute. I had no skin left on my elbows at all. But I stuck it out. That way, I attracted attention and got myself promoted.

So it wasn't the hard life in Dachau that made me think:

How am I going to get out of here? It was the crushing monotony. When I heard that the Reichsführer's SD was taking men, I said to myself: This looks good to me.

LESS: The Reichsführer-SS was Heinrich Himmler?

EICHMANN: Right! I thought: There I'll be where the action is, I'll have to keep my eyes open, I'll see all sorts of things, I'll be here and there and everywhere. I applied for a pass to Munich. Motive: to apply to the SD for admission. They made me fill out a questionnaire. Then I was sent back to Dachau. For a long time I didn't hear anything and I thought my application had been passed over.

The SD began with a mistake. When Hitler and Himmler hit on the idea of setting up an intelligence service to combat enemies of the party and to spy on party members, they looked for a man with experience along those lines. One applicant, Reinhard Heydrich, a naval lieutenant with an administrative discharge from the service, described himself as a former intelligence officer with a knowledge of wireless telegraphy, encoding, etc. But Himmler believed at first that he had specialized in espionage. In June 1931, Heydrich was commissioned to establish and direct a Security Service, or SD.

EICHMANN: One day in Dachau I was summoned to the office of the battalion adjutant. There I received an order to report immediately to the Security Service of the Reichsführer-SS. I was given travel orders for Berlin. There I reported to 102 Wilhelmstrasse, no, not Prinz-Albrecht-Strasse—that was the Secret State Police [Gestapo].

LESS: Was that the central headquarters of the SD?

EICHMANN: The central headquarters was in the Hohenzollern Palace at 102 Wilhelmstrasse, Berlin. I was in for a big disappointment. I expected to see what I'd seen in the *Münchner Illustrierte*: SS commandos riding in cars behind high party leaders, men standing on running boards. That was an escort commando, I'd got the Reichsführer-SS's Security Service mixed up with the Reich Security Service [Reichssicherheitsdienst]. I had never even dreamed of anything like what I was getting into. Well, I got to Wilhelmstrasse early one morning—I had traveled all night —checked in, and was taken straight to the barracks.

LESS: To whom did you report in Berlin?

EICHMANN: I don't remember, but my immediate superior turned out to be an Untersturmführer Petersen. In the barracks I was given a bed with blue-checked blankets. They put me in the barracks because I was listed as "unmarried, therefore single." If I'd have been married, they'd have let me out. There were ten of us in the room. I wasn't the only one who had already done military service and was having to start all over again. I was taken to Untersturmführer Petersen, who warned me to keep everything absolutely secret. Then I was sworn in. I had to laugh when I thought of it later—much later—but for me, fresh out of training camp and used to the open air, it was comical having to walk around this palace, always on tenterhooks, always taking care not to slip on the parquet floors. I passed a coffin with some bones in it, that was the first thing I noticed. I didn't find out until later that they had been showing me through the Freemasonry Museum. I must have looked pretty dazed and flustered when they told me all this, because I couldn't make any sense out of it. I wanted to get into the escort commando [Begleitkommando] but I didn't know the word. My idea of the Reichsführer's Security Service was watching out that nothing should happen to him, attempts on his life, that kind of thing. That's what I imagined. We were taken to a great big room in the palace with enormous filing cabinets. A Scharführer was working at a desk. That was our boss.

Then I saw what we'd be doing and it gave me the creeps. We had to put the card files in alphabetical order. It was all about Freemasons. We sorted and sorted. Always taking care to keep the right letters together, the C's with the C's, and so on.

I'd never even heard of the Freemasons, I had no idea what they were. A Sturmbannführer kept coming through. He seemed to be the top boss. When a superior came in, from the rank of Sturmführer up, we had to spring to our feet, stand at attention, and wait for orders. Most of the time he would say: "Carry on."

With that kind of work, the day seemed to last forever. A Sturmbannführer with a goatee was sitting some distance away from us. He was almost deaf, he struck me as outlandish and very funny. Much later I found out that he was Professor Schwarz-Bostowitsch, the scientific director of Section I of the SD. Under the Tsar he'd served in the Kiev court of appeals; he was an expert on Freemasonry and had even published a book about it. That's why he'd been made an SS-Sturmbannführer. He had a few young men around him who were working on card files like us. One of them, whose name I shall often have occasion to mention, was Wisliceny.

LESS: Dieter?

EICHMANN: Dieter Wisliceny. At that time he was directly under Schwarz-Bostowitsch. During the two, no, three weeks that I worked there, there were several inspections. They were conducted either by the Reichsführer in person or by Kaltenbrunner. We hated those inspections. They'd come along every second or third day, usually in the late afternoon, and we'd have to stand there waiting until all the material was out of the building, or at least outside the jurisdiction of Section I. —Then I was transferred from the card-file room to the Freemasonry Museum. Nobody asked me, they just turned me over to an Oberscharführer Richter, a Berliner, who had had several terms at a university but had given it up because of political events. He was the curator, so to speak. His job was to build up a museum with the material taken from Masonic lodges all over Germany—libraries and so-called ritual objects such as aprons, medallions, seals, etc., in addition to photographs. One room was supposed to represent a St. John's Temple, and another a St. Andrew's Temple. My work was to classify, catalogue, and label thousands of seals and hundreds of medallions. It must have kept me busy for five months, until the museum, the whole department in fact, was moved to another part of Berlin. —But in the meantime I had made the acquaintance of an Untersturmführer von Mildenstein. He visited the museum one day, Göring and Goebbels had been there, too. I didn't know him. He was an Untersturmführer, I was a noncom, and at that time differences in rank meant a lot in the SS.

I had my desk in the St. John's room. He examined everything and asked me to explain a few things, which I did to the best of my ability. Then he said he had just organized a Jews department at SD headquarters, and asked me if I'd like to go in with him. I'd have gone in with the devil himself just to get away from that business with the seals. —I said yes, but I didn't hear anything for a while. As I've told you, the museum moved, and one day, at the new location, I received an order to report to Untersturmführer von Mildenstein in Department So-and-So, I don't remember the number, at 102 Wilhelmstrasse.

LESS: What was that department called?

EICHMANN: Jews. —In this Jews department I was given an entirely different kind of work. Untersturmführer von Mildenstein was an open-minded, friendly sort, a native of Austria. He seemed to have traveled a good deal. He was different from most superior officers. He didn't have that brusque, clipped way of speaking that overawed you so much that you didn't dare to say a word. I was soon on friendly terms with him. One of the first books he gave me to read was *The Jewish State* by Theodor Herzl.

This book, advocating the establishment of a Jewish state in Palestine, was the beginning of the Zionist movement, which soon found numerous adherents, especially in Eastern Europe.

EICHMANN: Von Mildenstein told me to read it through, and in the following days I read it carefully. The book interested me very much. Up until then, I had no knowledge of such things. Somehow—probably due to my romantic side, my love of nature, of the mountains, the woods—this book touched a chord in me and I took it all in. I had no idea what would come next. When I had finished reading, I was told to make an abstract of it to serve as an orientation booklet for the General SS and also for the specific use of the SD.

LESS: What year was that? Do you remember the exact date?

EICHMANN: I was transferred to the SD in September 1934. It must have been 1935, probably the second half. My abstract was submitted several times to the department head, he was a stickler for style, and it kept coming back with requests for changes. All changes in substance were made by von Mildenstein. This abstract was actually printed, in the form of an SS orientation booklet. In it I described the structure of the Zionist world organization, the aims of Zionism, its sources, and the difficulties standing in its way. I also stressed the need to encourage it, because it fell in with our own desire for a political solution: the Zionists wanted a territory where the Jewish people could finally settle in peace. And that was pretty much what the

National Socialists wanted. Hand in hand with this activity, I studied the new Zionist organization and prepared an abstract of that, too, but I don't know if it was published as a booklet. —In the ensuing period I came to know Untersturmführer von Mildenstein as a man who absolutely rejected *Stürmer* methods and favored a political solution.

Der Stürmer, *a rabidly anti-Semitic weekly, was published in Nuremberg by Julius Streicher, Gauleiter of Franconia. It was so outrageous that many National Socialists condemned it. After the war, Streicher was sentenced to death by the International Military Tribunal in Nuremberg and hanged.*

EICHMANN: I have always regarded Herr von Mildenstein as my mentor. He was the only man at Central SD Headquarters capable of providing me with reliable and thorough information about the Jews. The field assigned to me took in world Zionism, neo-Zionism, and orthodoxy. One of my colleagues covered the assimilationist organizations. That's all we had.

At that time, a man turned up who seemed to be a good friend of von Mildenstein, a certain Ernst von Bollschwingh. He had spent quite some time doing business in Palestine, in association with a certain Herr Bormann, who, if I'm not mistaken, sent a shipload of onions every year from there to some Scandinavian country. This Herr von Bollschwingh would often drop in at our office and talk to us about Palestine. He spoke so knowledgeably of the aims and situation of Zionism in Palestine and elsewhere that I gradually became an authority on Zionism. I also subscribed to periodicals, *Haint* [*Today*], for instance. I couldn't read the letters, so I bought Samuel Kaleko, which is a book for learning Hebrew. I started by learning the Hebrew printed alphabet. Some words, too. But mostly I wanted to be able to read the printed letters of *Haint*, which was written in Yiddish but with Hebrew letters.

LESS: That was in 1935?

EICHMANN: Right! But at the beginning of 1936 there was a change. Herr von Mildenstein was transferred to the highway department—the Todt Organization—and was sent to North America to study the highways. I forgot to tell you that he was a civil engineer by profession. My new boss was a much younger man, a Scharführer or Oberscharführer, an immature, arrogant fellow. Our department had no influence, it was small and unimportant; our office consisted of a single room, about twice as big as this one where I am now. But we didn't have to work together for long, because a few weeks later the young man was drafted into the army, and with that he was gone! My next superior was a new man, a certain Dieter Wisliceny, whom I've already mentioned. At the same time, we moved into a new office, consisting of two or three rooms. Wisliceny set himself up in one room, I was in the second, and a certain Dannecker, a Scharführer, I believe, occupied the third. I kept my specialty, Dannecker took assimilation, and Wisliceny reigned supreme. He was a pleasant superior. His corpulence, if nothing else, made for serenity. With him there was no excitement, no scenes. He knew a lot about history. He was marvelous to converse with. After a while I was allowed to look at the so-called daily input, which I'd never seen before. There were reports from the SD sections and subsections and from other offices, but the bulk of it was records of conferences held by Jewish organizations in different parts of the world. Sometimes it was scientific or supposedly scientific material that had been seized in raids, and since the Gestapo didn't know what to do with it, they turned it over to the SD. There were also reports from National Socialist organizations and various police administrations. The message center in our building sent everything connected with Jews to us. Wisliceny just had to decide whether it was for me or for Dannecker, depending on the subject matter.

By 1937, Theodor Dannecker, Dieter Wisliceny, and Adolf Eichmann, who would later send millions of Jews to their death, were all at work in Bureau II 112 of SD headquarters. In 1948, Wisliceny was sentenced to death and executed in Bratislava. Dannecker has not been heard of since the end of the war.

EICHMANN: It was about then that the various offices and departments were first required to supply monthly reports. The responsible head, in this case Wisliceny, had to work over and combine Dannecker's reports and mine. This bureau report went to our commanding officer, Standartenführer Dr. Six. He was a university professor, I believe.

LESS: What was the department called at that time?

EICHMANN: The department was still called the I Bureau, meaning Information Bureau. As far as I can remember, it took in churches, Jews, Communism, sects, and Freemasonry. Maybe something else, I can't be sure. Six tried to make certain changes. Mainly in the way the various SD subsections reported to the sections and the sections to central headquarters. The idea was to provide the sections with guidelines indicating what to report on and what was of interest. These guidelines would be passed on to the subsections, and from there, through the branch agencies, to the network of V-men.

LESS: What were these V-men? What was their function?

EICHMANN: Confidential agents [Vertrauensmänner]. Their function was to keep their eyes open and see what was going on, here a meeting, there a church, or maybe the

Jews would be holding a meeting to discuss questions of emigration, or some religious business, that kind of thing. Most of them were honorary V-men, but I think some were paid. We ourselves, at central headquarters, had nothing to do with V-men. We didn't know any, and none of them ever came to central headquarters.

In my section, the groundwork for our reporting was provided by the SS orientation booklet. I just had to consult it. This is what we want. The government wants emigration; whatever favors emigration must be done, nothing must be allowed to hinder it. Everything revolved around that. Naturally, I had to find out how many were emigrating. I heard that things were going badly. For the first time I heard about trouble with the tax-clearance certificate. Also with deadlines, because certain documents lost their validity after a short time and had to be renewed. I heard about the trouble it created when some local police authority, out of ignorance or stupidity, sealed up the offices of Jewish organizations, arrested their officers, and generally prevented them from functioning. That made for more delays. I heard that the Mandatory government in Palestine was creating difficulties by keeping immigration quotas too low. And that other host countries were making trouble. But there was nothing I could do, because the SD was exclusively an intelligence organization and we could only pass on our information to the competent authorities.

LESS: You say you "heard." Does that mean that you were personally in touch with various Jewish groups?

EICHMANN: Not really. Not yet with groups at that time. I first heard about them through the V-men's reports. I had acquired the *Encyclopedia Judaica* and quantities of other literature. I read a great deal on the subject. And of course all the Jewish newspapers I could get hold of. I also began to make contact with the Jewish department of the Gestapo, which implemented policy, and requested authorization to consult various officials now and then about certain questions that baffled me, not in our office of course, because we had no authority to take action or to summon or send for anyone. I obtained the authorization. In the ensuing period, I took to discussing anything that was unclear to me with a Dr. Eppstein. Either Dr. Eppstein would be called to 8 Prinz-Albrecht-Strasse or I would be notified when Dr. Eppstein had an appointment with the Gestapo. Evidently, Prinz-Albrecht-Strasse was in touch with this man at all times.

LESS: Had you received further promotion by that time?

EICHMANN: By 1936, I believe, I had acquired two stars, yes, '36. That made me an Oberscharführer, and in 1937 I became a Hauptscharführer. Hauptscharführer wasn't obligatory, that rank could be passed over. I don't know why, I had to sweat it out. Dr. Six, who was an "eager beaver," as we used to say, had a certain animosity toward the somewhat phlegmatic Wisliceny, who made us do the work while he himself read history books to while away the time.

LESS: Would you care for something to drink?

EICHMANN: Thank you, thank you very much. One day, Wisliceny was relieved and a friend of Six's was put in charge. What was the man's name? He had already served under Six in the press section of the SD—Hagen, that's it, Hagen was his name. Yes, this Oberscharführer Hagen was an intelligent man with a broad outlook. He had good general knowledge and he had a gift for assimilating brand-new material that he had never dealt with before. Up until then he hadn't the vaguest idea of Jewish affairs, of their organizations, aims, and purposes. The first thing he did when he came to us was to call me in and question me at length about my field. He wanted so much information that I had to scrape together everything I knew. He pumped me dry. And the amazing part of it was that he remembered it all. From then on, he knew as much about it as I did.

LESS: Cigarettes, please, for the prisoner. —If you please.

EICHMANN: Thank you very much. —I kept in touch with Herr von Bollschwingh. That was useful, because no one else could give me firsthand information about the country I was most interested in for my work.

One day I read an article about the Haganah in *Haint*. From it, I gathered that this must be a military-type, in fact a military Zionist organization. I questioned Dr. Eppstein about that. He denied it, but after all, I had seen it in black and white, and I must admit that my sympathies at the time were not with the Arabs but with the Jews. The Reich government was looking for a solution of the Jewish problem, and I, who after the most modest beginnings was getting more and more deeply involved in the subject, had no choice but to obey the orders of the Reich government; that is, after they had passed through the hands of the Lord knows how many intermediaries and finally come down to Six and Hagen.

In an attempt to minimize his importance and shift the responsibility for his crimes to as many superiors as possible, Eichmann affects to be no more than the last link in a long chain of command. Actually, this chain of command was extremely short. After a while, Eichmann himself replaced Hagen, his immediate superior, and it wasn't long before he was bypassing Dr. Six, the department head, and dealing directly with Müller, the top man at the Gestapo. And Müller was responsible only to Heydrich, commander of the RSHA, who in turn answered only to Himmler.

EICHMANN: I wasn't interested in the Arabs. I was interested in sending as many Jews as possible to Palestine. I was interested in every aspect of overseas emigration. But all that was only theory. The most I could do was state in my reports what was possible and what was desirable. What was really needed was a political solution. For that, it was necessary to combat *Stürmer* methods. When we had visitors in the office, men from the party or the government, we told them all that. Somehow the *Stürmer*, that is, the editors or managers of the *Stürmer*, must have got wind of these talks. The *Stürmer* was a paper, a weekly, devoted solely and exclusively to attacking the Jews. The stories it went in for could almost be called medieval, and its whole approach was just impossible. I can't think of any other word at the moment. Anyway, though that sort of propaganda may have appealed to some people, it couldn't contribute in any way to a solution.

One of the editors, Wurm was his name, Streicher's right-hand man, came to see me. He wanted to establish some sort of liaison, the idea being to feed the SD information emanating from *Stürmer* circles. I rejected his proposition both orally and in writing. Dr. Six and Hagen agreed with me that the *Stürmer* approach was no help toward a solution. So I was able to go on working as before, without benefit of *Stürmer* material. We never even received any. Instead, I was invited to the Reich Party Congress in Nuremberg. But I only spent one night there, or at the most two nights. Friends of the *Stürmer* from all over the country were holding a meeting at one of the hotels, and apparently Wurm was bent on drawing me into it. Actually, another specialist on the Jewish question was there, too, but since my department was Zionism and Zionism was the more timely topic, I was the more interesting, maybe because I had dug more deeply into the subject and knew more than Dannecker, who came from Tübingen and was rather lazy intellectually. But he copied down whatever he could and asked me about things he didn't know. In Berlin I made my report. Our relations with the *Stürmer* were unchanged.

At about that time, Herr von Bollschwingh arranged for the visit of a Jewish official from Palestine. I had read that article about the Haganah, and I said to myself, if that's the lay of the land, they'll use force against the High Commissioner, against the Mandatory government, against the Arabs. If that happens, the immigration quotas may conceivably be increased, and maybe we'll be able to send larger numbers . . .

LESS: Who was this gentleman?

EICHMANN: Herr von Bollschwingh told me a gentleman from the Haganah was in Berlin and arranged a meeting. First I must tell you that I had gone through official channels and asked in writing for written instructions about this particular case. I was in no position to decide anything for myself. Naturally, this decision didn't come from Hagen either. It came from Six, who may have talked it over with Heydrich. Anyway, I received authorization and was able to inform Herr von Bollschwingh that the gentleman could call at SD headquarters in Berlin. Of course, I've completely forgotten his name. We met—I seem to remember—at the Hotel Zur Traube near the zoo. I took the gentleman to lunch. He knew who I was and I knew that he was from Palestine. He told me all about the kibbutzim, about construction and development projects, things I already knew because I had read about them, but now I began to take a real interest. There was no hostility. We both said what we had to say, and neither of us—I had the impression—kept anything back, because we believed that our aims converged. After a second lunch, the gentleman invited me to Palestine. He wanted me to go and see the country for myself, and said they'd show me everything. I was more than willing. I reported that, too, and I submitted a report of our discussion, which went as far as Heydrich. And something I hadn't thought possible: Heydrich authorized me to accept the invitation. This came as a surprise to my colleagues. It sparked off a race between them: Wisliceny wanted to come along, so did Hagen. Hagen won out. We traveled under our own names, I as editor-in-chief of the *Berliner Tageblatt*, Hagen as a student. The SD made over a hundred English pounds to the *Berliner Tageblatt*. Then we picked up the money from the newspaper office, and left a receipt.

The choice of the Berliner Tageblatt *was a clumsy attempt to fool the British authorities. Until 1933, this world-famous newspaper had been published by Mosse Verlag. Hans Lachmann, its owner, and Theodor Wolff, its editor-in-chief, were both Jews, and outside of Germany the newspaper still enjoyed the reputation of an independent liberal paper, though it had long since been "coordinated"; that is, taken over by National Socialists. As subsequent events show, British Intelligence was not fooled.*

EICHMANN: We traveled by train through Poland and Rumania to Constanta. From there, we took the steamer *Constanta* to Haifa. While the ship was in the harbor, we got permission to go ashore. I took a cab to the top of Mt. Carmel. Back on board, I said to myself: We'll soon be in Cairo, and then . . .

LESS: When was this trip?

EICHMANN: About the end of 1937, I believe. Six had mobilized the DNB [Deutsches Nachrichtenbüro, or German News Bureau] for our trip and had instructed Dr. Reichert, the DNB representative in Jerusalem, to give us two greenhorns all possible help and advice. The same with the DNB representative in Cairo, I think his name was Gentz. In Alexandria we were guests for a few days at the home of an Egyptian we had met on shipboard. Then we went to Cairo to see Gentz. He notified Dr. Reichert in Jerusalem, through whom we were to meet the Haganah man. So one fine day we went to the British consulate in Cairo, and there we were told: "I'm sorry. Nothing doing." I seem to remember that there had been some kind of disorders in Palestine at the time, maybe bombings. It's also possible that British Intelligence had caught on to us. Anyway, they wouldn't give us permits to enter the mandate. So Dr. Reichert came to Cairo with the gentleman.

LESS: With the man from the Haganah?

EICHMANN: Right. But the real purpose of the trip, that I should see the country and the practical workings of Zionism, came to nothing. But as long as we were all there, we wanted to meet again. We invited the gentleman to dinner with the two DNB men. We were all friendly and polite, we had a nice time, we talked about one thing and another, but for practical purposes the trip was a failure.

The SD often mobilized DNB journalists accredited in foreign countries and used them for missions that had more to do with espionage than with journalism.

EICHMANN: Two weeks later we started back on an Italian ship. We had hardly put to sea when I came down with paratyphoid. I spent the whole voyage in the ship's hospital and was discharged in fairly good shape in Bari. That was the pathetic end of what had looked like a promising trip.

LESS: Did you write a report about it? About your trip?

EICHMANN: Oh, yes. A detailed report. Absolutely negative in substance. What else could I have said? I still remember that Heydrich wrote under it in pencil: Good. And his stamp.

LESS: In connection with your statements up to now, I'd like to ask you some questions if you don't mind. You have stated that you were discharged from the Vacuum Oil Company in Austria for reasons of retrenchment.

EICHMANN: That is correct. On the other hand, the German consul in Linz discovered somehow that I had been dismissed because of my membership in the SS.

LESS: In your curriculum vitae you wrote—I quote: "Up until June 1933, I worked for the firm in Upper Austria, Salzburg, and North Tyrol. At that time I was given notice because of membership in the NSDAP." Which of these two versions is correct?

EICHMANN: Before I left Austria for Germany, I was told at the German consulate in Linz that I had been dismissed because of membership in the SS. Since then, I have therefore supposed this to be the more correct version.

LESS: In speaking of your activities, you have many times referred to Jewish emigration, and called it advantageous both to the Jews and to the German government. Is that correct?

EICHMANN: Yes, sir.

LESS: A number of laws and decrees made it impossible for the Jews of Germany, and later of Austria and Czechoslovakia, to practice their professions. Grave financial burdens were imposed on the Jews. There was the flight-of-capital tax [Kapitalfluchtsteuer]; after the Kristallnacht, exorbitant fines were levied on all Jews, and in many cases their property was "Aryanized." Under these circumstances, how can you talk of emigration? Would it not be more accurate to say that they were driven out of the country?

EICHMANN: Yes, of course, strictly speaking, pressure was put on them to emigrate.

A forced emigration of this kind, namely, the mass expulsion of Polish subjects of Jewish faith to their country of origin, impelled Herschel Grynszpan, a seventeen-year-old Polish Jew living in Paris, to assassinate the secretary of the German legation in Paris. In retaliation, the Nazis organized an allegedly spontaneous outburst of popular indignation. On November 9, 1938, Jewish property was destroyed and looted, synagogues were burned, Jews were arrested, herded into concentration camps, brutalized, and killed. This was the Kristallnacht [Night of Broken Glass].

The Jews living in Germany were forced to pay an indemnity of a billion marks. Numerous firms were Aryanized, that is, seized in return for ludicrous compensation and taken over by Nazis, and a decree was promulgated excluding all Jews from economic life.

LESS: Have you read Hitler's *Mein Kampf?*

EICHMANN: Never all of it, and never carefully.

LESS: Were you in agreement with his doctrine?

EICHMANN: When I was still in Austria, on January 30, 1933, I heard Hitler's seizure of power on the radio in some village in the Tyrol, where I happened to be on Vacuum Oil business. I have to admit that I was enthusiastic at the time, because it is my policy now as always to tell the truth. In this seizure of power I saw, with my youthful, relatively youthful eyes and impulses, I saw—I saw a nationalism that appealed to me. Hitler fulminated against Versailles, work and bread were promised, and the promise was kept later on.

But this would take us too far, Herr Hauptmann. At the time I was happy about the whole development, because I thought to myself: Now things will change.

LESS: In other words, you supported Hitler's doctrine at the time.

EICHMANN: Yes, at the time I supported it.

LESS: Had you read the party program?

EICHMANN: The twelve points? Yes, I must have read them, but today I couldn't tell you what they were.

The program of the NSDAP, proclaimed on February 24, 1920, at the Hofbräuhaus in Munich, consisted of twenty-five points. It was never changed and it never affected the history of the party one way or the other.

LESS: How did you feel about the point denying Jews the right to be German citizens?
EICHMANN: When I joined . . . when I joined the NSDAP . . . I didn't give these details . . . these details . . . a thought. And these details were never discussed among, among so-called comrades.
LESS: Have you read Rosenberg's *Myth of the Twentieth Century?*
EICHMANN: No, I have not read it. To tell the truth, I never read any books about National Socialism either before or after. Before going into the SD, I didn't read at all—much to the dismay of my father, who often pointed out to me that he had an excellent library in the house, with all the classics, which he had built up in the course of his life, evidently to no purpose. When I was with the SD, it wasn't those books that I read but others, as I have already told you in part. I read specifically Jewish books; I read books about Freemasonry. I doubt if I read any other book in all that time—novels, for instance. I've never in all my life read crime thrillers or love stories, I still don't.
LESS: Those books you read about the Jews—were they critical?
EICHMANN: I only read books written by Jews. No others were of any use to me in my—in my study. My mind was not clouded by any previous knowledge.

LESS: Did you know that Hitler accused the Jews of causing the defeat of Germany in the First World War?

EICHMANN: At that time I belonged to the category of people who form no opinions of their own.

LESS: Did you read *The Protocols of the Elders of Zion?*

EICHMANN: No, I did not, but I heard about it and I couldn't imagine what it could be. When I asked Mildenstein and he described it as rubbish, I accepted that opinion and I disposed of it in more or less the same words—I remember that clearly—at the SD school in Bernau.

The Protocols are the alleged resolutions of a nonexistent Jewish conspiracy to subject the entire world to Jewish domination. This notorious forgery figured prominently in the propaganda of Streicher and his school.

LESS: When did you leave the Evangelical Church?

EICHMANN: It must have been in 1937. In those years, in 1935, I think, it had become fashionable for SD members to resign from the party . . . from the Church, I mean of course. But when it came to religion, I refused to be pressured, partly because I had always been deeply rooted in the Church, for one thing because my father had been an elder of the Evangelical congregation in Linz for years, and I didn't want to do that to my old father. Besides, I said to myself—especially in the years when I was reading scientific works on religion at the SD—I said to myself: This is a decision that calls for careful thought. And in 1935 I was married in church, though they tried to dissuade me. I wasn't forbidden, they just made fun of me. My wife herself wouldn't have married any other way, because she comes of a religious, that's right, a solidly Catholic peasant family.

LESS: Then why did you leave?

EICHMANN: More and more I came to the conclusion that God can't possibly be as small as in the Bible stories. I thought I had found my own belief. And I read Schopenhauer, who says the way of religious faith is safer and the way of freedom is a dangerous way, which the individual must perpetually work out for himself. I said to myself: The God I believe in is greater than the Christian God. Because I believe in a great and powerful God, who created the universe and keeps it in motion. No one influenced me—my wife tried to hold me back, but then I stopped telling her anything about my work. —And one fine day I went to the courthouse and had my records changed.

LESS: Did you join the German Church?

EICHMANN: No. I left the Church of my own free will, not because it was the thing to do, or because anyone made me. And I did not join any other church.

LESS: In your official records, your religion is down as theist. Doesn't that apply to the German Church?

EICHMANN: Everyone who left the Church at that time called himself a theist, because he had to call himself something.

There was never any such thing as a German Church. But within the Evangelical Church there was a splinter group of "German Christians." There was also a non-Christian, predominantly pantheist group that called itself the German Faith Movement [Deutsche Glaubensbewegung], but it never attracted many members. Since the party propaganda machine was constantly reviling atheist intellectuals and godless Marxists, the people who left the Church could not very well put down "none" under "religion."

LESS: Were you a loyal, unconditionally obedient SS man?

EICHMANN: Yes. I can say I was. I had taken the oath, and I obeyed orders. In the first years I had no conflicts, no inner conflicts of any kind. I sat at my desk and did my work. My unconditional, my absolute allegiance underwent a change when I . . . when the . . . the . . . the so-called solution of the Jewish question became more violent—I mean, that is—when the gassing and shooting started. I made no secret of the fact and I said—yes, I believe I said . . . to my superior, Gruppenführer Müller . . . I said, that is, I said, this isn't what I imagined, it probably isn't what any of us imagined, because it's not a political solution. We were still talking about a political solution . . . up until then, that was the approved line. But this wasn't a political solution. And then I . . .

LESS: In what terms did you state this opinion?

EICHMANN: I said the exact same words I've just said, the same sentence, when I came back from Minsk and saw what was going on. And from Chelm and those places, that's what I said.

LESS: Did you unconditionally support the National Socialist philosophy?

EICHMANN: Yes and no. In those years, the first years, I didn't give the National Socialist philosophy and such things a thought. In those first years, what mattered to me, as I've already said, was work and bread for seven million people, an Autobahn, and the fight against Versailles—in those matters my attitude was unconditional. And later on, in my military service—to all intents and purposes it was military service, and at first I liked it, until the time came when I wanted to get out and go into private industry but found myself behind a desk instead. And in this desk work, Herr Hauptmann, in the first place you weren't asked, and in the second place you didn't waste your time thinking about unconditional allegiances, unconditional loyalty, because you threw yourself head over heels into your—into your—work.

LESS: In other words, you were a convinced National Socialist, a loyal SS man, true to the oath you had taken. How then do you explain your contention that you have never hated the Jews and were never an anti-Semite?

EICHMANN: That is true, Herr Hauptmann. I would certainly have had conflicts sooner, in Dachau if for instance, instead of being in SS Battalion I, in the Austrian SS, that is, I'd been behind the barbed wire, serving as a concentration-camp guard. But since for many years I had no contact with such things, I didn't worry my head about them. Because I didn't have to do them.

LESS: But you must have had anti-Jewish opinions. Because they were required. A large part of the program had to do with the Jews.

EICHMANN: But not in the early period, Herr Hauptmann. In the early period the Jewish problem wasn't the main thing. What interested us in Austria was work and bread, freedom, an end to servitude.

LESS: But wasn't hatred of the Jews a leitmotiv running all through Hitler's *Mein Kampf*?

EICHMANN: That is possible. I've told you I never read it carefully, I never read it through, I didn't need to. Yes, Herr Hauptmann, of course there was hatred of the Jews in it. But in those days there were lots of party members with Jewish relatives by blood or marriage. I myself knew an SS-Scharführer who was a Jew.

LESS: What was his name?

EICHMANN: I don't know. But he came to see me one day in Berlin and asked me what he should do. He had been an Oberscharführer during the fighting days. I said to him: Good God, man, there's nothing I can do for you. The only advice I can give you is: Clear out, go to Switzerland or somewhere else, because it's no good for you here, it's no good, it's hopeless. Then he asked me to give the border

(41)

station between Austria and Switzerland instructions, so he could be sure of crossing safely without papers. So I instructed them to let So-and-So pass. This was a technique I had taken over from Section VI, which sent its agents across that way. I had adopted that technique.

LESS: As a loyal SS man, shouldn't you have reported him?

EICHMANN: Yes, I should have. I shouldn't have let my own cousin leave the country, and I shouldn't have let the Jews emigrate to Hungary unmolested. It struck me—pardon me if I give my private opinion—it struck me as too . . . as too persnickety to report these little things that I did on the side. In Vienna, for instance, I let out a Jewish couple as a favor to my uncle, who reminded me that he had helped me get a job with the Vacuum Oil Company, where I'd always been well treated, even though Popper, the president, was a Jew, and so was Weiss, the vice-president, and possibly Kannhäuser, the Linz manager, and certainly Blum, the Salzburg manager.

LESS: Do you remember the name of this Jewish couple?

EICHMANN: I don't know. No, I don't know.

LESS: You say that you submitted a detailed report to your superiors after your trip to Palestine.

EICHMANN: I can't remember today what I wrote, because not being able to visit Israel, I mean what was then Palestine, stripped the whole mission of its interest. And it's possible that the report was written not by me but by Hagen, my superior. Yes, it comes back to me now. It wasn't me, it was Hagen that wrote it.

LESS: If Hagen wrote it . . .

EICHMANN: I must have signed it, too. Yes.

LESS: You also said that your sympathies went more to the Jews than to the Arabs. Is that true?

EICHMANN: That is true. And in Haifa I didn't pick an Arab cab driver, I picked a Jewish cab driver to take me up Mt. Carmel.

LESS: Was this sympathy expressed in your report?

EICHMANN: I don't remember that, Herr Hauptmann. But it's quite possible, because I always said—and since then I've said it fifty or a hundred times—that in Palestine it's best to deal only with Jews, because an Arab is always holding out his hand and the one who gives him the last piaster is his friend.

LESS: I'm going to show you a sheaf of photostats connected with this report on the journey of SS-Hauptscharführer Eichmann and Stabs-Oberscharführer Hagen to Palestine and Egypt, begun on November 4, 1937.

EICHMANN: Yes. Hagen . . . as I've told you . . . Hagen [wrote] all that . . . It's not my report. It's Hagen's report.

LESS: But the report must have gone through your hands, you must have corrected it. These corrections, for instance, aren't they in your handwriting?

EICHMANN: No, that's Hagen's writing.

LESS: This, too?

EICHMANN: Yes, Hagen's . . . corrections —I can't be sure at the moment. That's a repetition . . . The T could be my T . . . Let's see now . . . Yes, that D could be mine. Yes, I recognize the D, it's my correction. Undoubtedly—unquestionably my correction.

LESS: Now I'm going to quote from the report: "Seen from the economic angle, Palestine presents a deplorable picture. We were told that most payments are made by bills of exchange, which no one redeems, but which nevertheless, though completely devaluated, are passed from hand to hand, because the protesting of bills of exchange has seldom brought results. Drafts on the German Templar banks are regarded as the safest means of payment, since those are the only solvent banks. This financial chaos is attributed to the fact that the Jews swindle one another and are unable to conclude their business deals with Aryans because there are not enough of them. Typical of the total incapacity of

Jews to maintain an orderly economy is the fact that in Jerusalem alone there are said to be forty Jewish banks, which live by cheating their fellow Jews."

Would you say that this passage expresses your pro-Jewish attitude?

EICHMANN: This whole thing is not by me, I solemnly swear it. Hagen dictated this document. Then, as I see here, he gave it to me to look through, and I corrected it. Hagen composed and dictated the whole thing.

LESS: In this report you have the following to say of the German Jews in Palestine: "Better to go back to Germany and be sent to a reeducation camp than to stay in Palestine." What did you mean by "reeducation camp"? Are reeducation camps identical with concentration camps?

EICHMANN: Herr Hauptmann, I don't know who wrote that.

LESS: My question was: What were reeducation camps? Were they concentration camps?

EICHMANN: Nothing else can be meant. There wasn't anything else.

LESS: If this report stemmed primarily from Hagen, who was your superior, it should logically have been titled: "Report on the Journey to Palestine and Egypt of Stabs-Oberscharführer Hagen and SS-Hauptscharführer Eichmann. Since you are named first, since it is you who were actually—

EICHMANN: Invited.

LESS: . . . who were the actual initiator of the trip, this whole document must have been approved by you. The words, the written words, may be Hagen's, but the content, the substance, the opinions must also have been yours, since the responsibility . . .

EICHMANN: Undoubtedly. Yes, today I am bound to say . . . I must bear the responsibility. I have no choice.

LESS: Would you say that the passages I have quoted show the Jews in a favorable light?

EICHMANN: No, those passages do not show them in a favorable light.

LESS: A proposition was made to you that fifty thousand Jews should be allowed to emigrate each year, each with a thousand pounds sterling. In a document rejecting this proposal, you give two reasons. I quote: "(a) Our purpose is not to have Jewish capital transferred abroad but primarily to encourage the emigration of indigent Jews. Since the above-said annual emigration would primarily strengthen the Jews in Palestine, this plan must be rejected in view of the fact that German national policy opposes the establishment of an independent state in Palestine. (b) Increased transfer of wealth to the Near and Middle East would mean the loss of those countries to the German Reich as sources of hard currency."

EICHMANN: This was exactly the position of the Reich Ministry of the Economy, which was consulted in this connection.

LESS: Now I will quote a record of your impressions on your journey through Rumania on the way to Palestine: "The rural population has lately been up in arms against the Jews, who travel around the country swindling the peasants in the usual way." Wouldn't you agree that this quotation is worthy of the *Stürmer*?

EICHMANN: Yes, but I didn't write that either.

LESS: No, but—as we said before—you approved it.

EICHMANN: I can't ... I ... I ... can't defend myself, because ... because I have no proof to offer.

LESS: What directives did your superiors give you before your trip to Palestine? Who was your immediate superior at the time?

EICHMANN: My superior was Six, Dr. Six. Directives, Herr Hauptmann, one can't really speak of directives.

LESS: Weren't you given this directive: to make a thorough study of the Jewish colonization effort in Palestine, knowledge of which seemed important, primarily because once a Jewish state or a Jewish-administered Palestine was proclaimed, German foreign policy would be faced with a new enemy, which would play a crucial part in the political development of the Near East. Furthermore, the establishment of a Jewish state would render the minority question acute in connection with the Jews living in Germany.

EICHMANN: Yes, that was the position of the Foreign Office—for a long time it was.

LESS: Then it may be assumed that the instructions given you before your trip were along those lines?

EICHMANN: That was none of my concern. Hagen was my superior. Our whole official mission was covered, so to speak, by his discussions with Six.

LESS: Still, when you received your instructions, you must have been called in and told: These are the guidelines, this is your mission.

EICHMANN: No! I am sure that was not the case. Certainly not. It wasn't customary. And there was no need for it. In an organization like ours, operated along military lines, the commanding officer gets the instructions. And that was Hagen.

LESS: And after the trip your work in Berlin went on as usual?

EICHMANN: Yes, sir. In January 1938, there began to be unmistakable signs of an imminent action in Austria. The action itself did not take place until March, but for weeks in advance every able-bodied man they could find was put to work in three shifts: writing file cards for an enormous circular card file, several yards in diameter, which a man sitting on a piano stool could operate and find any card he wanted thanks to a system of punch holes. All information important for Austria was entered on these cards. The data was taken from annual reports, handbooks, the newspapers of all the political parties, membership files; in short, everything imaginable. All the material that the so-called V-men had brought from Austria to Germany after the party was suppressed in Austria. Each card carried name, address, party membership, whether Jew, Freemason, or practicing Catholic or Protestant; whether politically active, whether this or whether that. During that period, our regular work was put on ice.

On March 11, 1938, Kurt von Schuschnigg, the Austrian Chancellor, resigned. He declared that he was doing so under German pressure, and was yielding to force because he did not wish German blood to be shed. On March 12, German troops marched into Austria, welcomed by jubilant crowds. The NSDAP had been suppressed on June 19, 1933, and had been prohibited ever since. Since the country was threatened from without by Hitler's demands for annexation and from within by the increasing activity of the illegal National Socialists, the governments of England, France, and Italy issued a declaration on February 17, 1934, guaranteeing Austrian independence. How justified this decision was is shown by the putsch of the Austrian National Socialists, who on July 25, 1934, occupied the Vienna chancellery and murdered the Chancellor, Dr. Engelbert Dollfuss. The putsch failed, but encouraged by Hitler's success in Germany, pro-Nazi sentiment grew steadily. In the end, the government had so few supporters that it could offer no resistance to National Socialist aggression.

EICHMANN: One fine day an SD team for Austria was sent to Vienna. I was sure I'd be chosen to go along, but I was not. Eager as I was to go home, there was nothing I could do about it. Orders are orders; you've got to obey, and that's that.

But about a week later I suddenly received an order to

report to the SD section in Vienna. Temporary detached service, I was told. Later on, it became a transfer. The SD section had set up its offices in the residence of a branch of the Rothschild family. I was assigned a small room with nothing in it but a desk, and told to take charge of Jewish affairs.

EICHMANN: I didn't know my way around Vienna. I had only been there three or four times as a child, just visiting relatives. The first thing I did was go to the headquarters of the Secret State Police and ask them who could give me information about Jewish affairs. Then I was—oh, I forgot to tell you, I'd meanwhile been promoted, on January 30, 1938, to Untersturmführer—and then I was taken to see a so-called Journalbeamter [duty officer], an old term from old Austria, a jurist, who introduced himself as Dr. Ebner. At the time he was still in Austrian uniform . . . of the Security Police. I told him I'd been sent down there to take charge of Jewish affairs, I had no idea what was going on and would he fill me in on the situation.

LESS: Well, what was the situation at the end of March 1938, exactly two weeks after the so-called seizure of power in Vienna?

EICHMANN: It was very simple. He told me they were all under lock and key, the Jewish officials were all in detention. For the first time, I was thrown into practical activity. Up until then, I'd been sitting at a desk. I told Dr. Ebner that in the Old Reich—as we called it at the time—the policy was to encourage emigration. Everything that favored emigration was allowed. In Germany, I told him, the Zionist movement was allowed freedom of movement, and the religious organizations were given their head, as long as they supported emigration. And I told him that somehow

(49)

Jewish political life had to be set in motion again in Vienna and Ostmark, as Austria was then called. He gave me a list of the former Jewish political functionaries, who were under arrest, and I asked him to bring me certain ones whom I judged to be the ranking leaders. You see, I wanted to talk to them, but I was still in the SD and had no authority to send for anybody on my own. When I wanted something, I had to go down on my knees to the Secret State Police. I don't know who it was who came; a few gentlemen, but they struck me as too old, not sufficiently energetic or intelligent. Anyway, that was my impression. Until I came across Dr. Löwenherz, Dr. Richard Löwenherz. Those first gentlemen, I can still see them standing in front of me, were let go, because they hadn't been locked up . . . hadn't been locked up . . . to stay locked up. They had been arrested in the excitement of the first week, during the days of upheaval, of revolution.

I gave Dr. Löwenherz paper and pencil and said: "Please go back for one more night and write up a memo telling me how you would organize this whole thing, how you would run it. Object: stepped-up emigration."

Here I must mention an incident that I've never forgotten. Dr. Löwenherz had been brought in from detention, so naturally he was excited and just at first he said something that was untrue. Anger got the better of me, I lost control—which very seldom happened—I don't know what got into me—I let myself go and slapped him in the face. It wasn't the kind of slap that hurt, I'm sure of that, I haven't got that much muscle; but I never concealed, never concealed that incident. Later on, when I was already a Sturmbannführer or Obersturmbannführer, I spoke of this incident in the presence of my subordinate officers and of Dr. Löwenherz, and begged his pardon. I did that deliberately, that's right, you must have ample means of checking, because in the department I ran later, I did not tolerate physical violence. That was why I apologized in uniform and in the presence of my staff.

From March 14 on, the supreme political authority in Austria was Josef Bürckel, Gauleiter of the Saar and the Palatinate. To the dismay of the Austrian party leaders, already devoured by envy of one another, all the important posts were occupied by "Piefkes"—as the Austrians called North Germans, especially Prussians—sent from Berlin. All the German anti-Jewish laws and decrees now became valid for "Ostmark." New ones were continually added. On March 28, the Jewish congregations lost their corporation status and were obliged to register as private associations. Persons regarded as Jews according to the Nuremberg Laws were obliged to declare all property, holdings, and liquidities to the authorities, and in August all Jews were required to indicate their origin by appending the first name Israel or Sarah to their family names.

EICHMANN: The next day, this Dr. Löwenherz brought me his draft. I found it excellent and we immediately took action on his suggestions. Dr. Löwenherz himself asked to be appointed director of the Jewish community, and I backed his proposal. I myself could not make the appointment, only the Secret State Police could do that. As was to be expected, the first days of the reorganization of Jewish life brought requests from Dr. Löwenherz and his associates. If I remember correctly, the funds that were still extant but under sequester were returned to their owners.

Youth organizations were approved. The community's education section was revived. Religious life was restored. In short, conditions were normalized, but of course everything was subordinated to the promotion of emigration. Emigration increased as the Jews wishing to emigrate became more nervous, more intent on escaping the pressure of the party and also in a certain sense of the government authorities. Because of this nervousness, many useless applications were made; it must be said, however, that from sadistic motives certain government officials, and unofficial employees as well, went out of their way to make it harder for a Jew wishing to emigrate. He'd be sent home on some stupid pretext.

One day Dr. Löwenherz and some of his associates said to me: Hauptsturmführer—or was I an Obersturmführer at the time?—this can't go on. And they suggested that I should somehow centralize the work, or that I myself should speak with certain officials and arrange to make things easier for Jewish petitioners. That same afternoon an idea took shape in my mind: a conveyor belt. The initial application and all the rest of the required papers are put on at one end, and the passport falls off at the other end. I then suggested to Regierungsdirektor Dr. Stahlecker, my immediate superior, that he should persuade Reich Commissar Bürckel to issue a decree establishing in Vienna a Central Office for Jewish Emigration to which the government departments—Police Presidium, Finance Ministry, State Police, Currency Control, in short, all departments concerned—should send representatives. They would all sit side by side at this long conveyor belt, under the supervision of a member of the Vienna section of the SD; namely, myself.

After the decree was signed, vetoes came in from Berlin, because no such thing had ever been seen in the whole history of the German bureaucracy. They compared me . . . in Berlin there was talk of a mini-council of state, where delegates of all the different departments would work together under police supervision. But these difficulties were ironed out in Berlin. In Vienna we didn't even notice these difficulties. All the departments worked together.

The Israelite community was also present at the conveyor belt, represented by six to fourteen delegates, depending on the amount of business to be handled. Some days we had as many as a thousand cases. A lot of people tried to make a good thing out of this stepped-up emigration. For instance, there were the lawyers of the National Socialist Jurists Association, who didn't want the Jews to come to the conveyor belt unattended; they wanted to be brought in as counsel, for an appropriate fee, it goes without saying. And there were the Aryanizers, who swooped down on Jewish businesses, ready to take them over.

It was therefore suggested that a so-called emigration fund should be built up from property that emigrants were not permitted to take with them, and that it should be entitled to incorporation.

LESS: Who financed—who provided the money for this emigration fund?

EICHMANN: The money came out of the property that wealthy Jews had to hand over. And I sent Dr. Löwenherz and other gentlemen, I don't remember their names, abroad at regular intervals to work out new avenues of emigration and to bring back foreign currency by giving lectures, which they did. I made an arrangement with the Vienna exchange office that the foreign currency brought back from abroad by these Jewish officials should be tax exempt. This foreign currency was to be sold by the Israelite community under the supervision of the exchange office at a rate that varied with the wealth of the emigrating Jew. If he had a great many schillings or marks, Dr. Löwenherz would demand a rate, let's say, of twenty marks to the dollar. With a poorer emigrant, he would demand proportionately less. In any case, the emigrant could buy his presentation money [the sum he would be required to show on arriving in certain foreign countries as proof that he would not become a public charge] from the community with internal currency,

(53)

and the community received a very, a relatively high yield for its foreign currency, with which to help finance its operations.

LESS: Was Dr. Löwenherz's dollar exchange rate fixed by the Finance Ministry?

EICHMANN: It was fixed by Dr. Löwenherz, because he knew the financial circumstances of the Jewish candidates for emigration.

Before a Jew could leave Germany, he was once again thoroughly milked. He was required to prove that he owed nothing to the state and that he had not made a secret of any property, by producing a tax-clearance certificate; and he was subjected to still other exactions. Because of the chronic shortage of hard currency in the Reich, he was made to surrender all foreign currency, and he needed special authorization to take German marks out of the country. A Jew selling his belongings was often beaten down by threats. If he wished to take valuable furniture with him, authorization was required. Since the host countries were unwilling to accept poor immigrants who would immediately become public charges, an immigrant was required to produce a certain sum of money in hard currency. The strict currency control prevailing in the Reich made it impossible to buy foreign currency from a bank. Consequently, the emigrant was obliged to buy at the extortionate rate which—under Eichmann's instructions—the Jewish community demanded of him.

LESS: Wasn't it the plan that the wealthier Jews should pay for the poorer ones?

EICHMANN: That's right, yes yes, that's the correct way to look at it.

LESS: In other words, this method was not Löwenherz's idea; it was imposed by you and your offices.

EICHMANN: Yes, Herr Hauptmann. In a way, yes. The money was brought in by Löwenherz and other functionaries, or was donated by foreign sources. This money should have been handed over to the Reichsbank and to no one else; then Löwenherz would have received the equivalent in marks, according to the value of the dollar. But Dr. Löwenherz had said to me: We can't pay our team any more, we need more and more men. We have no bureau to take care of the poor Jews. If we were exempted from the obligation to turn in these dollars, we could sell them. I said to myself: This is perfect. With or without these dollars, the Reich will be no richer or poorer, but with them the apparatus of the Vienna community will be able to muddle along. That's how the system got started at the time. Later on, though, we had endless difficulties. People started saying: Just the Jews, of all people, don't bother to turn in their foreign currency.

LESS: First, the Jews were compelled to raise foreign currency outside of Germany. Then at home they had to pay a staggering price for it. In the end, no one profited but the Reich government. The Jews were made poorer by having to pay thirty to forty thousand marks for a thousand pounds sterling, the true value of which was twelve thousand marks.

EICHMANN: That is true, Herr Hauptmann. Yes, that is clear, quite clear.

LESS: In June 1939, Dr. Löwenherz came to you again to complain about Jews being evicted from their homes. Absolutely impossible quarters were assigned to them. And Jews were being beaten up if they ventured into the few parks that were set aside for them. Dr. Löwenherz pleaded with you to do something about this.

EICHMANN: Lodgings, of course, were not in my department. Neither were beatings in parks. But you see that he came to me with all his problems.

LESS: Once more, Dr. Löwenherz called your attention to the

atmosphere of panic among the Jews, caused by arrests and evictions. The community was paralyzed, because it was impossible to obtain the necessary papers and permits in so short a time. The most desperate of the Jews, those who were Polish subjects or stateless, tried to leave German territory illegally, to escape to Poland or Belgium. Both countries sent them back, and their return trip from the border caused the welfare agency of the Vienna community unnecessary expense.

EICHMANN: About that, I have only this to say: It was none of my doing that they were deported or arrested. That wasn't in my department at the time. I might also state that the Central Office for Jewish Emigration was a first in the German administrative machine. This brought us numerous visitors from various departments in the so-called Old Reich, who came to Vienna for this express purpose. Heydrich, who was then head of the Security Police, came, too. The so-called Reich Kristallnacht—I don't know what else to call it—occurred during the period when this Central Office was active.

LESS: Do you remember exactly when?

EICHMANN: I regret to say I do not. It must—I believe—have been in the autumn. It must have been in 1938. The incidents of that night were not the work of the police or the SD. I still remember that I went to the community the next day to form an idea of the damage, because this, too, had a very bad effect on emigration. I can still see a certain Oberführer or Brigadeführer of the General SS picking up a typewriter, and before I could even ask him whether or not he was supposed to be performing police functions, the typewriter came crashing to the floor. Senseless destruction. I told him I was the head of the Central Office. At that he called me a—he used an obscene word. I told him government orders were not to obstruct emigration in any way and that I would report him to my superior officer, the head of the Security Police and the SD. Then he threw me out. I made the report. What came of it, I don't know.

It is impossible to believe that the former Jewish-affairs specialist of the SD and the Gestapo did not remember the date of the Kristallnacht, that state-organized, nationwide pogrom. Whenever that night was mentioned in the course of this hearing, Eichmann made a show of ignorance.

EICHMANN: After that night, we had more work on our hands than ever. By the time of my transfer to Prague, the number of Jews who had emigrated from Austria had risen to 150,000. Altogether, I believe I can remember, the figure came to 224,000 or 234,000.

In the spring of 1939, the so-called Protectorate of Bohemia-Moravia was established. Dr. Stahlecker, who had been promoted to SS-Oberführer in the meantime, was sent from Vienna, in his capacity as inspector of the Security Police and the SD, to take command of the Prague Security Police and SD. I was sure that once Dr. Stahlecker took up his new post, he would put through my transfer to Prague as soon as possible. Around April 1939, I was ordered to Prague. At first, I was reluctant to leave Vienna. When you've set up that kind of office, you don't like to give it up. I had no difficulty with the Jewish functionaries. And I don't think any of them would have complained about me. Not even today. I certainly don't believe so, because they knew I wasn't a Jew-hater. I've never been an anti-Semite, and I've never made a secret of the fact. I'm not trying to praise myself. I just want to say that our collaboration at the Central Office was decently businesslike. As a child in elementary school I had a Jewish friend and the last time we met we went for a walk together on the

Landstrasse in Linz. I already had the party badge in my buttonhole and he thought nothing of it.

Meanwhile, Hauptsturmführer Rolf Günther and the future Hauptsturmführer Alois Brunner took over the Central Office in Vienna. I wasn't in charge there anymore, only in Prague. The Prague Central Office was much smaller than the one in Vienna, but the system was exactly the same. The functionaries of the Prague Jewish organizations went to Vienna and the functionaries of the Vienna Jewish organizations came to Prague. That way, I had no need to take a hand; Prague simply followed the example of Vienna. That alone made for a smooth start, though I must also say that there was no one in Prague with Dr. Löwenherz's energy, far from it. The people in Prague were calmer and more easygoing, and for that reason neither side registered the same success as in Vienna. But it is also possible that it was too late for our foreign missions to accomplish much, because in many places most of the cream had been skimmed off by our agents working out of Vienna. In that respect, the gentlemen in Prague had a harder time of it. In Prague, too, an emigration fund was set up.

LESS: Who were your Jewish associates there?

EICHMANN: I got along best with Dr. Murmelstein, the rabbi. There was also a Dr. Weinmann and a Herr Epstein, I think his name was Epstein. Maybe it was their Czech accent that kept us from—how shall I say—making contact. Just with Dr. Murmelstein it didn't take long. Later on, it was he, Dr. Weinmann, and some other functionaries [of the Jewish organizations] they themselves chose who set up Theresienstadt. With Dr. Stahlecker I had a good personal relationship that went beyond our duty hours. We met privately on Sunday mornings, and naturally we spoke, among many other things, about the possibility of a solution, a political solution, because that was the beginning and end

(5 8)

of my whole career in the SD. Theresienstadt, where, as the Protectorate government had decided, the Jews of Bohemia and Moravia were to be concentrated, was much too small for the purpose. Give the Jews an autonomous territory, then the whole problem will be solved to the satisfaction of all. As long as the British are in Palestine and immigration is strictly limited, another territory must be made available. The Polish campaign was succeeding beyond all expectation. I don't remember whether the idea came from Stahlecker or from me; anyway, someone had it. The idea was that as soon as possible we, that is, the SD, should set aside as large a territory as possible as a protectorate.

LESS: Was that so urgent in the middle of the war?

EICHMANN: The war had reduced the possibilities of emigration. On the other hand, the Gauleiters, the Propaganda Ministry, in other words, Goebbels, and the Office of the Führer's Deputy, in other words, Bormann—were putting every possible pressure on us. They did not communicate directly with men of my rank. They addressed themselves to the chief, Himmler. He was the kind of man who always wanted to oblige the highly placed—then highly placed—leaders. It was considered the right thing to meddle in Jewish affairs. No sooner had Hitler made a speech—and he invariably touched on the Jewish question—than every party or government department felt that it was up to them to do something. And then Himmler authorized each one to attend to it. He'd pass the order on to Heydrich, head of the Security Police and the SD, who would pass it on to Müller, and then it came to me.

LESS: Who was Müller?

EICHMANN: He was my immediate superior, promoted to Gruppenführer a little later. I'll come back to Müller's Reich Security Headquarters. May I now continue where

I left off; namely, with Poland. Yes, there we were beginning to see daylight. One day my chief, Dr. Stahlecker, whom I've already mentioned, and I took a trip to Poland. We went as far as the San in southeastern Poland, a tributary of the Vistula.

When we got to the demarcation line, some Russian police guards led us a short way through Russian territory. We finally came to Nisko on the San. Nisko was in the Radom government; this I only knew from Jewish sources, because I had sent out some Jews to investigate settlement possibilities in that district. We went in; we saw an enormous territory, river, villages, markets, small towns, and we said to ourselves: This is perfect, why not resettle the Poles, seeing there's so much resettling being done in any case, and then move Jews into this big territory. The Eastern Jews are remarkably skillful craftsmen. If industries are set up, if Jews are brought in from Austria, Germany, Czechoslo —Bohemia and Moravia . . . Protectorate, plus agriculture— that might easily provide a temporary solution, sure to be good for quite a while. That would relieve the worst of the pressure. It would benefit all concerned. It would be a political success for the Reich government. And it would take care of one point in the party program: solution of the Jewish problem. We, the Security Police, would have nothing more to worry about. One thing at least would be settled. So Stahlecker submitted the proposition to Heydrich. It was approved, and I received an order to send five hundred, or maybe a thousand—I can't be sure of the numbers at this late date—Jewish artisans with a few train-loads of material to Nisko to put up a village of shacks, and using it as a center to settle Jews in proportion as the inhabitants were moved out.

LESS: On October 10, 1939, Dr. Löwenherz in Vienna was ordered to organize the first shipment of Jews to Poland. The community was to select a thousand to twelve hundred able-bodied men, mostly artisans, especially carpenters and mechanics. They were to take woodworking equipment with them, saws, axes, hammers, nails—

EICHMANN: Right. That was for Nisko!

LESS: . . . and food for three or four weeks. The report goes on to say that Dr. Löwenherz requested authorization to see SS-Hauptsturmführer Eichmann and state his misgivings—

EICHMANN: Right.

LESS: . . . about this shipment of Jews to Poland.

EICHMANN: Right . . .

LESS: On October 27, Dr. Löwenherz saw Hauptsturmführer Eichmann. Of course, he said, the community realized that it had to carry out the missions assigned to it.

EICHMANN: Right . . .

LESS: But met with difficulties among the Jewish population.

EICHMANN: Just as preparations were in full swing, the post of Governor General was created in the person of Frank. We called him the Polish Frank to distinguish him from K. H. Frank, the State Secretary in Prague. That was the beginning of heavy-handed obstructionism; a big tug-of-war set in. Frank raised a big hullabaloo in Berlin; he wanted to solve his own Jewish question and he didn't want any Jews sent to his Government General. The ones who were there had to clear out immediately. Frank ordered SS-Brigadeführer Streckenbach, commander of the Security Police and the SD in Cracow, to arrest me the moment I set foot in the Government General. Streckenbach told me about it. He had no right to arrest me without the authorization of his superior and mine, Heydrich. In his anger, Frank had probably overlooked this fact. Well, that put an end to our dream of a temporary solution.

If in those days Dr. Löwenherz of Vienna hoped to obtain help and sympathy from Eichmann, he would no longer have found him in Prague; he would have had to go to Berlin. With this change of function and of scene, the stage was set for Eichmann's future career of murder. Thus far, Eichmann, as an SD functionary, had been without executive powers. Now he was incorporated into RSHA, Reich Security Headquarters, which was established on September 27, 1939, and had as its function—to cite a decree issued by Himmler—"to merge the central offices of the Security Police and the SD." From then on, he enjoyed the advantages of a hybrid position: as convenient, he could act as a party functionary by virtue of his position in the SD or as a Gestapo official, endowed with executive powers.

EICHMANN: At the beginning of October 1939, I believe it was, Hauptsturmführer Günther, my permanent representative at the Vienna Central Office, and I were ordered by telegraph to report to the future SS-Gruppenführer Müller, head of the Secret State Police, in Berlin. Supposedly, I was to brief Göring on the Jewish question. In reality, Günther and I were transferred to Berlin to set up a Central Office for Jewish Emigration. I pointed out that I was indispensable in Prague and tried to get out of it on various pretexts. For instance, I had just been transferred from Vienna to Prague. They didn't say yes and they didn't say no, and I was beginning to think I had won out. But a few days later I received a telegram informing me—this time explicitly—that I was to be transferred as of such and such a date. After delegating my duties in the Protectorate, I went to Berlin with Hauptsturmführer Günther. The headquarters assigned to us were in Kurfürstenstrasse, number 116, I think it was—a building that had formerly belonged to some Jewish institution. There had also been a restaurant in it. The place was a complex of marble stairways and enormous rooms. It would be hard to imagine anything more unsuitable for administrative quarters, but we managed to set up a business office. Little by little, we brought in the people we needed from Prague and Vienna to set up a conveyor belt of the kind already functioning in Prague and Vienna. A Dr. Eppstein of the Reich Association of Jews in Germany [Reichsvereinigung der Juden in Deutschland]—that, I believe, was the name of the official umbrella organization—had roughly the same function in Berlin as Dr. Löwenherz in Vienna. The government departments concerned sent their delegates and the work got started. Of course, it was late in the day, I'm referring to the shutdown of emigration that would become definitive with the onset of war against the Soviet Union. Already, emigration had become exceedingly difficult, and as far as I know, the only avenue that remained open was to the south. And also to the east via Rumania. At the Central Office, in short, we were hanging on by the skin of our teeth. The mood, I might say, was one of discouragement on both sides. With the Jews, because it was really hard to find any possibilities of emigration worth mentioning. On our side, because nothing was going on and we weren't getting any callers at our office.

LESS: But wasn't it one of your duties to clear Vienna, at least, of Jews by the end of 1940?

EICHMANN: Not only Vienna, Herr Hauptmann. I had been given all sorts of deadlines and I had to proceed accordingly —at this point, I can't help saying that it has always been easy to give orders. But these deadlines were never met, because the implementation of our program depended on many factors, which went far beyond my sphere of action.

LESS: Now let me read from a report of the Vienna Central Office. "On December 2, 1939, Dr. Löwenherz reported to Hauptsturmführer Eichmann"—he must have gone to see you in Berlin—"that the American Joint Distribution Committee had informed him that foreign exchange would be supplied only on the basis of continued emigration . . . If, from March 1940 on, shipments of Jews to Poland were resumed, the payments would stop . . . Hauptsturmführer Eichmann authorized Dr. Löwenherz to inform the Joint that the shipments to Poland would be stopped if the Joint declared its readiness to supply the community with foreign exchange until the end of 1940, and if the community committed itself to inducing a corresponding number of Jews to emigrate, so that the emigration program might be liquidated by the end of October 1940."

EICHMANN: I communicated these conditions to Dr. Löwenherz in Berlin. From then on, I did nothing in the Secret State Police office there without clearing it with the head of Section IV. I no longer had to consult the inspector in Vienna or the commanding officer in Prague. I must certainly at that time have approached Heydrich, not orally, but in writing, through the head of Section IV. I said: We will get so and so much foreign exchange if the shipments of Jews to Poland are stopped. The answer seems to have been: No more shipments. At about that time there was a big shakeup at the Secret State Police, and I was put in charge of Bureau IV B 4. Evidently Müller said to himself: They have nothing to do in their emigration office, I can cut down on personnel. That was the Jewish office, which up until then had been located at 8 Prinz-Albrecht-Strasse, along with Section IV. Himmler and Heydrich under him were my top superiors. Section IV at Security Police Headquarters was headed by Gruppenführer Müller. Between him and my department there was yet another Gruppenleiter for Group B. Naturally, all papers had to go through him to be countersigned, but he was not exactly burdened with knowledge of what we were doing, so I always tried to go directly to Müller. Altogether, Section IV had roughly from eighteen to twenty-two bureaus. For lack of space, the bureau assigned to me stayed on Kurfürsten-strasse. In addition to Günther, I had a few men from Vienna and Prague at the Central Office for Jewish Emigration. In taking over Bureau IV B 4 from the Secret State Police, I acquired the entire staff, except for the director.

LESS: When you speak of Günther, which Günther do you mean? There were two brothers.

EICHMANN: Hauptsturmführer Günther, Rolf Günther. He was my "permanent representative" [Ständiger Vertreter]. We didn't use the word "deputy" [Stellvertreter]. So the routine work of the bureau went on as before, because the personnel had only changed their place of work. Günther attended mostly to this new Gestapo work, which we were both completely unfamiliar with, though he really didn't have to, because the original staff—if I may use a vulgar expression—worked their balls off anyway, that was their idea of duty. I myself concentrated on the Madagascar plan.

LESS: How did you hit on that?

EICHMANN: Emigration had dropped to practically nothing as a result of the war. If you don't mind my going back again: Theresienstadt had not been a solution, and the Nisko on the San experiment had failed, too. Then the French campaign got under way, and that gave me new hope of at least a temporary solution. I remembered Theodor Herzl's efforts to bring about a Jewish state, described by Adolf Böhm, and that at one time Herzl had considered plans for Madagascar. I also remembered that in this connection he had met with considerable opposition in his own ranks. I said to myself: It's all the same to me how we get soil and living space, the main thing is to do something. The situation was getting more and more acute as the Jews were driven out of one part of the country after another, on the one hand by legal restrictions, and on the other by party pressure on the non-Jewish population to boycott the Jews.

It was plain as day, you didn't have to be a genius to see that if things went on that way, the result would be turmoil, the nature of which I didn't really foresee at the time. I certainly suspected nothing like what happened later on. But something had to be done, I said to myself, because a boiler full of water, with a fire under it and no safety valve, is bound to explode. I, in my little job, wanted to help look for that valve, and it seemed to me that my efforts to find ways and means of resettlement were just such a safety valve. The Madagascar plan struck me as a new hope for a solution.

The French campaign, beginning with the German offensive of May 10, 1940, ended on June 25 of that year with the total victory of the Wehrmacht and an armistice, by the terms of which half of France was subject to German military occupation. The island of Madagascar was at the time a French colony, with 3.5 million inhabitants and an area more than twice the size of the Federal Republic of Germany.

EICHMANN: By then I had learned from Theresienstadt that ghettoization accomplished nothing. The way I planned it, it would have offered a relatively satisfactory partial solution for about ten thousand people, but too many people were shipped in. Many of the Gauleiters wanted to rid their territories of all Jews too old to emigrate. They kept after Himmler to ship *their* Jews—as they called them—to Theresienstadt. On the other hand, the Gauleiter of Saxony opposed this ghetto on the grounds that Jews so close to the borders of his Gau [territory] were a hotbed of infection and a center of black marketing. I continually referred to these difficulties in my reports, though they were not in my jurisdiction, because the ghettoization program was under Himmler's personal command. For a long time Himmler was under the influence of Streicher-*Stürmer* ideas, in sharp contradistinction to Heydrich, his Security Police and SD chief, who had no use for this unrealistic, fool's wisdom, as I called it on one occasion.

LESS: You thought Madagascar more realistic?

EICHMANN: I first went to the Reich Office for Emigration at the Ministry of the Interior and made inquiries about the geographical, climatic, geological, and other conditions. I obtained detailed information from the Tropical Institute in Hamburg, and the picture did not seem too unfavorable. From the juridical point of view, I had in mind an autonomous Jewish region of Madagascar.

Up until then, I had always functioned as a kind of specialized assistant, hiding behind the broad back of a superior. In Berlin, that changed. Now I was in charge, and I was brought into contact with an administrative machine such as I had never encountered before or even heard of. You can't imagine the difficulties I ran into, the tedious, tooth-and-nail negotiations, the thousands of objections raised by the various agencies. They all felt it was their business. For instance, the Foreign Office claimed that the Security Police should have no say in the matter, because Madagascar wasn't Germany. None of these people understood our aims or intentions. They had never read, studied, assimilated any basic work on the subject. They had no contact, no inner contact, with the question. They didn't throw themselves into the problem as such. A Regierungsrat* Lischka, for instance, would never have concerned himself with such a matter. A Regierungsrat Lischka, a Regierungsrat Lange, a Regierungsrat Suhr, a Regierungsrat X Y Z, not one of them, I tell you, no dry-as-dust office manager would have bothered about Nisko on the

---

* Roughly, the second secretary of a government department. Here the term expresses a Nazi's contempt for the government bureaucracy.—*Trans.*

San or Theresienstadt, he wouldn't have bothered with any of that, because he wasn't interested, because it's not in the files, not in the registers, so he won't touch it. Such people, of course, lead a quieter life, they make things a good deal easier for themselves. These people had never read, studied, assimilated a, let's say, a basic work. They had no contact, no inner contact with this thing. By the time the plan seemed fully clarified and none of the departments had any more changes to suggest, it was too late. The German army had long been in Paris, but by then nothing could be done about Madagascar. When the French fleet put out to sea and Germany occupied the previously unoccupied zone of France as far as the Mediterranean seaboard, Madagascar was out of the question. It was all over, the plan had been wrecked. I capitulated. The dream was over. That must have been in 1940.

Once again, Eichmann has his dates wrong. The Western Allies landed in North Africa on July 11, 1942. It was then that the German High Command thought it necessary to occupy all of France, especially the Mediterranean seaboard. This was done on November 11, 1942. The French warships concentrated in the harbor of Toulon had been neutralized in accordance with the terms of the armistice. Their crews now scuttled them to prevent them from falling into the hands of the Germans. This cut off all possible communication between the German masters of France and such distant outposts of the French colonial empire as Madagascar.

LESS: Was the Madagascar plan supposed to account for all the Jews? Your records always speak of four million Jews.
EICHMANN: Well, it certainly never went beyond the theoretical stage, because no one knew whether or not there would be room for four million Jews on Madagascar.

LESS: But the plan was supposed to contribute to a solution of the Jewish question?

EICHMANN: To a considerable degree—mainly at first with regard to the Jews located in Germany, Austria, and Czechoslovakia. What would have been possible after that remained to be seen.

LESS: How about the Jews in the Government General? Were they taken into account?

EICHMANN: Undoubtedly. I had started that in Radom.

LESS: Have you ever heard of a report by a Polish commission of inquiry that visited Madagascar in 1937?

EICHMANN: No, never, never, never. I got the idea from Theodor Herzl.

LESS: Are you aware that Madagascar had previously been investigated by this Polish commission, for instance—

EICHMANN: No, I am not, no, I didn't know.

LESS: . . . which came to the conclusion that a maximum of fifteen thousand European families could be settled there, while certain members of the commission thought that figure far too high?

EICHMANN: No, Herr Hauptmann . . . no . . . I never heard about that. I relied on what the Ministry of the Interior told me . . . the Reich Office for Immigration and Emigration. I believe it was during my Madagascar efforts that an evacuation action from the Baden area was undertaken. This was the situation: Himmler informed the head of the Security Police and the SD that Gauleiter So-and-So, I forget his name, had petitioned him to get rid of "his Jews." It seems that Himmler consented and gave orders that these Jews should be shipped to unoccupied French territory. My organization, Bureau IV B 4, had to requisition the trains from the Reich Transportation Ministry. A so-called scheduling conference was held at the Ministry, and an itinerary via Châlons-sur-Marne was decided on. Here I have the following to say. During the war, one of the first measures taken by the Transportation Ministry was to rationalize the utilization of rolling stock. An agreement was reached with Heydrich. The Ministry said: All requisitions of rolling stock for Security Police missions must be channeled through one bureau; then, if we get an order, we'll know it's necessary. Then we'll know the order is "war-important." Later that term was replaced by "war-crucial." That applied to all departments, and in our department it was decided that Bureau IV B 4 should handle these requisitions. It made no difference whether it was Poland or gypsies, building materials or prefabs, everything went through my bureau. Müller or Heydrich might just as well have chosen some other bureau; clothing supply, for instance.

Châlons-sur-Marne, I believe, was the last station in occupied France, then came the unoccupied zone. It was dinned into me that these trains must not stop anywhere in the occupied zone. But at the border station I couldn't help seeing that it would be absolutely impossible to move a convoy of four to six trains—passenger trains they were—across the demarcation line. In the first place, it was guarded by police, and in the unoccupied zone the French were autonomous. In the second place, the tracks were blocked by signals. How I got the idea of telling the stationmaster at the last station in the occupied zone that these were Wehrmacht troop trains and why the stationmaster believed me and sent the trains through after he had seen them, I couldn't tell you today. I only know that it would have turned out very badly for the Jews and for me, too, if the trains had been stopped at that point. They couldn't have gone ahead and they couldn't have gone back. When the last train had passed, I got into my car, I was bathed in sweat, and drove off as fast as I could. After that, there were difficulties with the French government in Vichy, but the Foreign Office had to straighten them out.

LESS: How many Jews were evacuated in this way?

EICHMANN: There were four to six trains. Roughly thirty-five hundred to four thousand Jews, I should say.

Eichmann makes this episode sound like a schoolboy prank. In reality, it meant disaster for 6,504 Jews of both sexes and every age. Alsace had been attached to the jurisdiction of Gauleiter Robert Wagner (Baden) and Lorraine to that of Josef Bürckel (Saar-Palatinate). According to the peace treaty, the Jews residing in these territories were to be admitted to France. But on this occasion both Gaus were totally "cleansed of Jews." At the end of October, over 6,500 Jews from Baden and the Palatinate were dragged out of their homes in the early morning hours and herded into trains, each with a maximum of fifty kilos of baggage and a hundred marks. Their property was confiscated by the German government. There were nine trains. After four days and three nights, the deportees were removed from the cars—to French concentration camps. Less than a thousand managed to emigrate or otherwise escape. Two thousand died of starvation and disease in the French camps. All the rest were later, on Eichmann's orders, shipped to the East, where they were murdered. This action was by no means the first of its kind. After a conference in Katowice on October 10, 1939, Eichmann noted: "For the present the Führer has ordered the redistribution [Umschichtung] of 300,000 Jews from the Old Reich and Ostmark." The first large-scale action took place on the night of February 12, 1940, in Stettin [now Szczecin]. Twelve hundred Jews of both sexes and of all ages were taken out of their houses and, outfitted only with warm clothing and a suitcase, herded into freight trains. Germans who had fled the Baltic provinces to escape the Soviet occupation took over their

property. The shipment went to the Government General.
Seventy-one persons froze to death en route. Two hundred
thirty more died in camps within a month, and the rest dis-
appeared into the death camps.

EICHMANN: These shipments to France are a typical example
of Himmler's impulsive reactions and how, out of the blue,
he would issue orders that led to impossible situations.
Himmler was greatly feared for this reason. Just one little
example: If Himmler sent for an officer who was a smoker,
pumice stone and lemon would be put into the toilet of his
special train or command post. Because if Himmler saw
nicotine stains on the man's fingernails, he was perfectly
capable of taking his hand and saying: "No smoking for
three months, six months! Your word as an officer. That's
an order! Dismissed!"

Seeing I had nothing interesting to do after the
Madagascar plan fell through, I asked Gruppenführer
Müller to transfer me to some city as police president. His
answer: A soldier can't decide where he chooses to fight.
Later on, I tried several times to be sent to the front, always
with the same negative result.

Toward the end of 1940, the ghettoization measures in
the Government General went into an intensive, or you
might say final, phase, and also in Warthegau [from the
Warta River in southwestern Poland], an action which did
not concern Bureau IV B 4.

Both Gauleiter Greiser in Posen, for his formerly Polish ter-
ritory in West Prussia, and Governor General Frank, with
headquarters in Cracow for West Poland, had been empowered
by Hitler to concentrate the Jews in their territories in ghettos,
and to have those unfit for work killed. For this, they did not
need Eichmann. Nevertheless, his bureau was not inactive.

EICHMANN: At this time, Gruppenführer Müller, my immediate superior, sent me on frequent trips to Poland, with instructions to inspect one thing or another and report to him. He himself never left Berlin, but he insisted on being thoroughly informed. So I inspected the ghetto of Litzmannstadt—now it's called Lodz again—and the Warsaw ghetto, too.

LESS: You might tell me what the functions of your department were at this time.

EICHMANN: Yes, sir. Yes, sir. Bureau IV B 4 had undergone a number of slight changes. When I took it over, it was simply called Jewish Affairs. I can't say for sure whether over the years, before it acquired the official title Weltanschauliche Gegnerbekämpfung [Defense Against Ideological Enemies], it ever bore the title Final Solution of the Jewish Question. Originally, the words "final solution" had nothing to do with physical extermination, of which I shall have more to say. I already had the words "final solution of the Jewish question" in mind when I took up the Madagascar project.

LESS: Was it already called Final Solution of the Jewish Question at that time?

EICHMANN: Herr Hauptmann, I am certain that the term "final solution" was usual even before that. It was one of the terms employed by Heydrich and Himmler. When I took over the bureau, it handled withdrawal of nationality and citizenship and the confiscation of property. That was a complicated business. The State Police never saw the property, only the orders.

LESS: Were the orders countersigned by you before being sent on?

EICHMANN: Often they were initialed at the bottom by the post office. These were routine papers. The whole process was automatic, printed forms, you didn't have to read them.

LESS: Now tell me about the deportation of Jews from Western and Eastern Europe.

EICHMANN: As far as I can remember, Jews were deported from Holland, Belgium, France, from Greece, Slovakia, and Rumania. Whether any were deported from Croatia, I don't know. From, what's the name of that country up there, Denmark, I believe. From Hungary. I don't know if I've forgotten some country.

LESS: Italy?

EICHMANN: Italy proper, no, but possibly from places in the Côte d'Azur region that were somehow connected with border disputes. *(Less offers Eichmann a cigarette)* Thank you. Gracias.

Of course I haven't the faintest idea how many were evacuated from these countries, how many shipments were sent out. I'd have to make up figures, but that wouldn't do anyone any good. I'll do it of course, if you wish. Yours to command.

LESS: Very well. We'll come back to that. You have touched on the final solution of the Jewish question. Would you like to speak about that now, or about the war with Russia first.

EICHMANN: The final solution depends . . . it's mixed up with . . . something that happened after the start of the German–Russian war.

At that time Reich Marshal Göring issued a document conferring a special title on the head of the Security Police and the SD. I'm trying to remember the wording. Was it "Deputy Charged with the Final Solution," or was it "with the Solution of the Jewish Question"?

LESS: Wouldn't this document relate to the period prior to the outbreak of the Second World War?

EICHMANN: We can only be sure that it relates to the period when emigration had ceased to be possible and the more radical solution was resorted to. The war with the Soviet

Union began in June 1941, I think. And I believe it was two months later, or maybe three, that Heydrich sent for me. I reported. He said to me: "The Führer, well, emigration is . . ." He began with a little speech. And then: "The Führer has ordered physical extermination." These were his words. And as though wanting to test their effect on me, he made a long pause, which was not at all his way. I can still remember that. In the first moment, I didn't grasp the implications, because he chose his words so carefully. But then I understood. I didn't say anything, what could I say? Because I'd never thought of a . . . of such a thing, of that sort of violent solution. And then he said to me: "Eichmann, go and see Globocnik in Lublin."

LESS: Who?

EICHMANN: Globocnik, the former Gauleiter of Vienna, was then head of the SS and the police in the Lublin district of the Government General. Anyway, Heydrich said: "Go and see Globocnik, the Führer has already given him instructions. Take a look and see how he's getting on with his program. I believe he's using Russian anti-tank trenches for exterminating the Jews." As ordered, I went to Lublin, located the headquarters of SS and Police Commander Globocnik, and reported to the Gruppenführer. I told him Heydrich had sent me, because the Führer had ordered the physical extermination of the Jews.

LESS: The Gruppenführer?

EICHMANN: I beg your pardon?

LESS: The Gruppenführer?

EICHMANN: The Führer. The Führer was Hitler. Yes, the Führer was meant. I've only quoted Heydrich's . . .

LESS: Heydrich's.

EICHMANN: . . . Heydrich's words. He said: "The Führer has ordered the . . . that is . . . Hitler has ordered the physical extermination of the Jews."

(75)

Globocnik sent for a certain Sturmbannführer Höfle, who must have been a member of his staff. We went from Lublin to, I don't remember what the place was called, I get them mixed up, I couldn't say if it was Treblinka or some other place. There were patches of woods, sort of, and the road passed through—a Polish highway. On the right side of the road there was an ordinary house, that's where the men who worked there lived. A captain of the regular police [Ordnungspolizei] welcomed us. A few workmen were still there. The captain, which surprised me, had taken off his jacket and rolled up his sleeves, somehow he seemed to have joined in the work. They were building little wooden shacks, two, maybe three of them; they looked like two- or three-room cottages. Höfle told the police captain to explain the installation to me. And then he started in. He had a, well, let's say, a vulgar, uncultivated voice. Maybe he drank. He spoke some dialect from the southwestern corner of Germany, and he told me how he had made everything airtight. It seems they were going to hook up a Russian submarine engine and pipe the exhaust into the houses and the Jews inside would be poisoned.

I was horrified. My nerves aren't strong enough . . . I can't listen to such things . . . such things, without their affecting me. Even today, if I see someone with a deep cut, I have to look away. I could never have been a doctor. I still remember how I visualized the scene and began to tremble, as if I'd been through something, some terrible experience. The kind of thing that happens sometimes and afterwards you start to shake. Then I went to Berlin and reported to the head of the Security Police.

LESS: Müller?

EICHMANN: Yes, Müller, of course.

LESS: Not Heydrich?

EICHMANN: Yes, Heydrich, but Müller was my immediate

superior. I told him what I've told you now. Maybe I'm getting some things mixed up. Do you mind if I put down . . . *(Takes paper and pencil)*

LESS: Go right ahead.

EICHMANN: . . . dates, a few notes, because I'm trying to keep things straight. That was . . . yes, as I said before, it must have been late summer, autumn . . .

LESS: Of what year?

EICHMANN: After the war broke out between Germany and Russia. That would make it the autumn of 1941. Then I was sent on to Kulm [Chelmno] in Warthegau. I received orders from Müller to go to Litzmannstadt and report back to him on what was going on there. He didn't put it the same way as . . . as Heydrich . . . not as crassly. "An action against the Jews is under way there, Eichmann. Go take a look. And then report to me." I went to Gestapo head-quarters in Litzmannstadt—now it's Lodz again—and there I was told. It was a special team, put in by the Reichsführer [Himmler]. And they told me exactly where this Kulm is situated. I saw the following: a room, perhaps, if I remember right, about five times as big as this one here. There were Jews in it. They had to undress, and then a sealed truck drove up. The doors were opened, it drove up to a kind of ramp. The naked Jews had to get in. Then the doors were closed and the truck drove off.

LESS: How many people did this truck hold?

EICHMANN: I don't know exactly. The whole time it was there, I didn't look inside. I couldn't. Couldn't! What I saw and heard was enough. The screaming and . . . I was much too shaken and so on. I told Müller that in my report. He didn't get much out of it. I drove after the truck . . . and there I saw the most horrible sight I had seen in all my life. It drove up to a fairly long trench. The doors were opened and corpses were thrown out. The limbs were as supple as if they'd been alive. Just thrown in. I can still see a civilian with pliers pulling out teeth. And then I beat it. I got into my car and drove off. I didn't say another word. I sat there for hours without saying a word to my driver. I'd had enough. I was through. The only other thing I remember is that a doctor in a white smock wanted me to look through a peephole and watch the people inside the truck. I refused. I couldn't, I couldn't say another word, I had to get out of there. In Berlin I reported to Gruppenführer Müller. I told him the same as I've told you now. Terrible, an inferno. I can't. It's . . . I can't do it . . . I told him.

LESS: What did Müller say?

EICHMANN: Müller never said anything. Never! Not about these things and not about other things. He was always very terse and unemotional, he only said what was strictly necessary. He'd say yes or he'd say no. And when he didn't say yes or no, he usually said: "Eichmann, my friend . . ." That wasn't yes and it wasn't no. He was a man of few words.

LESS: Did you report on this in writing?

EICHMANN: No, I couldn't do that. I was expressly forbidden to; by Heydrich, I believe. Müller wanted especially to know how long it takes; I wasn't able to tell him that, I couldn't hear. I should have gone out there a second time, but naturally I didn't volunteer, and nothing was said to me.

LESS: Did you also see Jews being gassed with a submarine engine by Globocnik's outfit?

EICHMANN: No, I did not see that, but I'll come back to it. I was sent there another time. Let me think a moment, Herr Hauptmann. I was sent there after the following places: the two I've mentioned, and then Auschwitz, Auschwitz [Oswiecim], and then I was sent to Treblinka. And then to . . . what's the name of that double battle near Minsk? . . . near Minsk. Anyway, to Minsk, Auschwitz, Treblinka,

Minsk . . . That's all, I believe. Oh, yes, and Lemberg [Lvov], Lemberg. That's it. Those are the six places.

LESS: Were these just information-gathering missions? Or did you have some special assignment?

EICHMANN: No assignment, no assignment. I had no orders to give or anything else. No instructions about who to gas, or whether anyone was to be gassed, whether the gassing could or should be stopped, or started, or intensified, I never had anything to do with all that, Herr Hauptmann. If the newspapers said I did, it's a lie, I'm telling you the whole truth.

LESS: What was the function of your bureau within the framework of the extermination program?

EICHMANN: Evacuation. But not in the Government General of Poland. And later on I hope to speak of the occupied Russian territories, where the situation was different.

LESS: Herr Eichmann, you wished to speak of your visits to the extermination camps.

EICHMANN: Yes. That's right. Müller said to me: "In Minsk the Jews are being shot. I'd like a report on that." So I went to Minsk. I had nothing at all to do there, I didn't know anybody. I went to the command post—what was it called again? . . . Commander Security Police, or could it have been Action Team Security Police?—and asked for the commanding officer. I still remember, he wasn't there. I spoke to someone else and told him I had orders to see what was going on. I spent the night in that town, and next day I went to the place, but I got there too late. The work for that morning was already done, almost done—and I was very glad of that. When I got there, I was just in time to see some young riflemen, I believe they were riflemen, with the death's-head collar patch, shooting into a pit . . . maybe four or five times as big as this room. Maybe bigger, say six or seven times. I . . . I . . . my orientation in this case is unreliable, because I saw this thing without thinking, I didn't think anything at all. I just saw it, and that's all. They fired into the pit, I can still see a woman with her arms behind her back, and then her knees crumpled, and I cleared out . . .

LESS: The pit was full of corpses?

EICHMANN: It was full. It was full. I went to my car, I got in and drove away. I drove to Lemberg. I had no orders to go to Lemberg, I remember now. Somehow I went to Lemberg and found the man in charge of the Gestapo command post and I said to him: "It's horrible what they're doing there. They're training young men to be sadists." I told Müller the exact same thing. I told Günther, too. I told everybody. I told them all. And I said to that SS officer in Lemberg: "How can they stand there firing at a woman and children? How is it possible? . . . It's just not . . . Those men will either go mad or they'll turn into sadists . . . our own men." He said to me: "They're doing the same thing right here, shooting. Want to see?" "No," I said. "I don't want to see anything." "We're driving past there anyway," he said. There had been a pit there, it was already filled in, and blood was gushing out of it . . . how shall I say? . . . like a geyser. I've never seen anything like it. I'd had enough of that mission. I went back to Berlin and reported what I'd seen to Gruppenführer Müller. I said to him: "This is no solution to the Jewish question. And besides, we're training our men to be sadists. We shouldn't be surprised if they all turn out to be criminals, all criminals." I still remember Müller looking at me with an expression that said: Eichmann, you're right, that's no solution. But there was nothing he could do about it. Müller definitely couldn't do a thing. Not a thing. Not a thing. Who gave the orders for those actions? The orders, the orders. Obviously, the orders were given by the head of the Security Police and the SD, namely, Heydrich. But he must also have had his instructions from the Reichsführer-SS, namely, Himmler; on his own hook he can't . . . he could never have done such things on his own hook. And Himmler must have had express orders from Hitler. If he hadn't had orders from Hitler, he'd have been out on his ear before he knew what hit him.

LESS: Didn't Himmler give written orders about this final solution of the Jewish question?

EICHMANN: Writ . . . for extermination, physical extermination?

LESS: For physical extermination.

EICHMANN: I never saw a written order, Herr Hauptmann. All I know is that Heydrich said to me: "The Führer has ordered the physical extermination of the Jews." He said that as clearly and surely as I'm repeating it now. And those were the first, the first results . . . small-scale results . . . that I'm telling you about now. I implored the Gruppenführer: "Please, don't send me there. Send someone else. Someone with stronger nerves. They never let me go to the front. I was never a soldier. There are plenty of other men who can bear to see such things, who won't keel over, I can't stand it, I can't sleep at night, I have nightmares. I can't stand it, Gruppenführer." But it didn't get me anywhere.

LESS: Were Jews from the Reich, from Austria and the Protectorate of Bohemia and Moravia sent to Riga and Minsk in the autumn of 1941?

EICHMANN: In 1941, Herr Hauptmann, that is possible. I don't know. I only know that there were trains going to Minsk and Riga.

LESS: Did you know that, in the autumn of that year, action groups [Einsatzgruppen] liquidated Jews by shooting, both in Riga and in Minsk?

EICHMANN: I didn't know about it at the time, but of course I heard about it later.

LESS: You say you inspected Minsk?

EICHMANN: I have already said that IV B 4, my bureau, had nothing to do with the activity of the action groups in the East. We neither directed them nor gave them orders. Nor did we send any, how shall I say, any observers or advisers.

LESS: Did you receive periodic reports about the action groups, so-called occurrence reports, hence communications about the liquidation of the Jews in Russia?

EICHMANN: Yes. About the liquidation of the Jews along with other activities of the action groups. I never claimed not to know about this liquidation. I only said that Bureau IV B 4 had nothing to do with it. Here I must add something that chronologically speaking should have been mentioned before: the conference about the Barbarossa project. Shortly before the start of the German–Russian war, a conference was held in Berlin which all the top men at Reich Security Headquarters were obliged to attend. There for the first time I heard the code name for the war preparations against the Soviet Union. Someone read an organizational paper, prepared long before, and it mentioned the action groups and action teams in the East. As the German troops advanced, action groups under the commander of the Security Police and the SD [Heydrich] moved up right behind them and took over police power. The leader of one of these action groups was Ohlendorf, who testified at the war crimes trials in Nuremberg that his group shot eighty-four thousand, or maybe it was ninety-four thousand Jews.

LESS: Was it stated at this conference what the mission and function of these action groups was to be?

EICHMANN: No, it was not stated. I thought it was something military, something to do with the offensive, with the Waffen-SS, and I was upset about it at the time, because I thought I'd been passed over. My advancement had been relatively rapid and I said to myself: Now I'm an Obersturmbannführer, but if they send me to the front I'll be promoted to Standartenführer in no time. As it happened, I stayed an Obersturmbannführer until May 8, 1945. I couldn't be promoted any more. A bureau head [Referent] was equivalent to Regierungsrat or Oberregierungsrat in the government service, and I had already made the corresponding SS rank.

LESS: You were also in Auschwitz?

EICHMANN: I kept getting orders to visit Auschwitz. Müller told me they were expanding the plant, and he wanted me to take a look and report back to him. Herr Hauptmann, those fellows were very cruel, describing those things as gruesomely as possible to a man accustomed to desk work, putting it to him as abruptly as possible. Naturally, they laughed their heads off when my nerves broke down and I couldn't keep up my military dignity—that's what they called it—the way they did. Höss told me Himmler had been there and taken a good look at everything. He told me the Reichsführer himself had gone all weak in the knees. He meant that, meant that, in a disparaging sense, because Höss himself was thoroughly hardened. That was the day when Himmler, after seeing that—undoubtedly to screw up his own courage and hide his weakness from his concentration-camp men—told Höss that those were battles the coming generation wouldn't have to fight. When I visited the installation, Höss sent for an all-terrain car. We drove to a certain place—I don't know my way around Auschwitz. I never got any further than the command post at the main entrance. Had no desire to. As we were driving, I saw some big buildings. Almost like factories. Enormous chimneys. Höss says to me: "Working to capacity! Ten thousand!" A job was under way. They were separating the able-bodied from the ones who were supposedly unfit for work. I didn't watch the gassing. I couldn't. I'd have probably keeled over. And I thought: Whew, I've got it over with again. But then he drives me to a big trench. It was very big, I can't say exactly how big, maybe a hundred meters long, maybe a hundred and fifty or a hundred and eighty. And there was an enormous grating, an iron grating. And corpses were burning on it. Then I got sick to my stomach. Sick to my stomach.

LESS: But you were in Treblinka again?

EICHMANN: I'd like to say something about this last, about this last point of this terrible, terrible business. I mean Treblinka. I was given orders. I went to see Globocnik in Treblinka. That was the second time. The installations were now in operation, and I had to report to Müller. I expected to see a wooden house on the right side of the road and a few more wooden houses on the left; that's what I remembered. Instead, again with the same Sturmbann-führer Höfle, I come to a railroad station with a sign saying Treblinka, looking exactly like a German railroad station— anywhere in Germany—a replica, with signboards, etc. There I hung back as far as I could. I didn't push closer to see it all. I saw a footbridge enclosed in barbed wire and over that footbridge a file of naked Jews was being driven into a house, a big . . . no, not a house, a big, one-room structure, to be gassed. As I was told, they were gassed with . . . what's it called? . . . potassium cyan . . .

LESS: Cyanide.

EICHMANN: Potassium cyanide . . . or cyanic acid. In acid form it's called cyanic acid. I didn't look to see what happened. I reported to Müller and as usual he listened in silence, without a word of comment. Just his facial expression said: "There's nothing I can do about it." I am convinced, Herr Hauptmann, I know it sounds odd coming from me, but I'm convinced that if it had been up to Müller it wouldn't have happened.

Hydrocyanic, or prussic, acid is a colorless liquid which boils and becomes a gas at room temperature. When inhaled, sixty milligrams of it are fatal. It was used in the gas chambers in the form of Zyklon B, a commercial product designed for the extermination of vermin. The National Socialists' first experiments with poison gas as a means of mass murder date from the so-called euthanasia campaign, when mental patients were done away with on the alleged grounds that they were a useless burden to the national community.

LESS: What do you know about Zyklon B gas?

EICHMANN: I don't know anything except what I heard there, that it's contained in beer . . . I mean, I've heard today for the first time that it's called Zyklon B. Then I was told that it came in tablets that looked like beer mats, cardboard coasters. But whether it was Zyklon B or prussic acid, I have no idea.

LESS: I am now going to quote from the German edition of the proceedings of the trial of the leading war criminals before the International Military Court in Nuremberg. From the sworn testimony of Rudolf Höss, who was camp commander at Auschwitz from 1940 to 1943. He said: "Eichmann was repeatedly in Auschwitz and knew exactly what was being done."

EICHMANN: Herr Hauptmann, I knew no more than what I have said. I knew the killing was done with those round cardboard things. Höss told me that. He even showed me one. Then I saw the outside of that big building. Neither in Auschwitz nor anywhere else did I observe the extermination process. It was only in Minsk that I got there while the shooting was going on. Everywhere else I refused, because the burning, the burning of the corpses was as much as I could stand. I wasn't up to it.

LESS: When Rudolf Höss was under arrest in Poland, he made

autobiographical notes. Here I have his book: *Commandant of Auschwitz*. I'm going to read a passage: "Eichmann told me about the killing by exhaust fumes in trucks, as had been practiced in the East up until then. That, however, would not have been possible for the mass shipments that were to be expected. Killing by spraying with carbon monoxide in a bathroom, as had been done with the mentally ill in some places in the Reich, would have required too many buildings. Moreover, it was questionable whether sufficient gas could be procured for such a vast number of people. We left the matter unresolved. Eichmann undertook to find out about a gas that was easily obtainable and required no special installations, and report to me about it." Have you a comment to make?

EICHMANN: Yes, sir! The overwhelming majority of these assertions are pure invention. It is obvious to me that he was interested in only one thing: clearing his own department, the SS Administration and Supply Headquarters, commanded by Obergruppenführer Pohl. Precisely in connection with the technical details, which the Gestapo had nothing to do with, he is trying to clear the technical sections of the SS Administration and Supply Headquarters, keep them out of it for reasons unknown to me—still, to all intents and purposes, known. I never in any way—and to this I will take any oath, Herr Hauptmann—discussed this matter with Höss. On the contrary, when Müller sent me to Auschwitz for the first time, it was Höss who showed me those cardboard mats.

LESS: I will now show you a document presented by the prosecution at the first Nuremberg war crimes trial. It is a statement by Dr. Kurt Gerstein, former head of the technical disinfection service in the SS Command Headquarters, Group D, Hygiene, concerning the utilization of the poison gas that had been ordered from him in July 1942 by

Günther, your permanent representative. Would you care to read this document through?

EICHMANN: Yes, sir. *(Bends over the document and reads)* It deals first with the delivery of prussic acid to Hauptsturmführer Günther on July 8, 1942, specifically of one hundred kilograms of prussic acid. Next comes a report on his participation in killings in the Government General. And at the end Gerstein states that early in 1944 Günther ordered more prussic acid from him, and asked whether he had a poison with which one could take advantage of the wind for killing people in Theresienstadt. I must say that all this is news to me. Of all the persons mentioned here, only one is known to me, Hauptmann Wirth—I'd forgotten the name, but quite possibly it's the same captain I told you about. All the names are unknown to me; never heard them, never pronounced them, never had anything to do with any of these people. I know nothing about Günther taking delivery of prussic acid in 1942. I must say it's odd, very odd, that Günther should be mixed up in this business, when I'm not even—I ask you, it's not that I attach any importance to it, Herr Hauptmann—isn't it odd that I'm not even mentioned if I had anything to do with it. Anyway, I don't know anything about it. I wasn't involved in it, and if I wasn't involved, I can't very well say that I was. If I had had anything to do with it, my name would be mentioned here, as was everywhere customary.

LESS: You gave Günther the order. He certainly didn't act on his own hook.

EICHMANN: No, no, no! That I must deny, Herr Hauptmann. I did not. Of course Günther didn't think up this thing on his own, he must have received an order. That's plain. But he didn't get the order from me. I know nothing about it. A hundred kilos of prussic acid . . . I haven't the faintest idea. I don't know. I don't know.

LESS: You recall Höss's statement about the preparations for the gassing and your telling him that you'd find out about a gas. If you now consider what Gerstein says here, that suddenly on June 8, 1942, Günther ordered the gas— doesn't that hang together very nicely?

EICHMANN: Herr Hauptmann, a lot of things have happened that hang together very nicely . . . If I had had anything to do with it, Gerstein would certainly have mentioned me by name. Of course, some sort of order must have been given. Maybe it came direct from Müller, because by and large Müller had come to know me for . . . for a more sensitive person than Günther. I don't mean to say that I . . . that I'd shown girlish squeamishness, but I was a lot more sensitive than somebody like Günther, for instance.

LESS: For that very reason it's hard to believe that Müller would go over your head in giving Günther a special order.

EICHMANN: I absolutely refuse to be identified with that affair. Because I had nothing to do with it. If I had had anything to do with it, all right, I'd admit it. Then I'd say to myself: After all, Himmler himself was in on it, what can I do? I received orders, and it doesn't . . . it doesn't matter, do what you like with me. Because I couldn't help myself, I had orders. But I had nothing to do with that business.

LESS: Do you remember the Wannsee Conference? It occurs to me that you were present.

EICHMANN: Yes, sir. I even had to write the invitations to the state secretaries; that is, Heydrich told me briefly what he wanted me to say.

LESS: Why were you invited if you played so subordinate a role?

EICHMANN: Herr Hauptmann, I had to write the invitation. I had to supply Heydrich with the data for his speech, all the emigration figures. I was in charge of that department in the Secret State Police.

LESS: Müller was there too?

EICHMANN: Yes, sir. It was a . . . a high-level conference, as they said then. Nothing below state secretaries.

LESS: Why did they bring little Eichmann in? Heydrich couldn't have wanted to keep asking you at the conference whether he was saying the right thing.

EICHMANN: No; he did that beforehand. Things connected with emigration. Because at the time of the Wannsee Conference the killing had just begun.

LESS: Yes, officially. There had been killing before that. You claim that in 1941, around November, in Auschwitz, those gassing machines were already at work.

EICHMANN: Yes, that's right. At this conference Heydrich made known his authorization. I'm wondering: If the killing had already started—and it had started—this probably meant a tighter organization of the program. He was appointed by Göring. Up until then, the obstacles had been too great. Too many departments involved.

On January 20, 1942, at the invitation of SS-Obergruppen-führer Heydrich, fifteen of the leading officials and function-aries of all the departments concerned with the Jewish question met in a villa at 56 Am-Grossen-Wannsee. The only important department not represented was SS Administration and Supply Headquarters, which controlled the labor and extermination camps. This department had already received its instructions and orders directly from Reichsführer-SS Heinrich Himmler. Originally, the conference was to take place in December. It was delayed by the United States' declaration of war. At this conference, classified as "top secret," Heydrich announced that the aim in view was no longer the emigration but the extermination of the Jews. And the first sentence of the record of the conference, kept by Eichmann, reads: "At the start, Heydrich announced his appointment as special deputy charged with the preparation of the final solution."

LESS: I regard the fact that you were brought into the Wannsee Conference as an indication that you played a more prominent role in the final solution by extermination than you admit.

EICHMANN: No, no, Herr Hauptmann. I would admit it, I wouldn't hesitate to admit it, but I had always been bureau chief [Dezernent] of Bureau IV B 4, and a bureau chief in the Gestapo absolutely cannot break out of the frame in which he has been placed. If I had spoken up even once, Herr Hauptmann, I would have said yes, sir. But I had to keep my mouth shut. They kept me . . . I don't know, Herr Hauptmann, if you can put yourself in my place—I sat in the corner with the stenotypist, and no one bothered with us. No one. We were much too insignificant. They paid no attention to us. Not even Heydrich.

LESS: That gives me the impression that they were planning a more prominent role for you in the future.

EICHMANN: In that case, I must have given myself that role, because it was I who put myself on the list of those present. No, no, it's really a . . . I'd have the courage to come straight out with it—after all, what can happen to me?

LESS: I'm going to quote from your record of Heydrich's speech: "Emigration has now, with the Führer's approval, been replaced by another solution, the evacuation of the Jews to the East. The present actions, however, must be viewed as mere expedients, but they offer a source of practical experience of the utmost importance with a view to the final solution to come." What *does* all this mean?

EICHMANN: Since emigration was prohibited, they were to be deported to the East. This was the new—er—conception in behalf of which the conference of state secretaries was called . . . The new conception that Himmler discussed with Göring, undoubtedly in Heydrich's presence.

LESS: What is meant by "practical experience"?

EICHMANN: The Wannsee Conference—we called it the Conference of State Secretaries—was held on January 20, 1942. Two months later, I was sent to see Globocnik. It is quite possible that the killing there had already begun.

LESS: I see. So you think "practical experience" refers to the killing of the Jews, which had already begun?

It's true that action teams were already at work at the time.

EICHMANN: They started in . . . Of course, there was killing.

LESS: Here, on page 7 of your record, Heydrich says: "Under appropriate leadership, the Jews should be put to work in a suitable way within the framework of the final solution. In large labor columns, with separation of the sexes, the able-bodied Jews will be made to build roads as they are led into these territories. A large percentage of them will undoubtedly be eliminated by natural diminution." What is meant by "natural diminution"?

EICHMANN: That's perfectly normal dying. Of a heart attack or pneumonia, for instance. If I were to drop dead just now, that would be natural diminution.

LESS: If a man is forced to perform heavy physical labor and not given enough to eat—he grows weaker, he gets so weak that he has a heart attack . . .

EICHMANN: That would undoubtedly have been reported as natural diminution.

LESS: Heydrich goes on: "Since the ultimate survivors will undoubtedly constitute the most resistant group, they must. be treated accordingly, since this natural elite, if released, must be viewed as the potential germ cell of a new Jewish order." What does "treated accordingly" mean?

EICHMANN: That . . . that . . . that comes from Himmler. Natural selection—that's . . . that was his hobby.

LESS: Yes, but what does it mean here?

EICHMANN: Killed, killed. Undoubtedly.

LESS: The record continues: "State Secretary Dr. Bühler, from the Office of the Governor General, declared that the Government General would be glad to see steps taken toward the final solution in the Government General, because there the transportation problem was not of paramount importance and labor considerations would be no obstacle. He held that the Jews should be removed with all possible dispatch from the territory of the Government General because there more than anywhere else the Jew represents an eminent danger as a carrier of disease, and furthermore is constantly disrupting the economic structure of the country by his black-market activities. Moreover, the majority of the two and a half million Jews in question were unfit for labor." What is he suggesting?

EICHMANN: He is suggesting that they should be killed.

LESS: Now I am going to show you a document produced by the prosecution at the ninth Nuremberg war crimes trial. It is a special-delivery letter, dated Berlin, September 21, 1939, signed Heydrich and addressed to the commanders of all the action teams. It concerns the Jewish question in Poland, which had just been occupied. Is there anything you would like to say about it?

EICHMANN: At that time my duties had nothing to do with those things. This order, of which I was unaware, or which at least I no longer remember after all these years, fills in a gap in my knowledge of the ghettoization process. This order lays the groundwork for ghettoization in the Government General. At the very beginning it says: "A distinction must be made between (1) the ultimate aim, which requires longer periods of time, and (2) the segments in the implementation of this ultimate aim, which are to be carried out on a short-term basis."

After reading this now, I have this to say. To judge by this document, the order concerning the physical extermination of the Jews was not, as I formerly believed, issued or promulgated by Hitler at the outbreak of the German–Russian war. On the contrary, this, call it basic, conception was already firmly established at that date. I can think of no other interpretation for the words "the ultimate aim, which requires longer periods of time . . ." When I came to the Gestapo, all that was . . . under way. I still remember that, after the Wannsee Conference, Heydrich authorized Brigadeführer Globocnik, who had that killing installation in Lublin, to kill Jews, and even made the authorization retroactive.

LESS: Who conveyed this supplementary order to Globocnik?

EICHMANN: At that time Heydrich ordered me to draft the following letter: "I authorize you to subject another 150,-000 Jews to the final solution." Those Jews were already dead. Actually, I think there were 250,000. He, Globocnik, arranged to have the order given to him a second time.

LESS: Where did you keep Himmler's letter of April 1, 1940, to the head of the Security Police and the SD, in which he issued the order concerning the final solution of the Jewish question?

EICHMANN: An order from Himmler to the head of the Security Police? You say there was something in it about killing Jews?

LESS: About the final solution of the Jewish question, which the Führer had ordered . . .

EICHMANN: Herr Hauptmann, I can't imagine Himmler putting that in writing. To me, that is inconceivable.

LESS: We know from the Wannsee Conference that Heydrich also put it in writing. It's in the record of the Wannsee Conference.

EICHMANN: Herr Hauptmann, Heydrich did not at the time of the Wannsee Conference speak of killing. He spoke of putting Jews to work in the East. That was his way of camouflaging it.

LESS: If you read through the record of the Wannsee Conference, you'll see what he meant. True, he expresses himself very euphemistically.

EICHMANN: Well, I suppose so, if it's one of those documents that don't come out with the naked, brutal words. It's possible, Herr Hauptmann, but I can't remember that letter of Himmler's. If it ever existed, it was certainly kept in our top-secret file.

LESS: I will now read you parts of the statement made under oath by your onetime subordinate Dieter Wisliceny on January 3, 1946, at the Nuremberg war crimes trials. Asked what his particular duty was, Wisliceny replied: "Eichmann was responsible for the so-called solution of the Jewish question in Germany and in all territories occupied by Germany." When asked about certain phases of anti-Jewish activity, Wisliceny replied: "Up to 1940, the bureau's general guidelines provided for settling the Jewish question by systematic emigration. The second phase, which began at that point, provided for the concentration of all Jews in Poland and other German-occupied territories— and this in the form of ghettos. This phase lasted roughly until the beginning of 1942. The third phase was the so-called final solution; that is, the systematic extermination and destruction of the Jewish people. This phase continued until October 1944, when Himmler gave orders to stop the killing."

EICHMANN: Wisliceny says here that ghettoization came under the bureau's jurisdiction. That is not true. He says the killing began in 1942. That, too, is untrue. It should be autumn 1941.

LESS: I continue to quote Wisliceny: "Up to the spring of 1943, I was in Bratislava, at the German embassy. In the spring of 1942, roughly seventeen thousand Jews had been sent from Slovakia to Poland as laborers. At the time, Eichmann gave the Slovakian government the assurance that these Jews would be given decent, humane treatment in the Polish ghettos. As a result of this assurance, approximately thirty-five thousand more Jews were shipped from Slovakia to Poland. Premier Tuka repeatedly sent for me and expressed the wish that a Slovakian delegation be permitted to visit the territories where the Slovakian Jews were located. Eichmann told me that he could not under any circumstances authorize such a visit. When I asked him why, he replied, after various evasions, that a large part of these Jews were no longer alive. I asked him who had given him such an order. He said the order came from Himmler." So much for Wisliceny. And now your comment.

EICHMANN: Herr Hauptmann, Wisliceny was obviously trying—as he had every right—to distance himself as much as possible from the whole business. I can only repeat that I had no power whatsoever over what went on in the Government General.

LESS: Did you, as Wisliceny testified, discuss this problem with him?

EICHMANN: Of course we discussed it. I believe . . . though I can't really remember . . . it's not . . . it's been too long . . . but I believe we discussed the problem.

LESS: I shall quote again from Wisliceny's testimony: "Eichmann then said he could show me this order from Himmler in writing, if it would put my conscience at rest. He went to his safe, took out a thin file, and showed me a letter from Himmler to the head of the Security Police and the SD. The gist of this letter was that the Führer had ordered the final solution of the Jewish problem. The head of the Security Police and the SD and the Inspector of Concentration Camps were entrusted with implementation of this final solution. Pending the final solution, all able-bodied concentration-camp inmates of female or male sex should be employed on labor projects." Have you any comment?

EICHMANN: Yes, Herr Hauptmann. As I hear it now, it's possible . . . I won't deny it, there may have been an order from Himmler. As I hear it now—not in the crude form I had in mind before, with extermination and so on, but these circumlocutions, labor projects, etc.—it's possible, I don't . . . don't deny it . . . though I never saw this paper with my own eyes.

LESS: Wisliceny was asked about the date of that order. His answer: "The order was of April 1942 and was signed by Himmler in person. Eichmann told me that he personally had been charged with carrying out this order at Reich Security Headquarters. I said to Eichmann: 'God grant that our enemies never get an opportunity to do the same to the German people.' To that, Eichmann replied that I shouldn't get sentimental, that it was a Führer's Order and had to be carried out." Have you any comment?

EICHMANN: Yes, Herr Hauptmann. According to this statement, I had a special mandate, mand . . . er, er . . . to direct, to take complete command of the whole business, the evacuation and killing of the Jews. That is not true. That is not true at all. Wisliceny made it up out of whole cloth. I never had any special mandate and had—I cannot insist too much—nothing to do with the killing. With the evacuation, yes—I can't wriggle out of that, I have to admit it. But once a shipment was delivered to the designated station as per the decisions of the scheduling conference, my powers ceased.

LESS: So you were responsible for the shipments, but if the shipments hadn't got there, the killing wouldn't have been possible. With regard to the killing of the Jews, you say . . .

EICHMANN: I'm not . . . it's not . . . it's not possible. The Security Police had no authority, Reich Security Headquarters had no authority.

LESS: But isn't it strange that both Höss, the camp commander at Auschwitz, and Wisliceny, your co-worker, who advised the government in Bratislava on Jewish questions, should make almost identical statements? I don't believe they had a chance to compare notes.

EICHMANN: No, neither do I. But isn't it just as strange that even Pohl, head of the SS Administration and Supply Headquarters—who, after all, held the rank of general—should try to wriggle out of the whole business like a born coward? It's beyond me how, when things get rough, a man of his rank can shamelessly try to clear himself at the expense of men of lower rank. I've read in the papers that General Pohl blames everything on Reich Security Headquarters. At the height of their power, these generals have courage to spare, but when facing a court, they lose their nerve and try to shift everything . . . everything to somebody else's shoulders. I'm not calling anyone else to account for the evacuations. I was responsible. I'm ready to take my punishment. I'm not short on courage. Of course, it's a . . . sad kind of courage I need now. But in those days I had the gumption to say "Yes, sir!" and today I have the gumption to say: "All right. I'm ready. Here's my head . . . ready to go where it belongs."

HOFSTAETTER: This is June 6, 1960. It is now 2:10 p.m. You know who I am?

EICHMANN: Yes, sir, Colonel, sir.

HOFSTAETTER: As your statements up to this point show, you committed crimes against the Jewish people and against humanity during the period of National Socialist rule. I wish to make it clear to you once again that you are testifying of your own free will. You are aware that your statements can be used as evidence. What have you decided?

EICHMANN: I wish to continue testifying.

LESS: Then we shall proceed. You were going to speak about Himmler.

EICHMANN: Whenever Hitler made a speech in which he was particularly violent about the Jews, we knew something would come from Himmler. Something would come. He didn't always take the initiative on his own. I believe in fact that the Office of the Führer's Deputy—as the department under Reichsleiter Bormann was called—would notify Himmler that not enough had been done. I remember Himmler flying into a rage with Kaltenbrunner and wanting to know why things weren't moving ahead in France . . . or Holland. I don't remember which. The way they were dawdling, he'd say, had they forgotten there was a war on?

LESS: What was he referring to?

EICHMANN: To evacuation. Evacuation. I can only give you

the gist, but it hits the nail on the head. In such cases, the best I could do was say to Gruppenführer Müller: "Please send a telegram to the local officer in charge of Jewish affairs, tell him to come to Berlin and give a report." His report would go to Gruppenführer Müller in charge of Section IV, with a request to take note of it and decide whether to submit it to C. C meant the head of the Security Police and the SD. It was up to Müller to decide whether the report should go further. Often it came back with the comment: "C has taken note. Forward to Reichsführer-SS."

An example: Himmler ordered the evacuation of the Jews from France to the Litzmannstadt or Warsaw ghetto. In this case, the order went first to the higher-ranking SS and police officers and second to the head of the Security Police in Paris. If Himmler had previously settled the matter at some meeting with the Reich Foreign Minister, there was no need to worry about the approval of the Foreign Office. But if it was one of Himmler's impulses, the head of the Security Police had to obtain the approval of the Foreign Office. The administrative machinery began to grind. It took weeks to get all the necessary go-aheads. Then the French government in Vichy had to be notified and the Military Commandant of Paris drawn in. All this seemed worth mentioning because it shows that evacuations were not so easy to carry out. No matter how large a German force was present, they couldn't just round up people, put them in freight cars, and ship them out. The whole evacuation process in the European countries required stubborn, long-drawn-out negotiations. We had to requisition the trains from the Reich Transportation Ministry and contact Administration and Supply Headquarters. It was there that the destinations were decided on, because we . . . we didn't know where they were going. It was not in my province to decide where the shipments should go.

LESS: I assume you told the Jewish-affairs advisers in foreign countries—in the occupied territories—where these shipments were going.

EICHMANN: Yes. I told them, I told them when they asked me why it was being done. And I didn't lie. I'm the kind of man who can't tell a lie. Let me get ahead of myself. During my stay in Hungary, Dr. Kastner, the spokesman for the Jews in Hungary, often came to see me. One day he said: "Obersturmbannführer, stop the extermination machine in Auschwitz." I said to him: "Herr Dr. Kastner, I can't stop it, because I didn't set it in motion." And then another time he said: "Stop the extermination machine." I said: "Herr Kastner, I can't, I can't, I can't. I, I, it's not in my province, I have no powers. It's the same as if you tried to stop it. You stop it, I can't, I'm too small, I have no means, it's not in my power. The extermination machine is under Administration and Supply Headquarters, Gruppenführer Pohl." That's what I told Dr. Kastner in Budapest.

LESS: I see.

EICHMANN: That's what I told him. He certainly reported it. Certainly, because before that no one could have told him who was in charge of the administrative . . . the extermination machine, and I'm sure he reported it. In his place I would certainly have passed it on, because it was something . . . something new. Because now they had a man who was in charge. The concentration camps were under his authority. The Reichsführer, Himmler, that is—I keep using the old word "Reichsführer," though it's stuck in my craw for a long time. For years now, I've hardly spoken that word. Himmler gave this order to the head of Administration and Supply, because the concentration camps were under him. That was Pohl. They were under him. They weren't under Heydrich. And Heydrich wouldn't have been able to turn it off, Herr Hauptmann, not even he could have. Much less Müller. The orders went to Pohl, and I told Dr. Kastner that. I'm convinced—that was in 1944, about summertime—and I'm convinced that Dr. Kastner reported that to his superiors. And I had, I had no scruples about telling him, because why keep it secret? It was common knowledge. Not the names, of course, that's obvious, but after he'd pleaded with me like that, I had to tell him, and I did. I have a lot on my conscience. I know that, Herr Hauptmann. But I had nothing to do with killing the Jews. I never killed a Jew, but I never killed a non-Jew either—I've never killed anybody. And I never ordered anybody to kill a Jew, or ordered anybody to kill a non-Jew. No, never.

LESS: In the English edition of Rudolf Höss's book—*Commandant of Auschwitz*—there are some things about you that are missing in the German edition. I've translated them for you and I'm going to read them to you: "I became acquainted with Eichmann after I received orders for exterminating the Jews from the Reichsführer-SS. He came to see me in Auschwitz to discuss the details of the extermination process with me. Eichmann was a lively, active man in his thirties, always bursting with energy. He was always hatching new plans and always in search of innovations and improvements. He could never rest. He was obsessed with the Jewish question and the order that had been given for its solution. He had regularly to give the Reichsführer-SS direct, oral reports about the preparation and implementation of the various actions. Eichmann was convinced that if he succeeded in destroying the biological foundation of Jewry in the East, Jewry as a whole would never recover from this blow." Do you wish to say something?

EICHMANN: Basically, I reject all that as untrue, totally untrue. I'm covered with guilt, Herr Hauptmann, I know that. But I had nothing to do with killing Jews. I've never killed a

Jew. And I've never ordered anyone to kill a Jew. And I know that no one can produce a document proving . . . that I've ever done such a thing. I never did. Maybe that's what gives me a certain peace of mind. I'm guilty, because I helped with the evacuation. I'm ready to pay for that. For me it was a kind of inner tranquilizer—so to speak—to say to myself: Yes, I know, enormous shipments are going out for labor service, but after all, an age limit has been set. Later on, everything went topsy-turvy, they just crammed the evacuees in—but it wasn't in my province. I wasn't responsible for the detailed implementation . . . the practical details of the evacuations, only for carrying out the order from above . . . that an evacuation should take place. And I had to set up the guidelines for implementation, because those were the Reichsführer's orders. For instance, he said: "No one is to take any more with him than the Germans who were driven out by the French." After the First World War, he meant, from Alsace-Lorraine, or later from the Rhineland and the Ruhr. I had to find out; at that time, fifty kilos of luggage were allowed.

In referring to measures taken by the Allies, primarily by the French in their occupation of the Rhineland and the Ruhr in the years after the First World War, Eichmann was deliberately disregarding the fact that, for one thing, the two "deportations" ended very differently. The deported Germans were not sent to a foreign country; they were not prisoners, let alone forced laborers, and could be sure of finding help in unoccupied Germany.

LESS: We possess the minutes of a conference held at Reich Security Headquarters. At that conference, someone said that a thousand Jews should be loaded into trains with a capacity of seven hundred. It is not clear whether you personally gave the order that a thousand instead of seven hundred Jews should be packed into every shipment to the extermination camps.

EICHMANN: Obviously, I was responsible. But I did not say those things; that was my transportation officer, Hauptsturmführer Nowack.

LESS: You keep trying to convince me that in Reich territory it was the Gauleiters who pressed to have the Jews in their Gaus evacuated as quickly as possible. I'm going to read from the minutes of a meeting: "Gauleiters or Kreisleiters are to be informed of the evacuations, because several Gauleiters complained that they have received no notice of such crucial measures."

EICHMANN: Naturally, with so many actions under way, the local evacuation authorities didn't always observe the guidelines. The bureau never took it on itself to say: Look here. There are still . . . two thousand or five thousand Jews here . . . in, say . . . Rhineland-Westphalia, we want to get them out of here, and on the double. That wasn't the province of Bureau IV B 4. It never did anything like that, because so many orders were always coming in from the Reichsführer and the head of the Security Police that we were glad if we could just get half enough transportation for those jobs and arrange the routing and scheduling with the Transportation Ministry. We, the bureau I mean, really had no need to make extra work for ourselves. We already had it up to here.

LESS: You keep saying that this, that, and the other thing weren't in your department. There are hundreds and thousands of details which you took an interest in but which were not in your department. If they were not in your department, why do we find time and again, in all these documents, that you did take a hand in them?

EICHMANN: Well, Herr Hauptmann, all those things were inseparably connected with evacuation.

LESS: That's just it. One might say, for instance: no evacuation, no gas chambers.

EICHMANN: Yes . . . you could put it that way . . . though I had nothing to do with that sector.

LESS: You say you had nothing to do with the killing?

EICHMANN: That's right.

LESS: But you delivered the people to be killed.

EICHMANN: Yes, sir, that is true, insofar as I received orders to evacuate them. But not all the people I evacuated were killed. I had no knowledge whatever of who was killed and who was not. Otherwise, 2.4 million Jews would not, according to one count, have been found alive after the war.

LESS: It's no thanks to you that any Jews were found alive after the war. If the war had gone on longer, those two million would in all likelihood have been killed. Your plan called for total extermination of the Jews.

EICHMANN: Not my plan. I had nothing to do with that plan, Herr Hauptmann.

LESS: You certainly had the plan in your possession, because—

EICHMANN: I am obviously guilty of complicity. That is plain. I've said so before. To that extent, Herr Hauptmann, I cannot deny my responsibility, and any attempt to do so would be absurd. Because from a juridical point of view I am guilty of complicity.

LESS: We're not talking about the juridical point of view. We're talking about cold facts.

EICHMANN: Yes, but I mean, on the strength of these cold facts, I am guilty of complicity . . . from the standpoint of jurisprudence. That's obvious. I realize that, and I'm not trying . . . I can't try . . . to sidestep . . . to talk myself out of it.

LESS: Very well, but in all your statements you keep hiding behind "it wasn't in my department," "it wasn't in my province," "the regulations" . . .

EICHMANN: Yes, Herr Hauptmann, I have to do that, because as head of Bureau IV B 4 I was really not answerable for everything, but only for my rather narrowly circumscribed department. And this narrowly circumscribed sphere is easily definable, because we were a central office.

LESS: In the course of time, I shall show you documents that make many things clearer. Here is a photostat of a letter to Sturmbannführer Zöpf, who worked with you in the occupied territories. Would you care to read it?

EICHMANN: Yes, sir.

LESS: I'll turn off the recorder for a moment.

EICHMANN: Yes, sir.

LESS: Have you read the document through? Do you wish to say something about it?

EICHMANN: Yes. It was written by me. It has to do with a report from the commander of the Security Police and the SD for the Dutch territories, stating that certain Jews had obtained citizenship in a neutral country. With regard to this, I wrote: "Undesirable as it is that Jews who are deportable in the light of existing regulations should acquire the nationality of a neutral country whose subjects cannot be deported, deportation in their cases must be waived for diplomatic reasons, if their acquisition of the new nationality is legally valid . . . When it is known that a Jew is in the process of acquiring a new nationality, this need not be taken into consideration. Such persons should, on the contrary, be given priority for deportation to the East."

LESS: What was the purpose of that last sentence?

EICHMANN: To make Jews stop trying to acquire a foreign nationality . . .

LESS: . . . and have them deported before they could carry out their design?

EICHMANN: Yes, that's right.

LESS: Now I'm going to show you a letter written by your department. Re: Deportation of Jews from Norway. This letter is signed by you.

EICHMANN: Signed by me. Yes.

It's about the wish and attempts and . . . efforts of Sweden to give Swedish citizenship to Jews in Norway. Here it's written that this was not permissible, because it countered the Reich's measures concerning the Jews. Here it says: "Of this I hereby inform you, with the observation that it is our aim to include Jews who have been precipitately naturalized by the Swedish government, in the peculiarly tendentious way described above, in the current measures relating to the Jews."

LESS: What you are saying here is that the attempt of the Swedish government to save Jews by providing them with Swedish passports must be thwarted at all costs.

EICHMANN: Right! . . . However, it's not me personally that's saying it, but the subordinate charged with that particular transaction. Of course, I signed it.

LESS: What exactly were your activities in the "politicized churches" sector, which you took over in 1943?

EICHMANN: Ah yes, politicized churches. I did next to nothing. That was a dead department. What particular cases were handled, I don't know, Herr Hauptmann. I don't know. Sturmbannführer Jahr took care of that.

LESS: But arrests were ordered by your department?

EICHMANN: No, Jahr took care of that.

LESS: All right, but it *was* your department.

EICHMANN: It was the bureau. But they had no need to consult me, because the matter was covered by law, and Jahr acted accordingly. Just once I called in an Evangelical pastor—what was the man's name? I don't remember—he became Provost of Berlin later on, Provost of Berlin after '45—I called him in three times, because he had . . .

The Reichsführer had issued an order forbidding members of the clergy to intercede with the authorities in favor of Jews. This Evangelical clergyman—he had a little pointed beard—attracted attention at one of the State Police stations, I don't remember where, it must have been near enough, in the Berlin area or maybe even in Berlin proper, so there was no difficulty in my asking him to report to my office. I said to him: "A report has reached us." He should have been locked up. I told him it was my duty to confirm the order for his protective arrest demanded by the competent authority. I said to him: "I'm reluctant to arrest a clergyman, because my father was an elder of the Evangelical congregation in Linz." So I gave him an official warning and said: "If another report comes in, I'll have to take you into protective custody, because we have an order from the Reichsführer." He was reported again. I don't remember whether it was the second time or the third, when my superiors held the knife to my throat, and I had to take him into protective custody. I still remember his wife calling up and pleading with me to release her husband; but there was nothing I could do, though I'd have liked to with all my heart, but I had my orders. There was nothing I could do. I hadn't reported him.

LESS: What had he been reported for?

EICHMANN: For intervening in favor of Jews, I believe.

On this occasion, Eichmann's victim was the theologian Heinrich Grüber, then pastor in the Dahlem district of Berlin, who helped endangered Jews and, through an organization he himself had founded, actually saved a number of Jews from deportation and death by hiding them in the homes of members of his congregation. He survived his stay in the concentration camps and at the end of the war became the leading representative of the Evangelical Church in the German Democratic Republic.

LESS: What were the duties of Bureau IV B 4 in relation to Auschwitz?

EICHMANN: Strictly speaking, none, Herr Hauptmann, only when the man in charge of these things at Administration and Supply Headquarters, usually a certain Liebehenschel, was consulted about the destination of the shipments from one place or another ordered by the Reichsführer. This was a purely technical question of scheduling and routing.

LESS: What does "special treatment" mean, and who was subjected to it?

EICHMANN: Special treatment is . . . Hmm, who thought up that term, I wonder?

LESS: And what does it mean?

EICHMANN: Special treatment was killing. Who thought up the term—I don't know. Must have been Himmler, who else could it have been—but then, I have no proof, maybe Heydrich thought it up after Göring gave him his authorization. But I don't really know. I'm just trying to puzzle it out.

LESS: But you knew special treatment meant killing?

EICHMANN: Everybody knew that, yes, Herr Hauptmann, everybody knew. When a shipment was marked "for special treatment," they decided at the point of arrival who was fit for labor and who wasn't.

LESS: In other words, special treatment was given to those who were declared unfit for labor?

EICHMANN: By the doctor, yes. But there were also certain groups that Himmler put down for "priority accommodation."

LESS: Who drew up the lists of Jews to be sent to Auschwitz and given special treatment?

EICHMANN: That must have been the evacuating authority. That's my guess. Because IV B 4 didn't evacuate; it only transported.

LESS: Did you receive copies of the lists?

EICHMANN: No, never a list.

LESS: You only set up shipments?

EICHMANN: Set up shipments? No, Herr Hauptmann, only the schedules for the shipments. The shipments themselves were set up by the evacuating authority.

LESS: Was special treatment given in other places besides Auschwitz? What were those other places?

EICHMANN: Yes. In the Government General there was Kulm and there was Treblinka. No shipment was ever run to Kiev or Lemberg; in those places, people were shot.

LESS: Who drew up the lists of Jews to be deported for special treatment?

EICHMANN: There again, Herr Hauptmann, it was always the evacuating authority.

LESS: Was it the duty of Höss, the Auschwitz camp commander, to record the number of Jews sent to Auschwitz?

EICHMANN: I don't know that, Herr Hauptmann. I am not informed about his official duties, and if I had asked him I don't believe he would have given me truthful answers. Those Auschwitz people always kept you at a distance— Höss, too, at first—because they didn't want anyone to see their cards, and I was from a different outfit. They had the death's-head on their collar patch, and I didn't have anything.

LESS: How many Jews were gassed and killed at Auschwitz?

EICHMANN: Herr Hauptmann, I've read, and Höss is supposed to have said, that he killed four million Jews. Up to now, I've thought that figure exaggerated. But if we're going to talk about figures, whether it's one million or four million or a hundred amounts to the same thing in principle. In these last fifteen years, I've done some figuring myself. At the end of the war, I spoke to my officers of five million. I saw that figure as a kind of cloud in my mind's eye. In that brief—hmm, how shall I put it?—apocalyptic speech, or whatever you may choose to call it, I wasn't looking for exact figures.

I don't remember whether the *Jewish Year Book* published at that time gave the figure of ten million Jews for Europe, or whether that figure covered the German-occupied Russian territories. In any case, I tried to work out a basis to figure on. I've read that a few months after the war the Allies reckoned that 2.4 million Jews were still in existence. I read that somewhere. Emigration from Austria, Germany, the U.S.S.R.—I said to myself, let's say that 1.2 million Jews emigrated. Then comes natural diminution. I'm no statistician. I just figured that out for myself. So on that basis I said to myself: Yes, one way or another, about six million Jews must have been killed. Whether I was right or not, I don't know, Herr Hauptmann.

LESS: Were the names of the dead Jews registered by your department?

EICHMANN: Of the evacuated Jews? Or of the . . . the total . . . the total number? I never had them. Never had them.

LESS: Why, then, when deaths occurred, were requests for information and death certificates addressed to you?

EICHMANN: Inquiries were addressed to me. But there weren't any lists. There's no point in denying what happened. I'd have had to keep an enormous, or anyway let's say an extremely conspicuous, file. There was no such file.

LESS: If the concentration camps sent reports of deaths to Reich Security Headquarters, and if the deceased were Jews, wouldn't those reports have come to you?

EICHMANN: In the case of the Jews, there were no reports. In the case of individual executions, naturally a record was kept, but lists of all those deaths, imagine the sheer bulk . . . We had no lists.

LESS: But this document shows that lists . . .

EICHMANN: . . . yes, that lists were made. Of Jews, too. Comprehensive lists. But I had no such lists. I wouldn't hesitate to admit it if I'd had the lists, because I, I didn't kill them, did I? I didn't hang them and I didn't shoot them.

LESS: It says here that in cases of death the relegating authority had to notify the next of kin, and in the case of Jews you were the relegating authority.

EICHMANN: No, the Gestapo and the Gestapo branch offices, not Reich Security Headquarters. Hardly ever. To my knowledge, in only one instance, that of the Evangelical pastor . . .

LESS: Who became Provost later on? The one we've already talked about?

EICHMANN: Right! What lists of Jewish detainees were drawn up concerned Jews and Jewesses in protective or preventive custody, not Jews who, let's say, were included in the evacuation measures.

LESS: Didn't you say before that they were all in protective custody, including the mass deportees?

EICHMANN: Hmm . . . mass deportees were not in protective custody.

LESS: What were they, then?

EICHMANN: It . . . it was a special order. It . . . They were all shipped by special order.

LESS: Special treatment?

EICHMANN: Special order! Special order meant special treatment. Naturally, because here again a distinction must be made between individual cases and the general order, which came from above.

LESS: Didn't the commanders of the extermination camps send reports on their activities, giving figures, and didn't those reports come to your bureau?

EICHMANN: No. I never received any reports. They must have

sent reports to Administration and Supply Headquarters. One day a statistician came to see me. A professional statistician. His name may have been Zacharias or some such thing. I have an idea that it began with a Z. You can surely find out. My immediate superior, Müller, told me a report to Hitler, to the Führer as he said at the time, had to be made, on orders from Himmler, and it had to be typed on a Führer machine. I'd never heard that term before. It was a typewriter with outsized characters. When the statistician finished his report, I had to borrow one from Gestapo headquarters on Prinz-Albrecht-Strasse, because the Security Police had only one machine. Well, this man, this statistician, came to my office. He had been given instructions by the Reichsführer to compile exact statistics on the progress of the solution of the Jewish question in Europe; we were told to make everything, all our top-secret documents, available to this man. He seemed well informed. That was my impression from the start. He wrote to all the Security Police commanders.

LESS: What figure did he arrive at?

EICHMANN: He covered the whole extermination process in the East. It came roughly—taking account of emigration, and including the figure for natural diminution, as he called it—to 4.5 or 5 million. That figure stuck in my memory. Thus—the report concluded—thus the Jewish problem in Europe was to all intents and purposes solved.

LESS: You're not sure about that statistician's name?

EICHMANN: It began with a Z. Why do I keep thinking of Zacharias?

LESS: Dr. Korherr?

EICHMANN: Korherr? Good God, how can I have been so mistaken? Korherr, Korherr? Yes, I've heard that name.

LESS: What material did you give this statistician?

EICHMANN: All our top-secret stuff. That was the order. All the shipments, insofar as they had been reported to us.

LESS: Did this material also include figures on the extermination of the Jews?

EICHMANN: No. Not the extermination. I never had those figures.

LESS: Only the evacuation figures and the shipment figures? A report was sent to you when a shipment went out?

EICHMANN: We received those reports. That was the only figure I knew. And from those figures Günther drew up a graph on the wall of his office—Dr. Löwenherz must have seen it a dozen times, everyone who came into that office could see it, a long thick line. I'm sorry, I don't remember the final figure.

LESS: Had you, before that, drawn up a report on the number of Jews deported?

EICHMANN: Before the statistician came? I don't know, Herr Hauptmann. I'm sure I did if I was ordered to. But I don't remember. With all the paper work we had—because all our work was paper work—it's really very hard for me today to vouch for details.

LESS: Did the statistician come to see you because Himmler was dissatisfied with the extermination rate?

EICHMANN: No. That statistical report was drawn up so Himmler could fill Hitler in. Because I got the report back with a notation by Himmler: "1. Führer has taken note. 2. Destroy document." Or maybe it didn't say document. Just "2. Destroy."

Dr. Richard Korherr was not a member of the SS. He was a noted statistician. Himmler made use of Dr. Korherr because he thought statistics might help him to unmask the failings and misdeeds of his subordinates. In addition, he hoped to impress Hitler with the progress of his extermination program. But, to his dismay, he was unable to submit the report in person to his Führer and was obliged to leave it with Reichsleiter Martin Bormann, the Führer's deputy. It was returned to him by

Bormann with the remark that it could not be submitted to Hitler in its present form. The words "liquidation" and "special treatment" had to be replaced by others. Even when this was done, Bormann delayed submitting the report to Hitler. He was well aware that Hitler wanted the Jews to be exterminated, but officially and ostensibly without his knowledge.

LESS: Now I'm going to show you a photostat of a letter from the Reichsführer to the head of the Security Police and the SD in Berlin. Top secret. Can you tell me whose initials those are at the bottom?

EICHMANN: That's Himmler's signature, H.H. A top-secret communication from the Reichsführer's field headquarters. "I have received the statistical report of the Inspector for Statistics concerning the final solution of the Jewish question. I consider this report satisfactory as material for possible use at a later date, for purposes of camouflage . . . For the time being, it must be neither published nor passed on. The essential, in my opinion, remains that as many Jews as humanly possible should be shipped to the East . . ."

LESS: What? What does "for purposes of camouflage" mean here?

EICHMANN: I don't get it either, considering that the statistician pretty well—why do I say pretty well?—considering that he calls a spade a spade and gives figures, as you might expect of a statistician.

LESS: Maybe Dr. Korherr's report didn't give the figures for Jews killed. Maybe that's what was meant by "purposes of camouflage."

EICHMANN: Hmm, that doesn't seem likely. That would mean that in preparing his report the statistician made no use of the figures procured from, from the East. And after all, this . . . this report was for the Führer, and in a report for the Führer he wouldn't, he wouldn't—let's say—tone things down like that. "Purposes of camouflage"! No, I don't get it.

LESS: Here in the last sentence it says: "I want the short monthly reports of the Security Police to inform me exclusively of how many Jews have been shipped each month and of how many remain at the time of writing." So you provided monthly reports on the deported Jews?

EICHMANN: Oh, yes. Because, you see, reports, monthly reports, were part of the job; obviously. He probably thought the monthly reports were getting too long. I can imagine that.

LESS: Then your reports had previously contained more?

EICHMANN: Yes, they covered the whole situation, all the difficulties encountered in the various countries. An overall, how should I put it?—comprehensive work report, naturally in appropriate, hmm . . . appropriate telegraphic style. But about how many were killed I had no figures. When the statistician was with me, a week or maybe two, in my office, day after day, making his inquiries, he sent telegrams et cetera all over the place . . . So I believe . . . the following may be possible . . . Yes, now, now it's plain to me, why the letter says "for purposes of camouflage." Most likely I supplied the statistician with the figures shipped, but not the figures killed.

LESS: Since when had you known Dr. Wilhelm Höttl?

EICHMANN: I met Höttl in Berlin, I don't remember the circumstances. I believe he, too, was with the SD.

LESS: Was he with the SD the whole time? Was he in Hungary, too?

EICHMANN: I can't say at the present moment whether Höttl was in Hungary. But if he was, I must have spoken with him there.

LESS: Did you tell Höttl that you supervised and organized the deportation of the Jews in Hungary to the death camps?

EICHMANN: Supervise and organize—I would never have told Höttl anything like that.

LESS: What would you have told him?

EICHMANN: I'd have told Höttl the truth, because at that time —I think—Höttl had long been a department head in Section VI of Reich Security Headquarters. He knew as much about the business as I did. Section VI was an intelligence outfit. So naturally they knew all about the activities of their—well, of their own organization.

LESS: Did you tell Höttl how many Jews had been exterminated?

EICHMANN: My estimation? If he asked me, I may have given him an estimated figure—yes, I may have.

LESS: I shall now read you a quotation from the 31st volume of the Proceedings of the International Military Tribunal in Nuremberg, the sworn statement of Dr. Wilhelm Höttl. I quote: "My name is Dr. Wilhelm Höttl, SS-Sturmbann-führer, major in the SS. My occupation up to the German collapse was that of department head and Deputy Gruppen-leiter in Section VI of Reich Security Headquarters. Section VI was the so-called foreign department of the SD and busied itself with intelligence in all countries. It corresponded more or less to the British Intelligence Service."

And further on: "At the end of August, I had a conversation, at my home in Budapest, with SS-Obersturm-bannführer Adolf Eichmann, whom I had known since 1938. At that time, to the best of my knowledge, Eichmann was a department head in Section IV, Gestapo, of Reich Security Headquarters. In addition, he had been charged by Himmler with apprehending the Jews in every country in Europe and shipping them to Germany. At that time, Rumania's dropping out of the war had made a deep impression on Eichmann. He expressed his conviction that the war was lost for Germany and that he personally had nothing to hope for. He knew the Allies regarded him as a leading war criminal, because he had millions of Jewish lives on his conscience. I asked him how many that might be, and he replied that the figure was a state secret but that he would tell me, since the matter was sure to be of interest to me as a historian. He told me that he had sent a report to Himmler only a short time before, since Himmler wished to know the exact number of Jews exterminated. In the various extermination camps, he told me, some four million Jews had been killed in different ways, for the most part shot by the action teams of the Security Police during the campaign against Russia. Himmler, he said, had been satisfied with the results, since in his opinion the number of Jews killed must have been over six million. Himmler had said he would send a man from his statistical bureau to Eichmann, to draft a new report on the basis of material provided by Eichmann. I must assume that the information Eichmann gave me was accurate, because of all those involved he had the most comprehensive view of the number of Jews exterminated. In the first place he, through his special teams, delivered the Jews to the extermination facilities, and second, being a department head in Section IV, and as such in charge of Jewish affairs, he must have known the figure better than anyone else. Furthermore, the frame of mind into which recent events had put Eichmann makes it seem unlikely that he would have deliberately told me an untruth."

So much for Höttl. Have you any comment to make?

EICHMANN: I do! Höttl's statements are a miscellaneous mishmash from God knows where. Yes, sure, some of those things are perfectly true. When I say . . . that he says . . . I delivered the shipments . . . well, all right . . . delivered . . . we won't . . . I won't argue about the word. Insofar as . . . because it was the agencies, the Jewish-affairs advisers

(1 1 7)

in the different countries—except for the Government General and the occupied Russian territories—that actually attended to the shipments and then reported to IV B 4. To that extent, I did have a view of the whole process.

LESS: You knew how many Jews were shipped to the camps over the years?

EICHMANN: To the camps, yes, I can't deny that.

LESS: You also knew that the camps were synonymous with final solution. That is, extermination. Consequently, you had every reason to believe that the Jews you shipped had been exterminated. Even when you said labor service, you probably knew that no one could survive such treatment for long. Whether a forced laborer dropped dead at his work or was clubbed, or whether he starved to death or was gassed—in any case, he was dead.

EICHMANN: All the same, Herr Hauptmann—I believe—as I said before, that 2.4 million Jews were enumerated by the Allies after the end of the war. And hundreds and hundreds of thousands came out of the concentration camps. And some had been in labor service. Anyway, those things weren't in my province, I had nothing to do with the concentration camps. Once the guidelines for shipment were sent out, the bureau's responsibility stopped. If I wanted to go a step further, I might say—though there's room for argument—that at the very latest my responsibility ceased when the military police took over the shipments at the evacuation stations.

LESS: Do you in general accept what Höttl says here?

EICHMANN: Not everything, Herr Hauptmann, I can't . . . that is . . .

LESS: What he says about your giving him the figure of roughly four million Jews killed and . . .

EICHMANN: No!

LESS: . . . another two million dead from other causes.

EICHMANN: I must have told him the contents of the statistician's report. I must have told him that. I think the comprehensive report ended with a total of five million. That's what I seem to remember.

LESS: I shall now read from an affidavit sworn by Walter Huppenkothen at the Nuremberg war crimes trials. I quote: "The Bureau for Jewish Affairs and its head Obersturmbannführer Eichmann occupied a special position in Section IV. Gruppenführer Müller stressed several times in my presence that Eichmann was immediately under him and not under any Gruppenleiter. I often saw him in Müller's waiting room when he reported for conferences. After my appointment as Deputy Gruppenleiter of IV A, this continued unchanged. Eichmann and his associates never spoke of their duties. I also know from conversations with comrades that Eichmann often went to see Himmler and received personal instructions from him." Have you any comment?

EICHMANN: That is a . . . a mixture of truth and poetry, but there's more truth than poetry. About my special position, he is right insofar as . . . when he says that the Gruppenleiter—and there of course he's trying to clear himself, because he himself was a Gruppenleiter—that the Gruppenleiters initialed documents, but that I didn't consult them but submitted my projects directly to Gruppenführer Müller and discussed them with him. Because in such matters the word of my immediate superior, that is, of the Gruppenleiter, would not have been enough for me. Of course, I took a good many trips. Often went to see Himmler? That, on the other hand, is not true. Altogether, I was called in to see Himmler three times. The whole purpose of Huppenkothen's affidavit is of course to distance himself as a de facto Gruppenleiter from me. That's all there is to it.

LESS: I shall now, again from the record of the Nuremberg trials, read the statement of Bruno Waneck, whom you knew at Section IV of Reich Security Headquarters.

He was asked: "Is it true that after Heydrich's death Himmler put Eichmann in exclusive charge of the solution of the Jewish problem and that Eichmann, to the exclusion of all other departments, carried out this order in the utmost secrecy?" He replied in a sworn statement: "Yes, that is absolutely true. Even in Heydrich's lifetime, Eichmann occupied a dominant, not to say absolute, position, which increased steadily in scope. At Reich Security he handled the whole Jewish sector independently. From Heydrich's death to the end, he was directly responsible to Himmler. This was generally known at Reich Security."

EICHMANN: I was never directly under Himmler. I was ordered to Himmler three times. My superior, my immediate superior, was Gruppenführer Müller. I never let myself be guided by Gruppenleiters, because they could never have given me reliable instructions; for that, they were too far below me both in rank and in function. Waneck's statement is extremely farfetched.

LESS: At the war crimes trials, Höss was asked: "Is it true that you yourself have no exact notes about the number of your victims, because you were forbidden to make such notes?" "Höss: This is correct. That is quite correct." Question: "Is it also true that only a certain Eichmann had notes on this? The man who was charged with organizing the deportations and rounding up the people?" Höss: "Absolutely!" Question: "Is it also true that Eichmann told you that a total of more than two million Jews had been exterminated in Auschwitz?" Höss: "Yes!" Have you any comment?

EICHMANN: Yes, Herr Hauptmann. About the figure of two million. Höss must have known that better than me, because the shipments went to him, not to me.

LESS: Höss testified further: "I met Eichmann about four weeks after receiving the extermination order from the Reichsführer. Eichmann came to Auschwitz to discuss the implementation of that order with me. He had been charged by the Reichsführer, as the Reichsführer had already told me when I conferred with him. I received all further instructions from him. From Eichmann."

EICHMANN: At this point, Herr Hauptmann, I must say that this whole business from A to Z can't possibly be true. It assumes that I had some order from Himmler. That is not true. At that time, I had had nothing whatever to do with Himmler. I was under orders, as I have already had the privilege of stating, from Heydrich, at the time when he told me that the Führer had decided on the extermination of the Jews.

LESS: Höss was asked: "Was the Gestapo in any way involved in the extermination of the Jews?" Höss: "Yes, insofar as I received all my orders with regard to the implementation of the action from Obersturmführer Eichmann."

EICHMANN: In the first place, Herr Hauptmann, I was not an Obersturmführer; I was an Obersturmbannführer. While we're about it, I believe I'm entitled to set the record straight. In the second place, I provided no guidelines for implementation. The technical aspect, Herr Hauptmann, was handled by the Inspection of Concentration Camps Department at Administration and Supply Headquarters, never by the Gestapo, never, never at any time, at any time!

LESS: I shall now read you a passage from Höss's memoirs: "Eichmann came to see me in Auschwitz and acquainted me with the plans for action in the various countries. First, Upper Silesia and the adjoining parts of the Government General were to be drawn upon. Then, proceeding geographically, the Jews from Germany and Czechoslovakia, then those from the West—France, Belgium, and Holland.

We went on to discuss the extermination process. It transpired that only gas could be considered, because to eliminate the masses that were to be expected by shooting was absolutely impossible and also too hard on the SS men involved, having to shoot women and children."

EICHMANN: I will not shoulder the blame for things I didn't do, Herr Hauptmann. All that stuff was made up by Höss; it has nothing whatever to do with me.

LESS: Other people made similar statements, not just Höss, and there is no reason to suppose that their stories were made to order. They had no means of getting together and saying: Now let's all of us save our skins by testifying against Eichmann. Every one of those who testified knew what was in store for him.

EICHMANN: Herr Hauptmann, I myself have read a good deal about it, and I've always wondered: Why is it always me? The only explanation I can think of is that I was always at the focal point, at the center of everything connected with Jewish affairs. Höss knew that, so he lumped everything together in his statement, said he got his instructions from Eichmann rather than Administration and Supply Headquarters. That's what he said in Nuremberg, and he hoped people would swallow all the details he gives in his book at the same time.

LESS: Höss made that statement at a time when he had no reason to conceal or embellish anything. His situation was a foregone conclusion.

EICHMANN: My situation is pretty much the same. There's so much against me that my rejection of Höss's monstrous lies can't have much effect on my punishment.

LESS: I would like to quote one more short passage and hear your answer to it. He writes in his book: "As I once heard from Eichmann, the jewelry and foreign currency were sold in Switzerland; in fact, they swamped the whole

Swiss jewel market. Ordinary watches were brought to the Sachsenhausen concentration camp by the thousands."

EICHMANN: I had no more to do with the property of those killed, Herr Hauptmann, than with the rest of it. A department of Administration and Supply Headquarters took care of the, the, how shall I say, the realization of valuables and all that. After the war, a member of the Adolf Hitler Leibstandarte [Body Regiment], and Obersturmbannführer Kuhlmann, living in Brazil under the name of Geller, told me these watches came from Administration and Supply. He said it made the troops sick to be given watches for special achievements.

LESS: You keep trying to make it look as if you were nothing more than a transportation officer.

EICHMANN: That was true as a rule, Herr Hauptmann.

LESS: The documents thus far produced show that your duties went much further. Whether or not you were acting under orders is irrelevant in my opinion. The fact is that along with the transportation problem, the technical problem of transportation, as you call it, you were involved in other areas that certainly had nothing to do with transportation.

EICHMANN: May I . . .

LESS: Please do. Do you acknowledge that?

EICHMANN: Herr Hauptmann, Bureau IV B 4 never received extermination orders. Never! Its work was transportation and nothing else, subject of course to certain conditions. For instance, it could never send out an order to Paris or The Hague or Brussels saying: "Load a thousand people into a train." There were always guidelines to be followed. The evacuating authority had to know what was being done and what people were involved. Naturally, Bureau IV B 4— this I must admit—had to pass on this information in accordance with orders from above.

LESS: And that was purely a matter of transportation?

EICHMANN: Of course not. But no implementation was possible without guidelines.

LESS: It just happened to be a special mission. Right? A special problem—the extermination of the Jews—had to be solved, and, as you say, this problem was imposed on you from above.

EICHMANN: One thing is certain, Herr Hauptmann: IV B 4 never decided anything on the strength of its own judgment and authority. It never would have entered my head to mess myself up with a decision of my own. And neither, as I've said before, did any of my staff ever make a decision of his own. All decisions were based on (a) the relevant Reich laws and accompanying implementation orders; (b) the police regulations, the decrees, orders, and instructions of Himmler and the head of the Security Police—those were our legislative bases—if you don't mind the term—in quotes, of course. The loyalty oath in itself called for unquestioning obedience. So naturally we had to comply with the laws and regulations.

LESS: Did the law of the Reich provide for the final solution of the Jewish question?

EICHMANN: The final solution itself—I mean, the special mission given to Heydrich—to put it bluntly, the extermination of the Jews, was not provided for by Reich law. It was a Führer's Order, a so-called Führer's Order. And Himmler and Heydrich and Pohl, the head of Administration and Supply—each had his own part in the implementation of this Führer's Order. According to the then prevailing interpretation, which no one questioned, the Führer's orders had the force of law. Not only in this case. In every case. That is common knowledge. The Führer's orders have the force of law.

LESS: You wanted to say some more about the implementation of evacuation orders. At the time when you were in France.

EICHMANN: Oh, yes. There was trouble in France because certain elements in the French government created difficulties for the German authorities, either for chauvinistic reasons or because they didn't want the Jews to be evacuated. An action would get started, then it would stall. The German authorities would make an enormous effort and the Foreign Office would exert pressure. Then there'd be just a little progress. Forgive me for putting it so crudely, but I'm trying to make things sound as rough as they were in practice.

LESS: Now I'm going to show you a document bearing the signature of Theo Dannecker, your agent in France. On March 10, 1942, he wrote: "Re: Deportation of 1,000 Jews to the East. At the conference of agents for Jewish affairs held on March 4, 1942, at Reich Security Headquarters in Berlin, I once again stressed the urgency of immediately deporting the Jews concentrated in Compiègne. Obersturmbannführer Eichmann agreed to the removal of these Jews before the end of March. I have arranged the following: A telegram will immediately be sent from here, informing Reich Security IV B 4 of the following: who will defray the cost of transportation to the Auschwitz concentration camp considered as an intermediate station, and whether a military police escort to that destination can be provided. The Jews being deported are permitted to take a maximum of 50 kilos of baggage with them and must be given rations for three weeks. Above all, each Jew must have at least one blanket with him, and his footwear must be in good condition. The question of funds remains to be negotiated with the office of the military commandant. In accordance with special instructions from SS-Obersturmbannführer Eichmann, Jews living in mixed marriages are to be exempted from deportation until further notice." Would you care to look through this document and comment?

EICHMANN: This is a memorandum from Hauptsturmführer

Dannecker in Paris, then adviser on Jewish questions on the staff of the Security Police and SD commander in Paris. With regard to Jews living in mixed marriages, I certainly had no . . . no instructions . . . I must have inquired in connection with this affair, through some sort of official channels. Compiègne must have been a camp . . . a . . . a . . . or an assembly point where Jews were . . . somehow . . . detained by the French police.

LESS: Are you still of the opinion that you were informed only at the last minute about the destination of these shipments, namely, Auschwitz?

EICHMANN: Naturally, Herr Hauptmann, I had to inquire where the shipments were going. What has Dannecker written here? Auschwitz concentration camp, how much baggage, etc.? Bureau IV B 4 didn't decide these things on its own. It couldn't. It always received basic instructions from Himmler.

LESS: What is meant by "Auschwitz considered as an intermediate station"? Intermediate station?

EICHMANN: I presume, Herr Hauptmann, that they were sent on to labor service, etc. You see what it says about footwear, and that every Jew must have a blanket. So I presume that SS Administration and Supply Headquarters . . . somehow . . . sent this shipment on . . . for labor service. I presume . . . of course, I can't be sure.

LESS: How many cars were provided for shipping a thousand Jews?

EICHMANN: I really can't tell you that, Herr Hauptmann. I never once made those phone calls to the Ministry of Transportation. My colleague Nowack did that. Some sort of norm had been established.

LESS: What was this norm?

EICHMANN: If I only knew. I remember that a shipment came to a thousand Jews . . . Come to think of it, we had some [shipments] from the southeast, from Greece I think, of two thousand and maybe a couple of hundred. The number of cars wasn't set by Reich Security but by the Ministry of Transportation. It was their business to know how many people would fit into a car. Though, with these shipments, of course, the official capacity of the cars wasn't taken too literally if the evacuating authority had trouble with the local Reichsbahn [German railways] administration and got less rolling stock than asked for or, as in Hungary for instance, where the Hungarian police had their own way of loading the cars.

LESS: What did the shipping lists look like?

EICHMANN: I never received a list of names. Dannecker, who was kind of meticulous, must have drawn up this list, because . . . I see a lot of foreign names here . . . and being on the cautious side, he must have said to himself: I think I'd better be careful, I'll put all these down separately. This isn't a shipping list, it's a breakdown of nationalities.

LESS: Weren't the shipping lists broken down by nationalities?

EICHMANN: Nationalities, Herr Hauptmann, were a very complicated business. We were always wrangling with the Foreign Office. We always had to get clearance from the Foreign Office.

LESS: It says here that a copy went to you.

EICHMANN: Right.

LESS: So you must have received it.

EICHMANN: Yes, normally I should have. But it seems to me that a . . . that a list of names would hardly . . . What could a central bureau do with individual names? We'd have needed a special filing cabinet for all those names, all those shipping lists.

LESS: How am I to understand: "In accordance with special instructions from SS-Obersturmbannführer Eichmann, Jews living in mixed marriages are to be exempted from deportation until further notice."

EICHMANN: Dannecker must have asked me: "What do we do

about Jews living in mixed marriages?" And I must have answered: "I don't know. I'll have to inquire." So then I must have inquired through official channels. If Heydrich was still there, he may have decided on his own authority. Or the question went to Himmler . . . to Himmler. The fact is that everything connected with mixed marriages . . . was handled by the Office of the Führer's Deputy.

LESS: Did these instructions have anything to do with technical transportation problems? The question of mixed marriages, etc.?

EICHMANN: No, not with transportation problems . . . This was a fundamental . . . a fundamental decision . . . It had to be taken somewhere. Because nothing had been decided.

In France, only a Gestapo group from Müller's Section IV had the authority to keep a lookout for enemies of the regime. But to make arrests, it was obliged to make use of the Secret Military Police, which was under the authority of the Military Commandant of Paris. According to the terms of the armistice, the French police retained the power to make arrests in German-occupied territories. As the SS increased its influence in France, Dannecker, the local agent for Jewish questions, and Eichmann, his superior, began to use the French police for rounding up Jews, and the Gestapo organized French anti-Semites and Fascists into special police commandos. It was then that the deportation figure rose abruptly. In 1940, only three trainloads of Jews were sent to the East. In 1941, there were nineteen; in 1942, a hundred and four; and in 1943, two hundred and fifty-seven.

LESS: In the second half of June 1942, three trainloads of evacuees left France for Auschwitz. On June 26, you wired Paris: "Re: Evacuation of Jews. Since no further obstacles have arisen here to the smooth and frictionless implementation of the planned evacuation measures, the projected conference with the Paris agent at Reich Security Headquarters is canceled. Instead of the projected conference, Obersturmbannführer Eichmann will go to Paris on orders from SS-Gruppenführer Müller, head of Section IV."

EICHMANN: I undoubtedly went to Paris. Naturally, I don't remember anything about it now.

LESS: What particular problems were involved?

EICHMANN: It must have been the whole business with foreigners . . . The treatment of Jews with foreign nationality. I suppose I said to myself: I'd better go and see what's happening there. Because when we had Jews of foreign nationality to deal with, we tended to use kid gloves. Because that was where we had the worst difficulties with the Foreign Office. The higher echelons of the Foreign Office would get in touch with the higher echelons of the Security Police, and they'd give us a good chewing out. Before doing anything, as a matter of principle, I'd provide myself with documentary cover. I mean, I'd try to get some hint, some answer, some instruction from my chief. Here I see that I didn't even take that trip on my own responsibility, I had Gruppenführer Müller certify its necessity.

LESS: Now I'll read excerpts from some memoranda dealing with your stay in Paris. "Memorandum re impending large-scale deportation of Jews from Paris. Regarding deportation of Jews from occupied territories, the special Reich Security agents for Jewish questions have been notified that 30,000 Jews are soon to be deported from the occupied zone of France. The necessary preparatory measures are to be taken at once. The special agents have once again been ordered to carry out the necessary actions with the utmost vigor and to report how many Jews are eligible for shipment and how many children will be left behind . . . In view of the dilatory and often negative attitude of the

French authorities toward the solution of the Jewish problem, uncompromising action on our own initiative is necessary. Ultimate goal: total cleansing of the provinces of Jews, with Jews remaining only in Paris, from which the rest will be removed in a final shipment. It has been clearly and definitely arranged with Hauptsturmführer Dannecker that the Jews en route to their final destinations will be considered stateless on their entry into Reich territory, and moreover that their financial affairs must be cleared up in every respect. It was further established that the timetable prevailing up to now, three trains weekly, each carrying a thousand Jews, would soon have to be considerably stepped up, with a view to ridding France totally of Jews as soon as possible." Do you wish to comment?

EICHMANN: I do. That makes it fairly clear why I went to Paris. In connection with an order from the Reichsführer-SS and chief of the German police, to the effect that all Jews resident in France should be deported as soon as possible. It must have come to Himmler's attention that things weren't moving ahead in France, so he sends out this order demanding to be notified at once at what date the de-Judification—to use his word—of France could be expected.

LESS: Have I understood correctly that the Jews' financial affairs were also handled by you?

EICHMANN: No. They were not handled by me. It was arranged with Dannecker that the deportees were to be regarded as stateless on entering Reich territory. The Foreign Office settled that with the French government in Vichy. If financial questions had not been settled in every respect, there would have to have been some sort of special office at the French headquarters of the commander of the Security Police and the SD. But really, nothing of that sort is known to me, and I am absolutely certain that those matters were handled by the French authorities.

LESS: From this, I gather that when these Jews crossed into Reich territory you automatically deprived them of their previous nationality and declared them stateless, because then you could claim that you only deported stateless people. Is that it?

EICHMANN: No, Herr Hauptmann. The Security Police could never have done that. That wouldn't have been legally admissible. The Vichy government, which was always making trouble in any case, would have created enormous difficulties.

LESS: But you still maintain that only technical transportation problems were involved?

EICHMANN: Yes, Herr Hauptmann. It's . . . it's perfectly obvious that all these problems are connected with shipping . . . not with killing. Evacuation and transportation . . . that's all there is to it, Herr Hauptmann . . . pure transportation. It has nothing to do with killing, Herr Hauptmann. It's a big distinction. I always made it and I must still make it now.

LESS: The final solution of the Jewish question mentioned in these documents is the extermination of the Jews in the death camps.

EICHMANN: Herr Hauptmann, as I've already had the privilege of saying . . . Final solution . . . that was a much-used expression. In the end, final solution meant extermination, but before that, it had other meanings, it meant exclusion of the Jews from the living space of the German people; that went under the name of final solution.

LESS: At the time of the conference, on July 1, 1942—

EICHMANN: . . . the killing had already begun.

LESS: . . . Heydrich was already dead. But you had heard about the murders from him. Consequently, whenever "final solution" is mentioned in these documents, it means physical annihilation.

EICHMANN: But, Herr Hauptmann, in that case the people wouldn't have needed good footwear or fifty kilos of baggage, etc. Would they? In other words, they were being shipped off to labor service. And then there's the question of age, Jews over a certain age, and then the question of children, etc., etc.

LESS: Maybe the preparations for the killing were so thorough that every conceivable moot question had to be settled neatly and thoroughly in advance, in the well-known German manner. The question of footwear, for instance: it wouldn't do to have these deportees looking untidy on their arrival. What happened next didn't matter.

EICHMANN: No, no, Herr Hauptmann. I don't believe that. After all, there were so many, so many Jews left after 1945. There were hundreds of thousands of them, Jews who had been in the concentration camps.

LESS: I wouldn't want to ask what would have happened if the war had gone on for another year. I will now read you a memorandum of July 15, 1942, from the Paris Office for Jewish Affairs. "Re: Shipment of Jews to Auschwitz. On July 14, 1942, Obersturmbannführer Eichmann telephoned from Berlin and asked why the shipment for July 15, 1942, had been canceled. I replied that the star-bearers in the provinces were originally to have been arrested, but on the basis of a recent agreement with the French government, only stateless Jews were to be arrested for the time being. The train had to be canceled because, according to the Bordeaux SD command, only 150 stateless Jews were available, and it was not possible to make up the deficiency in the short time remaining. Obersturmbannführer Eichmann pointed out that this was a matter of prestige. To obtain the trains, long discussions with the Ministry of Transportation had been required, and now Paris was canceling a train. Such a thing had never happened to him before. It was most embarrassing. He wouldn't tell Gruppenführer Müller about it for the present for fear of putting himself in the wrong. He would have to consider dropping France altogether as a deportation country. I begged him not to do that, adding that it was not the fault of this office and that the other trains would leave on schedule."

EICHMANN: Dannecker phoned me after that and somehow managed to dispose of all my complaints. From the contents of the memo, it can be gathered that three trains had been obtained from the Transportation Ministry with the utmost difficulty. And then this one train was canceled. Such incidents always brought a dreadful howl from the Transportation Ministry, because they disrupted its schedules.

LESS: I will now show you a telegram from Paris, dictated by Dannecker on July 10, 1942. "To Reich Security Headquarters, IV B 4, Berlin. Re: Deportation of Jews from France. Memorandum of a conversation between SS-Obersturmbannführer Eichmann and SS-Hauptsturmführer Dannecker. Stateless Jews in Paris are to be arrested by the French police in the period between July 10 and July 18, 1942. It is to be expected that after this arrest some 4,000 Jewish children will remain behind. These children will be cared for temporarily by the French Public Welfare Service. Since prolonged cohabitation of these Jewish children with non-Jewish children is undesirable, and since the Union of Jews in France can accommodate no more than 400 children in its own orphanages, urgent telegraph instructions are requested: Is it permissible, as of roughly the tenth, to deport the children of the deported stateless Jews along with their parents? per proc. Dannecker."

And now a memo from Dannecker of July 21, 1942. "Re: Deportation of Jews. On July 20, 1942, Obersturmbannführer Eichmann and SS-Obersturmführer Nowack phoned from RSHA IV B 4. The question of deporting children was discussed with Obersturmbannführer Eichmann. He decided that as soon as deportation to the

Government General becomes possible again, shipments of children can get under way. Obersturmführer Nowack promised to make possible some six shipments to the Government General, to comprise Jews of all kinds, including the old and infirm. Obersturmbannführer Eichmann was further informed that, for the present, only another ten shipments would be possible and that negotiations for the arrest of more Jews were pending with the French government."

Do you wish to comment?

EICHMANN: I remember now about the children; I remember hearing that. The general decision affecting those children was made by Himmler in person. Reich Security Headquarters, through Gruppenführer Müller, asked him for instructions in the matter. This thing wasn't decided by Müller and it wasn't decided by the head of the Security Police and the SD. It was submitted to Himmler, and Himmler's decision was: "Ship!" I remember now, Herr Hauptmann.

LESS: Was that decision a technical transportation problem? Sending four thousand children to the death camps?

EICHMANN: Yes, Herr Hauptmann. It was a question of guidelines for the handling of shipments. Our offices abroad had to be provided with guidelines, and I had to procure those guidelines.

LESS: One more document, please. I'll turn off the recorder for a moment.

EICHMANN: It's a telegram to Bureau IV B 4, my office in Berlin. Hauptsturmführer Dannecker informs us that his negotiations with the French government in Vichy have "made all stateless Jews in the occupied and unoccupied zones available for deportation. Premier Laval suggested that when Jewish families are deported from the unoccupied zone, children under sixteen should be taken along.

He is not interested in the question of Jewish children left behind in the occupied zone. I therefore request an urgent decision as to whether, as of the fifteenth, children under sixteen may be included in the shipments of Jews from France."

LESS: Do you believe that fourteen-year-old children are fit for hard labor and that they could survive in an extermination camp like Auschwitz?

EICHMANN: Herr Hauptmann, these guidelines were handed down by the Reichsführer, not by me.

LESS: I asked you whether you thought fourteen-year-old children were fit for hard labor.

EICHMANN: Of course not. Or only in exceptional cases.

LESS: Can't we infer that the plan was to gas these children the moment they arrived?

EICHMANN: I didn't give the order, Herr Hauptmann.

LESS: I will now read to you from a document in which a member of your Paris office reports on a conference on Jewish questions held at Reich Security Headquarters on August 28, 1942. "The RSHA pointed out that, for the present, only stateless Jews could be deported. Concerning other foreign Jews, discussions with the Foreign Office are in progress and have not yet been concluded. Under no circumstances is it desirable to return foreign Jews to their own countries. The request of the Swiss consulate that a number of Jewish families of Swiss nationality be deported to Switzerland cannot be granted. The property of foreign Jews cannot yet be confiscated, since the representatives of various foreign countries are interested in the property of their Jews."

There's one thing I fail to understand. Maybe you can explain it. What do the undesirability of returning foreign Jews to their homes and the confiscation of Jewish property have to do with transportation problems? All these documents indicate, time and again, that your bureau was concerned with a lot more than transportation problems.

EICHMANN: Yes, Herr Hauptmann, to the extent that such matters were the groundwork without which an evacuation could not be carried out. You couldn't have any old officials belonging to any old evacuation authority going out in the street and indiscriminately picking up every Jew they saw —just because they happened to belong to the "deportation of Jews" department . . . No, that wouldn't do . . . First, IV B 4 had to iron out all the difficulties with the various competent authorities, as I've already had the privilege of . . .

LESS: Now I'm going to show you another photostat. Of a document dealing with a shipment of children.

EICHMANN: This . . . Too bad we haven't got the whole document. Some official body seems to have notified Reich Security Headquarters in 1943 that a thousand Jewish children, accompanied by a hundred Jewish adults, wished, with the cooperation of the Wagons-Lits International Sleeping Car Company, to emigrate to Palestine by the land route via Bulgaria. Thereupon Bureau IV B 4 received instructions to give the Foreign Office a negative reply. At the end, it says: "You are requested as far as possible to prevent this projected emigration." The last sentence shows a certain lack of enthusiasm.

LESS: And here you have another three pages of photostats on the same subject.

EICHMANN: Yes, that was the usual position of the Foreign Office. They were always worried—rightly so, if I may speak objectively—about a new state being set up in Palestine, which would create all sorts of difficulties for the Foreign Office. That little preoccupation runs like a red thread through all the Foreign Office's activities in connection with the treatment of Jews when the question of emigration came up. It gave me all kinds of trouble, especially in Vienna, because of the stepped-up activities of the Zionist organizations.

LESS: Read this photostat. It's a telegram, dated Belgrade, September 12, 1941, addressed to the Foreign Office, and concerns the Jews in Serbia.

EICHMANN: The undersigned reports to the Foreign Office that "in view of present internal conditions it is not possible to keep the Jews in labor camps, because security cannot be guaranteed. The Jewish camps would only endanger the troops. It is therefore necessary to remove 1,200 Jews from the Sabac camp immediately, since subversive bands several thousand strong have been sighted in the region. The removal of all male Jews is essential if order is to be restored." The sender was probably a man from the Foreign Office. And then these penciled notes: "IV B 4 . . . As per information Obersturmbannführer Eichmann . . ." ". . . accommodation in . . ." What can this word be?

LESS: Russia.

EICHMANN: ". . . in Russia and the Government General impossible. Not even the . . . not even the Jews from Germany . . ."

LESS: ". . . can be . . ."

EICHMANN: "Can be accommodated there. Eichmann suggests shooting . . . suggests shooting." "Speak with RSHA . . ." Anyway, it says here clearly: "Eichmann suggests shooting." Well, I suppose I passed the matter on. Judging by the content, it's perfectly clear to me: it must have been decided that there was no other course than to shoot them. To set the record straight, I'd like to say here, though there's no need to, that I didn't give that order to shoot them on my own authority. I handled those matters through channels, and the order that came down from my superiors was: Shoot them.

LESS: Your agent in Holland wrote a letter from The Hague addressed to the Jewish camp in Westerbork: "Re: Filling the trains bound for the East." Have you read this document, and do you wish to comment?

EICHMANN: It should be possible to connect this memorandum about supplying a sum total of eight thousand Jews to fill six trains with a demand made by our superiors or by a scheduling conference and with a report of April 1943 on the de-Judification of Holland. The RSHA must then have made trains for a sum total of eight thousand Jews available to the commander of the Security Police in The Hague. And here the commander of the Security Police is wondering how he's going to round up that number.

LESS: Am I to understand that the RSHA demands that eight thousand Jews be shipped in the month of May at all costs; in other words, that you made the occupied countries supply monthly quotas of Jews to be deported?

EICHMANN: If I, for instance . . . Well, today I can't remember, but the important thing for the RSHA was the number of trains it obtained. The Reich Transportation Ministry had instructions from a higher echelon to do everything in its power. The Reich Transportation Ministry allotted the trains, let's say, en bloc, but then they were apportioned. And naturally they'd be apportioned in accordance with the reports that had come in. If, for any reason connected with the functioning of the Reichsbahn in Holland, empty trains were available, the RSHA would be expected to make use of this return freight.

LESS: Am I to understand that after rolling stock had been requisitioned and you knew how many cars were available, you would set the quota of Jews to be deported from the occupied countries accordingly?

EICHMANN: Well, yes, but . . . it wasn't me . . . I definitely had orders from the Reichsführer, who had been after the

(138)

Transportation Ministry to supply the maximum number of trains and was after us to evacuate without delay. If eight trains were made available to me for Holland, then The Hague would supply eight thousand Jews, because they knew that a thousand would be loaded into each train . . . But here I read that twelve hundred were shipped in one train, and on May 1 as many as 1,450 old and sick Jews. Now there's something I don't understand, unless . . .

LESS: Am I to understand that once the figure had been set at eight thousand, these eight thousand had to be shipped at all costs, even if only six trains were available?

EICHMANN: I don't know anything about their local arrangements. What it says here: sick and elderly Jews . . . they were . . . for the East . . . That was contrary to the regul . . . contrary to the guidelines . . .

LESS: But they were deported all the same.

EICHMANN: To the East? Could they really have been deported? And where . . . where did they end up? Sick and elderly Jews, that's contrary to the guidelines.

LESS: Your department insisted that eight thousand Jews should be deported in the month of May without fail. Wasn't that forcing the pace?

EICHMANN: Herr Hauptmann, Bureau IV B 4 had to speed up the rate of evacuation for two reasons. One was the Reichsführer's clear and inflexible orders. And in the second place, IV B 4 was dependent on the supply of rolling stock. At times when it was easily obtainable, IV B 4, on the basis of the general orders of the Reichsführer-SS and chief of the German police, had to strain every muscle to make the fullest use of that rolling stock.

LESS: Here I have a telegram from your Berlin bureau to your agent Zöpf in The Hague, dated January 22, 1944. Re: Jewish buyers of metals.

EICHMANN: This telegram contains an order to evacuate certain Jews named by name, who had evidently been active as buyers of metals for the Reich Ministry of Armaments and Munitions. Here I can only make the general observation that we had strict orders to finish the job in Holland with all possible haste.

LESS: Here's what it says: "In consideration of imminent total de-Judification of the Netherlands, the request of the agent for the Reich Minister of Armaments and Munitions to liberate the following Jews"—here the names are given—"to enable them to buy metals, cannot, for reasons already stated, be granted." In other words, this particular ministry was interested in having those Jews released and your bureau comes and says no.

EICHMANN: In addition to the already existing orders, the Reich authorities had issued a new order to proceed with special severity in Holland. I must have known all that at the time. We had the pertinent documents. But I know that —for a time, at least—very special attention was paid to Holland, because of the rotten situation there, with some sort of groups still running around free.

LESS: Can one infer from this document that certain German agencies in the Netherlands were trying to liberate Jews?

EICHMANN: Exactly. A representative of the Reich Minister of Armaments and Munitions.

LESS: Am I to take it that your bureau was opposed on principle to any liberation of Jews?

EICHMANN: Because there was an order from the Reichsführer. Of course. It had to.

LESS: Did you concern yourself with the personal fate of individual Jews and make decisions affecting them?

EICHMANN: Except for the Jewish functionaries, with whom I worked all those years, I did not decide a single personal fate; and as for the functionaries, I never decided their fate, I never had any of them evacuated, let alone killed . . . or anything of the kind.

LESS: Now let me show you a letter of December 2, 1942, from your bureau to the Foreign Office. "Re: The Jew and former French prisoner of war Roger Massé, born in 1884. The above-mentioned Jew was deported to the East—Auschwitz—on June 5, 1942. For reasons of principle, I cannot agree to having him shipped back. per proc. Eichmann."

EICHMANN: That's a normal routine communication, drafted by a clerk.

LESS: But it shows that you personally . . .

EICHMANN: Herr Hauptmann, it's a form letter. A routine communication. It's not a decision on my part.

LESS: But it says "I": "For reasons of principle, I cannot agree . . ."

EICHMANN: Yes, yes, of course. That's a bureaucratic . . . always the same old story . . . obviously. I was the bureau head. It had to have my name on it. This letter had no effect on the fate of the man concerned.

LESS: Of course not, because he wasn't sent back. Quite right. This next document concerns the owners of the Kapitol Cinema in Heidelberg. A letter of February 2, 1943, from you to the Foreign Office in Berlin. Is this your signature?

EICHMANN: My signature? Yes, it is.

LESS: It concerns the Jewish family of Jakob Hirsch, alias Eugen Romani, Hungarian national. From here on, I quote. "From the above, it follows that the motion-picture industry is almost completely Jew-contaminated. In the here prevailing view, this Eugen Romani is obviously a Jew, who appears to have managed, on the strength of his connections with influential Hungarian circles, to get himself transformed into an Aryan in return for bribes. It therefore seems pointless to ask him or his children for proof of their alleged Aryan descent. I therefore intend to give instructions not to renew the residence permit of Eugen Romani, his wife, and his son Rudolf, which expires on February 12,

1943, and to expel said persons from the Reich. Rudi Romani, because of his incredible conduct, is to be sent to a concentration camp. Before I have this measure executed, however, I should like to be informed as soon as possible whether there is any diplomatic objection. per proc. Eichmann." It seems to me that you decided that family's fate. Right?

EICHMANN: Right. Though the text as such was not drafted by me, but by one of the clerks. I signed for the head of the Security Police and the SD.

LESS: Here I have a letter of March 23, 1943, from you to the Foreign Office. Is this your signature?

EICHMANN: Yes, it's my signature.

LESS: I'm going to read you this document. "Re: The Jew Israel Hirschberg, residing at 34 Sodenerstrasse, Berlin-Wilmersdorf. According to his own statement, the Jew Hirschberg, of German citizenship, is employed by the Thai ambassador in Berlin as a language teacher and instructs both the ambassador and members of his family. Apart from the fact that suitable persons of German blood must be available for this activity, I am of the opinion that in employing the Jew Hirschberg the Thai ambassador's sole purpose is to shield him from difficulties. I should therefore be grateful if your office could persuade the Thai ambassador to dispense with the further employment of the Jew Hirschberg, and request notification of the results. per proc. Eichmann." Was your purpose in protesting Hirschberg's further employment to have him sent to a death camp?

EICHMANN: Herr Hauptmann, that was written in 1943 . . .

LESS: When you were involved in the final solution of the Jewish question . . .

EICHMANN: This, of course, is another one of the documents that I signed and that were submitted to me in accordance with the instructions and guidelines that had been given me for the bureau.

LESS: If the man was dismissed by the Thai ambassador, only one fate was open to him: deportation with the next or one of the next shipments.

This letter of September 27, 1943, concerns the Jewess and Dutch national Caroline Simons. It is a short letter. It says: "Due to recent political developments, I believe there is no further reason to favor the departure of said Jewess to Italy. I have therefore instructed my agency in The Hague to send Simons immediately to the East for labor service. per proc." Is this your signature?

EICHMANN: Yes. A clerk drafted it. It was written in answer to a letter of August 27, 1943, and I signed it, per proc.

"Due to recent political developments"—today, of course, I can't say what may have been regarded as a political development on September 27, 1943. In any case, the man who drafted this must have had certain documents before him, on the strength of which he . . .

On July 25, 1943, the Italian dictator Benito Mussolini was dismissed by his king and taken prisoner. The Fascist Party of Italy was dissolved. The new government under Marshal Badoglio broke with Germany and capitulated on September 8 to the Allies. Even under Fascist rule, the Italians had dragged their feet in applying the German anti-Semitic regulations. As long as Italy remained an ally, the Germans had had to put up with such laxity. But now, with the Italian capitulation, the German authorities had no further need to propitiate the Italians. The forty-year-old Caroline Simons must have had influential friends in Italy, who tried to save her from the Gestapo by getting her out of Germany, but in the new situation they were powerless.

LESS: And you . . . you sent out an order that this woman should be deported to the East. Labor service in the East, that meant a concentration camp. It meant Auschwitz. Yet at every one of our sessions you have insisted that your bureau was concerned with transportation and nothing else.

EICHMANN: That is . . . the . . . the . . . That was our job.

LESS: You have claimed that you never took a hand in the fate of individual Jews. But these documents speak for themselves. They show that you had full powers.

EICHMANN: That is true, Herr Hauptmann. But, on the other hand, these were not personal decisions. They were not personal decisions. If I had not been sitting there, someone else would have had to make exactly the same decisions on the basis of the instructions, regulations, and orders of the higher-ups. I wasn't expected to make any decisions at all. At the most, I wrote letters per proc. for somebody else, for the head of the Security Police and the SD. Not for IV B 4, because that was me.

LESS: The next document has to do with the evacuation of the Rumanian Jews. It's a telegram from Rintelen, the German Minister in Bucharest, to the Foreign Office.

EICHMANN: In it he says that the chief of the Security Police and the SD—he writes "Chief of the Security Police and the Sicherheitsdienst [Security Service]," that's wrong, of course, it has to be "Chief of the Security Police and the SD"—"has announced that the political and technical preparations for the solution of the Jewish question in Rumania have been completed and shipments can soon begin. It is planned to transfer the Jews from Rumania in a series of shipments beginning September 10, 1942, to the Lublin district, where the able-bodied will be assigned to labor service and the rest subjected to special treatment. It has been arranged that these Jews will lose their citizenship on crossing the Rumanian border. On instructions from the RSHA, SS-Hauptsturmführer Richter, adviser for Jewish questions in Bucharest, has requested and obtained a personal letter from Mihail Antonescu, the deputy premier. I request authorization to carry out deportation measures. Rintelen."

LESS: What does it mean that the rest will be subjected to special treatment?

EICHMANN: They will be killed. That's the technical term.

LESS: Am I to infer that in this case and others the Jews declared unfit for labor were automatically given special treatment?

EICHMANN: That's the way it was, by order of the Reichsführer-SS and chief of the German police. .

LESS: Was this order drafted by you?

EICHMANN: Yes. Yes, it was. It must have been signed by . . . by a superior. Kaltenbrunner or Müller.

LESS: The Bucharest agent of Reich Security Headquarters seems to have been one of your men. Richter, no doubt?

EICHMANN: Yes, it was Richter. But then we had to look into the matter and make sure all the requirements were met. Himmler couldn't simply give orders that all Jews were to be evacuated from Rumania, the able-bodied put to work and the rest subjected to special treatment. That wasn't a country where the Reichsführer-SS and chief of the German police only had to give an order and the trains would start rolling. In this case, all the requirements had to be met.

LESS: And what is the point of "It has been arranged that these Jews will lose their citizenship on crossing the Rumanian border"?

EICHMANN: Some bureau must have insisted on that.

LESS: Wasn't it *your* bureau? Once these people were stateless, it was all right to seize them and send them to the camps. Then no one could say: You've sent Rumanian citizens to the death camps. They were stateless.

EICHMANN: The Foreign Office must have imposed that condition. In such matters, the Foreign Office always took precedence. Müller and the chief of the Security Police and the SD were always extremely careful in such matters and insisted on things being settled at the highest level.

LESS: Because Herr Ribbentrop might otherwise have felt slighted?

EICHMANN: No, no. If the Foreign Office said no, the Security Police couldn't make a move in foreign countries. The various departments defended every inch of their competency tooth and nail. Otherwise, there'd have been no need for all this stupid paper work. The bureaucracy, the—what shall I call it?—the red-tape specialists stuck to the regulations with an obstinacy, a punctilio . . . That's why you've got these tons of documents.

LESS: The Germans have always been famous for their thoroughness. And that includes thoroughness in killing. On that score, one more letter from your bureau. Dated July 26, 1942, the very same day, to the Foreign Office. Re: Solution of the Jewish question.

EICHMANN: This is a letter from my bureau, stating that it is planned to send Jews from Rumania to the East by special trains as of September 10, 1942.

LESS: What sort of instructions did your bureau give your agents in connection with these shipments?

EICHMANN: They had to do with provisions for the trip, things like that. And then always and invariably the same identical sentence: "Avoidable cruelties are to be avoided."

LESS: When the authorities of the occupied territories addressed inquiries concerning the whereabouts of the deportees to your agents in those places, did you allow them, or forbid them, to provide such information?

EICHMANN: When questions were asked, the answer was: For labor service in the East. That was the official formulation. IV B 4 had no idea who was killed and who was sent to labor service. And . . . today I can imagine—since the answer was invariably "Labor service in the East"—that such questions were not often asked.

LESS: Here I have four pages of photostats on the subject.

EICHMANN: This is an inquiry from Paris to Reich Security Headquarters IV B 4, asking whether a reply could be given to the inquiry of the Union Générale des . . . Israélites de France, concerning the whereabouts of certain deported Jews, with a view to the payment of pensions, insurance indemnities, and other payments. To which Reich Security Headquarters replied in a telegram, signed by me, that the information was not to be given to the Jewish organization but to the French . . . er . . . the French police authorities. But, to avoid the misuse of such information for purposes of atrocity-mongering, no mention was to be made of evacuation or deportation. The reply was to state solely that the Jew in question had moved and that his present whereabouts were unknown. On the basis of this telegram, Paris communicated the relevant information to the Paris police prefecture.

LESS: What is meant by atrocity-mongering?

EICHMANN: Well . . . saying they'd been sent to concentration camps . . .

LESS: In the foreign press, you mean?

EICHMANN: Yes, of course, in the foreign press. Because they were always, and not just for that, criticizing the measures taken by the German government. All this kind of unfavorable publicity was known in the Reich as atrocity-mongering.

LESS: Even when it stuck to plain facts?

EICHMANN: Yes, yes . . . exactly.

It all went under the head of atrocity-mongering, even when it was true. Even when it wasn't connected with Jews but with something entirely different. It all went under the head of atrocity-mongering.

LESS: Didn't everything . . . everything connected with shipment to the camps pass through your bureau? Didn't your bureau . . .

EICHMANN: Not the killing! Not the killing! I . . .

LESS: . . . delivered the deportees to the camps?

EICHMANN: Yes, after Administration and Supply had told us where they were being sent.

LESS: Let's put it this way: the Jews were rounded up, deported, taken to death camps, killed.

EICHMANN: Right.

LESS: And you were the delivering agency.

EICHMANN: Yes, of course, the delivering agency. Yes, Herr Hauptmann, of course.

LESS: If, for instance . . . if some foreign power wanted a death certificate, then you would be asked for that document?

EICHMANN: By the Foreign Office, yes.

LESS: You were asked for it. Because you as the delivering, as the delivering agency, you were responsible for making out and issuing the death certificate.

EICHMANN: By the Foreign Office. They applied to us for it. And we had to apply to Administration and Supply, because we had no data about who went to labor service and who was killed.

LESS: Here is a letter of December 21, 1943, from your bureau to the Foreign Office. It concerns the Jew and Italian subject Bernardo Taubert.

EICHMANN: Yes, here the Foreign Office is informed that in the fifth year of the war there are more important things to do than investigating the whereabouts of an evacuated Jew. It is to be deplored that the embassy of republican Fascist Italy should continue to intercede for Jews in the same old way. Evidently, the embassy—yes, it can be inferred from this—demanded an inquiry into said Jew's whereabouts, and a negative reply was given on December 21, 1943.

Undoubtedly, he was evacuated. Either he was sent to Auschwitz or to one of the other destinations. It's possible that he was already dead and possible that he was still alive. But here, this sentence, saying there was no need to make such inquiries in the fifth year of the war, suggests to me that our bureau didn't even consult the records.

LESS: What did the life of a single Jew matter?

EICHMANN: Perhaps on this occasion I may be permitted to say a few words *pro domo*. I am neither a Jew-hater nor an anti-Semite. I said that to Dr. Löwenherz and Kommerzialrat* Storfer at the Vienna Central Office for Emigration and I said the same thing to Dr. Kastner in Budapest. I think I said it to everyone. Everyone heard it at least once. My men knew it. I never had any trouble with the Jewish functionaries. And I don't think any of them would complain about me. When during my absence in Hungary,

---

* Commercial Counselor, an Austrian honorary title given to successful businessmen.—*Trans.*

Kommerzialrat Storfer of Vienna was arrested by Vienna State Police Headquarters, by Dr. Ebner, and sent to Auschwitz concentration camp, I had words about it with Ebner, because he knew that Storfer, like Löwenherz, had been active in Jewish life for years and shouldn't have been sent to a concentration camp.

LESS: When were you in Auschwitz on Storfer's account?

EICHMANN: Kommerzialrat Storfer's account? That must have been . . . Right, and then I found a telegram waiting for me in Berlin, from Höss, the Auschwitz camp commander, saying that Storfer was begging to speak to me. So I said to myself: The man has always been decent, we worked together for . . . after all . . . we both held up our end. It's worth it to me. I'll go and see. In Vienna, Ebner said to me: "If only he hadn't behaved so stupidly. He hid and tried to run away. So the police arrested him and sent him to a concentration camp." The Reichsführer's orders were that no one who was in could be let out. Neither Dr. Ebner nor I nor anyone else could do a thing.

LESS: So you couldn't do anything for Dr. Storfer?

EICHMANN: I went to see Höss in Auschwitz. He said: "He has been assigned to a labor block." They brought Storfer in and he told me his tale of woe. I said: "Ah, my dear good Storfer, I really can't help you. What rotten luck we've had!" And I also said: "Look, I really can't help you, because by the Reichsführer's orders, no one can get you out." Then Storfer asked me if I couldn't get him off working, because it was hard labor, and I said to Höss: "Storfer doesn't have to work." Höss said: "Here everybody has to work." So then I said: "All right, I'll put in a note that Storfer should be given a broom and sweep the little gravel paths in the garden outside the Kommandantur"—they had these little gravel paths—"and that he's entitled to sit down on one of the benches at any time." I asked him: "Is that all right, Herr Storfer? Does that suit you?" He was delighted, we shook hands, they gave him his broom, and he sat down on his bench. That made me very happy.

LESS: Do you know what became of him?

EICHMANN: The next time I got back from Hungary, I heard that Storfer had been shot. And pretty much the same thing happened to Dr. Eppstein, whom I'd known since 1935 and worked with in Berlin. I had the impression at the time that they took advantage of my absence to do away with all the men I'd been working with for years, because I would never have done it.

LESS: In the Central Offices for Jewish Emigration in Berlin, Vienna, and Prague, did the Jewish functionaries sit with your men, or did they work separately?

EICHMANN: In Prague I can't remember, but I think it was the same as in Berlin and Vienna. In the Vienna office, there were maybe ten, twelve, fifteen co-workers, Jewish functionaries from the Vienna Jewish community. Stahlecker, my superior, often came to the office and inspected it, once he went over the whole conveyor belt. He shook hands with every one of the Jews, and so did the officials from the Finance Ministry, etc. About Vienna I'm sure, and since Prague was a replica of Vienna, I think it must have been the same.

LESS: And Berlin?

EICHMANN: In Berlin I can't tell you for sure, but I believe that officials from the Reich Union of Jews were put in there, were sent there, and they were certainly Jews.

LESS: Did you, in 1940, hold a conference in your office, which the Jewish functionaries from Berlin, Vienna, and Prague were ordered to attend?

EICHMANN: Yes. I had them come to Berlin a number of times when some new regulations went into effect. Once, the Jewish functionaries from all three cities were ordered to

Berlin; that time, I had the order from Müller. Yes, that's how it was. I even remember the date. It was right after that exhibition. "The Red Paradise," I think it was called . . . that's right, "The Red Paradise." There had been some act of sabotage. I don't remember what . . . and I was given the order . . . How was it? Yes, Dr. Löwenherz, I still remember, Dr. Murmelstein from Prague, Eppstein from Berlin. All in all, maybe six or eight functionaries were ordered to Berlin. Müller informed them that, on orders from the Reichsführer-SS and chief of the German police —I don't quite remember—certain Jews from the Berlin community, I believe—I may be mistaken, I'm not really sure—some Jews at any rate, were to be shot for sabotage at the exhibition.

LESS: Was the order carried out?

EICHMANN: Yes, it was carried out. And the functionaries were notified. That's all.

LESS: And now a few more documents relating to the Central Offices. Here is a letter of November 24, 1942, from your bureau. Top secret. To the Reichsführer-SS and chief of the German police, at his field headquarters. Re: Procurement of foreign currency for the enlisting of volunteers in the Waffen-SS in Hungary / funding of family allotments for the volunteers' dependents.

EICHMANN: In brief, here is what it's about: Jews were to be allowed to emigrate in return for appropriate payment, and the proceeds used to defray this expenditure for the Waffen-SS. The matter was undoubtedly broached to the chief of the Security Police and the SD by Chief Adjutant Gruppenführer Berger, who was in charge of all recruiting for the Waffen-SS. This is connected with the fact that the top leadership allowed certain Jews to emigrate for certain economic reasons, and so on.

LESS: Should this letter be taken to mean that your bureau

agreed, for the purpose of obtaining foreign currency, to let a few elderly Jews emigrate, in return for payments of a hundred thousand Swiss francs a head, instead of deporting them to the death camps?

EICHMANN: Yes. Basically, yes. When the Reichsbank and the Ministry of the Economy applied to Reich Security Headquarters, Bureau IV B 4 couldn't decide on its own; it had to go through channels for an authorization, because of the general order that no one should be allowed to emigrate.

LESS: And these elderly Jews were released in return for ransom?

EICHMANN: Once the Ministry of the Economy and the Reichsbank got the authorization, SS headquarters under Gruppenführer Berger would say to itself: I think we can approve this for the sake of the Waffen-SS. The purpose of this letter was to ask if it was all right with us.

LESS: Now I'm going to show you two photostats. One is a letter of December 14, 1940, from the German embassy in Afghanistan, concerning the attempt of Professor Emil Fleischmann of Vienna and Kapellmeister Otto Kollmann, also of Vienna, both Jews, to obtain teaching positions in Afghanistan with a view to emigrating to that country. The second document is a letter of February 28, 1941, from your bureau to the Foreign Office, concerning these two Jews. It says, in part: "Referring to your communication of February 18, 1941, I wish to inform you that in the meantime I have instructed the Central Office for Jewish Emigration in Vienna that, in the framework of the deportation of Jews from Vienna to the Government General, the Jews Fleischmann and Kollmann, mentioned in the letter of December 14, 1940, from the German embassy in Afghanistan, are being deported by one of the next trains. This would seem to settle the matter. per proc. Eichmann." This is your signature?

EICHMANN: Here I can only say that the question was decided in the negative. Since a professor was involved, they must have consulted the Reich Minister of Education and proceeded accordingly.

LESS: In your letter of February 28, 1941, did you write in "to the Government General" in your own hand?

EICHMANN: Yes. That is mine. I had to be exact about their destination.

LESS: How do you reconcile this letter with your repeated claims that even during the war you helped the Jews in their efforts to emigrate?

EICHMANN: Well, as I've said before: I did what I could. Here, obviously, there was nothing I could do. Here I had to . . . had to be guided by the decision of the Ministry of Education . . . I assume it was the Ministry of Education because of the . . . because of the circumstances . . . I had to go along with their decision. Once that sort of thing started through the . . . through the paper mill, it just went on rolling.

LESS: You were the competent authority. From this letter, only two facts can be inferred: that you had already, in the meantime, instructed the Central Office for Jewish Emigration to deport those two Jews to the Government General —and that "this would seem to settle the matter."

EICHMANN: Yes, but judging from all that . . . something must have happened first. You see, on February 28, 1941 . . . emigration was still possible and would be for some time to come. Unless it was one of those cases where a State Police office, a local State Police office, put in a veto.

LESS: No security reasons are mentioned in this letter.

EICHMANN: At any rate, as long as paper work was being done, it had to be done properly. Because a document from our bureau was taken seriously. Anything else is inconceivable. But here I read: "Minister of Cultural Affairs," their peti-

tions to the Minister of Cultural Affairs . . . Maybe that's
the . . . does he mean the Minister of Education?

LESS: The Afghan—

EICHMANN: The embassy—the German embassy in Afghanistan writes to the Foreign Office: "A letter addressed to the
Minister of Cultural Affairs has chanced to fall into my
hands . . . Two gentlemen from Vienna have written to the
Afghan Minister, inquiring about the status of the petition
they had addressed to the Minister of Cultural Affairs." Ah
yes, the Afghan Minister.

LESS: A letter written by German Jews had fallen into the
hands of the German embassy. This letter was passed on
through channels. Then the decision was taken: Government General.

EICHMANN: Well, it must have . . . it is . . . I can't . . . I
can't tell you any more about it, Herr Hauptmann, than
the way I figure . . . it must have been . . .

LESS: I'm going to read you a document. "Chief of the
Security Police and the SD, Berlin SW 11, October 9,
1941. To the Reichsführer-SS, SS Personnel Office, Berlin.
Re: SS-Sturmbannführer Adolf Eichmann, SS No. 45326.
I request the promotion of SS-Sturmbannführer Adolf
Eichmann to Obersturmbannführer, effective November 9,
1941. I propose this promotion on the strength of Eichmann's outstanding performance. As head of the Central
Office for Jewish Emigration, he has made an important
contribution to the de-Judification of the Ostmark. Thanks
to Eichmann's efforts, enormous amounts of money and
property have been secured for the German Reich. His
work in the Protectorate, performed with unusual initiative
and the requisite hardness, was also excellent . . . At present,
Eichmann is handling all questions concerning evacuation
and resettlement. Because of the importance of this work,
I regard Eichmann's promotion as desirable in the interest

of the service. per proc. Streckenbach, SS-Brigadeführer."
Do you wish to comment?

EICHMANN: That is a normal recommendation for promotion.
There's nothing I can say about it. It's normal.

LESS: What was your special contribution to the de-Judification of the Ostmark?

EICHMANN: Herr Hauptmann, that is, it's always like that in
recommendations for promotion, those are things that somehow naturally . . . The man has to be given special praise,
because without it he won't be promoted. That's how it is
with petty officers, with medium-level officers, and it's
exactly the same with high-level officers. Without such . . .
without this sort of special praise, you can't get a promotion. It's always been that way.

LESS: But the praise has to be based on something, it has to
have some basis in fact.

EICHMANN: That's true, Herr Hauptmann. In Vienna, and in
Prague as well, I did my job with unusual zeal. I've never
denied that. I regarded my work as a binding duty, and I
did my bit to make emigration from the Ostmark and . . .
from . . . from Austria and that part of Czechoslovakia as
it was then, from Bohemia and Moravia, proceed with all
possible dispatch. Of that, I made no secret to the Jewish
functionaries then, Dr. Löwenherz, for instance. So I can't
deny it today.

LESS: This document mentions "enormous amounts of money
and property." You speak of emigration funds. Did these
emigration funds consist of the assets of Jews who were
about to emigrate—and of what they could not take with
them?

EICHMANN: Yes . . . probably . . . yes. That's what they consisted of.

LESS: What is meant by the "requisite hardness" by which you
distinguished yourself?

EICHMANN: Herr Hauptmann, that was a catchword in the SS. That was . . . in the SS they always said . . . Himmler's instructions . . . an SS man was expected to be hard on himself and others . . . to do more than his duty . . . and these maxims—as we called them—of Himmler's, usually made their appearance around the turn of the year. At that time, new catchwords always caught on. For a long time it was Härte! Härte! [hardness, cruelty] . . . Later it was Durchhaltevermögen [endurance, ability to hold out]. All those slogans.

LESS: Will you agree that any sane person reading this document will take it to mean only one thing, namely, that you were promoted to Obersturmbannführer because you had distinguished yourself by sending large numbers of Jews to their death with the requisite hardness, and by stealing their money and property?

EICHMANN: Today, fifteen years later, it really does look that way.

LESS: Did you believe that the German nation could survive only if all the Jews in Europe were exterminated?

EICHMANN: Herr Hauptmann, if they had said to me: "Your father is a traitor," if they had told me that my own father was a traitor and I had to kill him, I'd have done it. At that time I obeyed my orders without thinking, I just did as I was told. That's where I found my—how shall I say?—my fulfillment. It made no difference what the orders were, Herr Hauptmann.

LESS: If they had told you your father was a traitor, wouldn't you have asked for some proof before proceeding to kill him?

EICHMANN: Herr Hauptmann, in those days I don't believe anyone would have asked for proof—I don't believe so, I don't. Death was all around us, and we had a view of life that people haven't got anymore.

LESS: Then you must have acquired the view that the salvation of the German people depended on the extermination of the Jews.

EICHMANN: Herr Hauptmann, we didn't have such opinions, we just didn't. Commands were given, and because they were commands, we obeyed. If I receive an order, I'm not expected to interpret it, and if I give an order, I'm forbidden to justify it. I receive an order and I'm expected to obey.

LESS: But not if you're ordered to do something blatantly illegal.

EICHMANN: You say illegal, Herr Hauptmann. Today I have a very different view of things . . . and in that I'm not alone . . . er . . . er . . . Probably just about everybody, except for the few wrongheaded oddballs you'll always find. But then? I wouldn't have considered any of those actions illegal. I'm being absolutely sincere with you, Herr Hauptmann, telling you how I felt then. If anyone had asked me about it up until May 8, 1945, the end of the war, I'd have said: This government was . . . er . . . er . . . elected by a majority of the German people . . . every civilized country . . . er . . . er . . . on earth had its diplomatic mission, and so on. Who is a little man like me to trouble his head about it? I get orders from my superior and I look neither right nor left. That's not my job. My job is to obey and comply.

LESS: If, for instance, an officer gives the order to shoot civilians—not hostages or anything like that—no, he just picks out these civilians and says, "Shoot them!" Must the subordinate carry out such an order?

EICHMANN: Yes, Herr Hauptmann. Same as the Allied flyers, who dropped their bombs on German cities and killed women, children, and old people. It's exactly the same. There's only one other thing he can do, and that's open to everyone. He can shoot himself.

LESS: A distinction can be made between war and peace.

EICHMANN: Yes, but all that happened during the war, Herr

Hauptmann. So I was never confronted with the alternative of shooting and giving orders to shoot.

LESS: But when a subordinate carries out a blatantly illegal order, doesn't he become responsible for it?

EICHMANN: In a war there's only one thing a man can do: obey orders. If you don't obey, you're court-martialed. If you obey and the order was a mistake, the commanding officer must answer for it. That's how it has always been. Little by little, we were taught all these things. We grew into them, all we knew was obedience to orders. We were chained to our oath.

LESS: What was the function of your co-worker Dieter Wisliceny in the framework of Bureau IV B 4?

EICHMANN: Wisliceny was attached to the German Ministry to the Slovakian government in Pressburg [Bratislava]. That was a kind of bastard arrangement, because primarily he took orders from Ludin, the German Minister. As far as the Security Police was concerned, his function was merely to keep us informed.

There were attachés of this kind in the chief cities of those countries which had not been conquered by force of arms but which, under German pressure, had accommodated themselves to the National Socialist system. The attachés functioned in part as intelligence agents, but primarily as so-called advisers on Jewish affairs. Almost all were SS officers. Technically, they were counted as personnel of the Foreign Office under Foreign Minister von Ribbentrop, who was in constant conflict with Himmler and the SS, often over questions of jurisdiction and over the allegiance of these attachés, most of whom were closer to the SS than to the diplomatic corps.

LESS: Were you in Bratislava, Pressburg as you call it, in May 1942?

EICHMANN: I may have been. I don't know.

LESS: Did you speak with Minister Mach?

EICHMANN: I believe he was Minister of the Interior. I think so, but I'm not sure. But I remember that name . . . Mach . . . Now I remember . . . Did I speak with him, did I . . . If he was Minister of the Interior, I must have. The Minister of the Interior invited me to dinner . . . one evening.

LESS: Did you on some occasion promise Mach and Premier Tuka that the Slovakian Jews—I am referring to seventeen thousand Jews, who were sent from Slovakia to Poland in the spring of 1942—that those Jews were receiving humane and decent treatment?

EICHMANN: I don't know . . . I don't know . . . I'm supposed to have said that . . . discussed that?

LESS: Were approximately thirty-five thousand Jews deported to Poland after that?

EICHMANN: From Slovakia? Thirty-five . . . ? Herr Hauptmann, if you say so, it must be true, because I really don't know how many.

LESS: I'm not saying. I'm asking you.

EICHMANN: Oh. Well, possibly . . . if . . . the figure is given . . . was somehow given . . . it must be right. Because I . . . I wouldn't dare to give a figure, because I haven't the remotest idea.

LESS: Did Wisliceny tell you the Slovakian government wanted to send a delegation to Poland to see how those Slovakian Jews were getting along?

EICHMANN: I won't . . . I won't deny it, Herr Hauptmann, but at the moment I can't tell you anything about it.

LESS: Were you officially notified by the Slovakian government that they were planning to send such a delegation to Poland?

EICHMANN: Was I notified? . . . Herr Hauptmann, I believe . . . now it comes to me. I wasn't notified. The Foreign Office was notified by the Security Police.

LESS: When Wisliceny was in Berlin at the end of July or the beginning of August 1942, did you discuss the fate of the Slovakian Jews in Poland with him?

EICHMANN: The Slovakian Jews in Poland? I don't know . . . I don't believe so.

LESS: Did you at that time inform Wisliceny that most of those Slovakian Jews were no longer alive?

EICHMANN: Just a moment, Herr Hauptmann. I'm trying to reconstruct . . . If the Slovakian government addressed such requests to the Security Police, I would automatically have made inquiries. I'd have asked: What became of those contingents? I'd have reacted automatically, it's possible that I approached Administration and Supply Headquarters. If so, I'd have seen Günther and Günther would have gone and asked Liebehenschel or Glücks: What's going on here? Obviously, neither Liebehenschel nor Glücks would have been able to answer off the cuff like that, they'd have had to make further inquiries. That's how it probably would have gone.

LESS: So it's possible that on the basis of your inquiries you did on some occasion tell Wisliceny that most of those Slovakian Jews were dead?

EICHMANN: If—if you don't mind, Herr Hauptmann, I'll go on with my story as it takes shape in my mind—if I had found out what had happened to those contingents of Jews, I'd naturally have told Wisliceny the truth about it.

LESS: When Wisliceny was put on trial after the war, he said: "In 1943 Eichmann summoned me to Berlin and told me to go to Salonika and there, in collaboration with the German military government, solve the Jewish question in Macedonia. Eichmann further informed me that he had charged Hauptsturmführer Brunner with the technical conduct of all actions in Greece. The Jews of Salonika were first concentrated in certain districts. At the beginning of March, when this concentration was complete, a telegram came from Eichmann to Brunner, ordering the immediate shipment of all the Jews of Salonika and Macedonia to Auschwitz. Over fifty thousand Jews, about fifty-four thousand, I believe, were deported." Do you wish to comment?

EICHMANN: Brunner operated independently? Obviously, Wisliceny, who outranked him, was in command in Salonika. That's as plain as day. You can't have two officers of different ranks running around in one and the same office in one and the same territory, in one and the same city, each doing just as he pleases. That simply doesn't happen. Obviously, Wisliceny . . . received the . . . how shall I say . . . the order.

LESS: Wisliceny was then asked: "Were there any sick among the Jews marked for shipment?" He replied: "In the actual camp . . . concentration camp, no particular cases of illness had been registered. But in the city districts inhabited by the Jews, there were cases of typhus and other contagious diseases, especially pulmonary tuberculosis. I informed Eichmann over the phone of these typhus cases. But he did not back up this objection; he ordered deportation proceedings to be initiated immediately."

EICHMANN: That is definitely untrue. I'd have gotten a terrible . . . a terrible chewing-out, as they used to say, if I had allowed cases of typhus or any other contagious diseases to be included in a shipment. I'd have been a devil—forgive the expression, Herr Hauptmann, if I'd allowed that . . . I could easily have drawn down the worst kind of official . . . official sanctions on my head.

LESS: When asked how many trains had been needed for the removal of the Jews from Salonika, Wisliceny answered: "There were between twenty, roughly between twenty and twenty-five trains. The load was at least two thousand, in some cases two and a half thousand, to a train. Closed freight cars were used. The evacuees were given provisions for about ten days, consisting chiefly of bread, olives, and other dry foods, plus water and certain sanitary equipment." About the usual shipment, wouldn't you say?

EICHMANN: Hmm. A pretty big load, it seems to me. But I don't know what reasons they may have had down there for putting in such loads. And I don't know what kind of cars were used.

LESS: Wisliceny was asked: "What was the destination of these shipments of Jews from Greece?" He replied: "Invariably, Auschwitz. These Jews without exception were delivered to the so-called final solution. By that I mean what Eichmann described to me as the final solution; in other words, they were biologically destroyed. As far as I could gather from conversations with Eichmann, this destruction was effected in gas chambers. The bodies were then burned in crematoriums." Did you ever speak to him about the manner of killing?

EICHMANN: That is possible. He knew about my visit, about my report to Müller . . . and as I've already said, I told my men all about it, just as it happened.

LESS: Wisliceny was asked: "How many Jews, concerning whose fate you personally are informed, were subjected to the final solution, that is, killed?" He replied: "I am very badly placed to give you an exact figure. All I have to go by is a conversation between Eichmann and Höss in Vienna, in which he said that only a very few of the Jews who came to Auschwitz from Greece had been fit for labor. Twenty-five to thirty percent of the Jews from Slovakia and Hungary were fit for labor. It is very hard for me to give a total. Eichmann himself always spoke of at least four million Jews; sometimes he went as high as five million. In my personal estimate, there must have been at least four million Jews." Have you any comment?

EICHMANN: I . . . I believe I did say that . . . in substance, Herr Hauptmann.

LESS: And it checks with what you had said at an earlier date.

EICHMANN: Approximately. That must have been in February 1945, what I said in the presence of several of my subordinate officers. It must be true in the main. Except that I absolutely can't remember that conversation with Höss in Hungary or Vienna. Or the percentages.

LESS: Wisliceny was further asked whether at the time you had said anything more about the number of Jews killed. He answered: "Eichmann put it in a particularly cynical way. He said that the knowledge of having five million Jews on his conscience gave him such extraordinary satisfaction that he would jump into his grave laughing."

EICHMANN: That is . . . theater, theater! That is . . . I can't think of anything else to call it but theater. All that is . . . it's . . . it's . . . this business here, Herr Hauptmann . . . this, this . . . this last passage . . . about suicide and so on . . . and so on . . . That was my . . . my, my, my last speech, my last speech to my men, as I've already told you. I may not have got the wording exactly right, but the meaning and substance, yes . . . exactly. Because that was my . . . my . . . summation in the . . . in the . . . how shall I put it . . . in the apocalyptic situation . . . which, which for a few days threw me into a state of shock . . . not nervous shock, but . . . moral shock: The Reich is kaput, it's all been a waste, it's all been for nothing, the whole war has been for nothing. That's what I said, that's what I told you. But this is theater! I never said it, never said it, Herr Hauptmann. The grave, yes, that's the only part that's right. The grave is right, I did say that . . .

LESS: Not in this context?

EICHMANN: . . . but not in this context. No, it wasn't cynical at all. On the contrary. I was . . . I was in a state of mind that left no room at all for cynicism; I felt . . . all I felt was deep sorrow, because of the millions of victims on our side . . . and the millions in the enemy camp . . . and there again

I mentioned the roughly five million . . . that's right. I gave the figure of five million, and I said it was . . . all for nothing . . . And then I . . . I said only one thing: For five years they had to batter the Reich. That was the one thing I said. But cynicism? Not a trace!

LESS: On the one hand, when Wisliceny says here: "The knowledge of having five million Jews on his conscience gave him such extraordinary satisfaction that . . ."

EICHMANN: No, no, Herr Hauptmann, that I must reject, that I must really reject. That sentence is not at all my style. And besides, it wouldn't have been true. My men would have taken me for a megalomaniac, because they knew I hadn't killed five million Jews. Wisliceny knew as well as I did that killing wasn't in our department.

LESS: In all your statements you keep hiding behind "That wasn't in my province, that wasn't my department, those were the orders I was given, the management of the German railways decided that," and so on.

EICHMANN: But you see, Herr Hauptmann, I have to say those things, because as head of Bureau IV B 4 I really wasn't responsible for everything, only for a rather narrowly circumscribed field. And that narrowly circumscribed field can be checked at any time. I wasn't free to do as I pleased.

LESS: Here I have a volume of the Nuremberg war crimes trials, volume 38. This document deals with the organization of SS Reich Security Headquarters as of October 1, 1943. Up here it says: "Secret." Here we have, among other things: Bureau IV B 1: Political Catholicism. Sturmbannführer Roth. IV B 2: Political Protestantism and sects [Hahnenbruch]. IV B 3: Other churches, Freemasonry [Wandersleben]. Under IV B 4: Jewish affairs, Evacuation, Confiscation of assets hostile to the nation and state, Annulment of German citizenship. —Is that your name?

EICHMANN: Yes. And it's correct.

LESS: Was the solution of the Jewish question regarded as crucial to the pursuit of the war?

EICHMANN: Seen from the top, undoubtedly, seen from the top—because it always . . . here I would like to specify, Herr Hauptmann. At first, from a certain date on, the word went out that no project could be undertaken unless it was war-important. As the war gathered momentum, the term "war-important" wasn't dropped, but it was complemented by another term, "war-crucial," and when a choice had to be made, it was the war-crucial projects that were given priority.

LESS: And the final solution of the Jewish question came under that head?

EICHMANN: Yes, it did. For one thing, Herr Hauptmann, because this concept . . . hmm, how shall I say? . . . and that's why I remember it . . . came under that head because applications to the Ministry of Transportation for rolling stock could be granted only if they were regarded as war . . . (Eichmann takes a cigarette) Thank you . . . only if they were declared to be war-important in the beginning and war-crucial later on.

LESS: Did your men, did men in your department volunteer for duty at the front?

EICHMANN: Oh, yes. Constantly, constantly. Like me. We all wanted to get out.

LESS: Did you sponsor such applications, or did you on principle reject them?

EICHMANN: Herr Hauptmann, these applications were not as a rule passed on through channels. Because through channels —everybody knew—it was nothing doing. They'd end up in the wastepaper basket. And anyway, it wasn't the thing to do, because we'd been ordered to this post and it was our duty to stick to it. All the same, a lot of men tried through personal contacts, through some superior they had come to think they had an in with . . . so they'd try to put in a word with him in the hope that this superior would make things easier for them. Like me. I tried it myself. If I'd applied through channels to be transferred to the front, they'd have made a howling example of me for insubordination, to frighten others. And the higher-ups would have treated anyone the same way.

LESS: But in general they released men who wanted to go to the front?

EICHMANN: Yes, but not from the office of the Secret State Police, Herr Hauptmann. They never let anyone out of there. I begged Müller most repeatedly . . .

LESS: Did you in the years from 1941 to 1945 consume larger quantities of alcoholic beverages than before?

EICHMANN: No, no, no. The most I can say is that the exact opposite was true. Because during the war—I was living in Berlin, you know—there were quite a few Sundays, I remember, when I'd have been glad to have a bottle and I didn't have one.

LESS: In conversations with other SS men, who did not belong to your bureau but with whom your work brought you into contact, did you advocate the total extermination of all Jews within reach?

EICHMANN: No! I never said that. And I'm sure no one can say I did. No one can say I did.

LESS: Did your work bring you into contact with Ahnenerbe [Ancestral Heritage], the Institute for the Scientific Study of Ends and Purposes, in Berlin?

EICHMANN: No, no, no!

LESS: Did you know SS-Standartenführer Dr. Sievers, the director of Ahnenerbe?

Ahnenerbe was a typical brainchild of Himmler's, a faithful reflection of his character. Its aims were at once chaotic and

romantic. It encouraged utter unscrupulousness on the grounds
that the end justifies the means. Its high-sounding title cov-
ered such diverse undertakings as experimentation on living
concentration-camp inmates and the study of Germanic pre-
history. Professor Dr. Wolfram Sievers was the director of
this obscure institute.

LESS: Did your duties bring you into contact with Dr. Sievers?

EICHMANN: No, no, no. Not that I remember. Not that I
remember.

LESS: Did you know SS-Hauptsturmführer Professor Dr. Hirt
of Strassburg University?

EICHMANN: Hirt? No, I didn't know him either.

LESS: Did you or your department have anything to do with
the transfer of detainees from one concentration camp to
another?

EICHMANN: No, no, no. From one concentration camp to
another?

LESS: Let's say from Auschwitz to Mauthausen. Or from
Auschwitz to Natzweiler?

EICHMANN: No, no. That wasn't my department. That would
have been the Protective . . . the Protective Custody Bureau.

LESS: Did your duties bring you into contact with SS-Obersturmbannführer Dr. Rudolf Brandt of the Reichsführer-
SS's personal staff?

EICHMANN: Dr. Brandt, the physician, oh yes, Brandt, he was
somebody's personal physician. I don't know if it was
Hitler's or . . .

LESS: Or Himmler's?

EICHMANN: That's it, Himmler's. No, I never had any connection with him.

Dr. Rudolf Brandt was not a physician. He was Himmler's
aide-de-camp, but his influence was far greater than that title

suggests. Dr. Karl Brandt, no close relation, was a doctor, one of Hitler's personal physicians.

LESS: Here I have some photostats of documents that were submitted in the first Nuremberg war crimes trial, the trial of the physicians. The sender of this letter is the business manager of Ahnenerbe. I'll read it to you. "Berlin, November 2, 1942. Secret. To SS-Obersturmbannführer Dr. Brandt. Dear Comrade Brandt: As you know, the Reichsführer-SS gave orders some time ago to the effect that SS-Hauptsturmführer Prof. Dr. Hirt should be supplied with everything he requires for his research. For certain anthropological investigations—I have already reported to the Reichsführer-SS on the subject—150 skeletons of prisoners or Jews are needed, and these are to be made available by the Auschwitz concentration camp." Etc., etc. It's signed: "With comradely greetings, Heil Hitler, Yours, Sievers."

The second document is a report by this Professor Hirt. "Re: Procurement of the skulls of Jewish-Bolshevistic commissars for scientific research at the University of Strassburg." I quote: "Extensive skull collections from nearly all races and people are in existence. It is only of Jews that so few skulls are available to science that work on them admits of no secure findings. The war in the East now offers us an opportunity to make good this deficiency. In the Jewish-Bolshevistic commissars, who embody a repulsive and characteristic type of subhuman, we have the possibility of acquiring a reliable scientific document by acquiring their skulls. The smoothest and most expeditious way of obtaining and securing this provision of skulls would be to instruct the Wehrmacht to hand over all Jewish-Bolshevistic commissars immediately to the military police. The person charged with securing this material (a young physician or medical student belonging to the Wehrmacht or better still to the military police) is to prepare a previously specified series of photographs and anthropological measurements. After the subsequently induced death of the Jew, whose head must not be injured, he will separate the head from the trunk and send it, immersed in a preserving fluid, in well-sealed lead containers made especially for this purpose, to the designated address."

And now the next document. A letter of June 21, 1943. From Ahnenerbe. Top secret. "To Reich Security Headquarters IV B 4, Attention: SS-Obersturmführer Eichmann. Re: Skeleton collection. With reference to your letter of September 25, 1942, and the consultations held since then regarding the above-mentioned matter, we wish to inform you that Dr. Bruno Beger, our staff member charged with the above-mentioned special mission, terminated his work in the Auschwitz concentration camp on June 15, 1943, because of the danger of an epidemic. In all, 115 persons, 79 male Jews, 2 Poles, 4 Central Asians, and 30 Jewesses, were processed. These inmates have been placed, men and women separately, in the concentration-camp sick quarters, and quarantined. For the further processing of these selected persons, immediate transfer to Natzweiler concentration camp is desirable and should be effected as quickly as possible in view of the danger of infection in Auschwitz. A list of the selected persons is appended. You are requested to send the necessary instructions."

And now for the last document. "The Reichsführer-SS Personal Staff, Field Headquarters, November 6, 1942. Secret. To Reich Security Headquarters IV B 4. Attention: SS-Obersturmbannführer Eichmann. The Reichsführer-SS has ordered that Dr. Hirt, head of the Anatomy Department in Strassburg, should be supplied with everything needed for his research. In the name of the Reichsführer-SS,

I therefore request you to help establish the projected skeleton collection. per proc. SS-Obersturmbannführer Brandt."

EICHMANN: I don't remember those names. Anyway, it's an order from the Reichsführer-SS and chief of the German police. The whole correspondence makes that clear enough. Of course, considerations of competence must have made me turn the whole thing over to Administration and Supply. Where could I have gotten all those skulls?

LESS: This is about skeletons, or rather, living people.

EICHMANN: Yes, that's a fact.

LESS: In other words, living people, who are to be transformed into skeletons.

EICHMANN: Yes, of course. The doctors are supposed to go to the concentration camp and select them. Why they apply to me, I can't make out. And there's no letter from me in the file, no answer or anything. So it's possible that I . . . not on my own authority, of course . . . submitted this whole thing to Müller and then, seeing it was an order from the Reichsführer, turned it over to Administration and Supply. Nothing else is conceivable, because I can't . . . I can't deliver skeletons . . . or living people. I . . . didn't have any camp . . . any camp where they could be selected. That could only have been done in a concentration camp.

LESS: Yes, but then you probably sent the camp instructions to . . .

EICHMANN: I can't give instructions, the instructions came from the Reichsführer.

LESS: Yes, but you did give instructions to send those people to Natzweiler.

EICHMANN: No, I can't do that either. The Protective Custody Bureau has to do that.

LESS: It's clear from Siever's letter to you . . . that . . . he was writing on the basis of a conversation with you.

EICHMANN: Yes, that's a fact . . .

LESS: What sort of conversation?

EICHMANN: . . . It's definitely true; I can remember discussing some such thing. But I didn't know . . . anything about skeletons. You see, I knew about skulls. Once I knew that this order came from the Reichsführer-SS and chief of the German police in person, I had to pass it on to the competent authority. That sort of thing wasn't in my department.

LESS: So you carried out the order?

EICHMANN: I couldn't carry it out, Herr Hauptmann . . . It had to be carried out by Administration and Supply Headquarters; it wasn't up to me.

LESS: So what did you do?

EICHMANN: Undoubtedly, I passed it on to Administration and Supply, because they were competent. Not on my own initiative, but because it was an order from the Reichsführer. I can't believe that I wrote to Camp Commandant Höss—Höss—in Auschwitz about it. I couldn't write to Höss directly about a thing like that. It's simply not true that Section IV, the Secret State Police, supplied those skeletons.

LESS: Those people . . .

EICHMANN: Supplied those people. Because in Auschwitz . . . in Auschwitz . . . because this was in Auschwitz, wasn't it? . . . So this doctor goes there and selects people. But there were tens of thousands of people in Auschwitz. I had no need to give any orders in Auschwitz if the Reichsführer-SS and chief of the German police had given them.

LESS: I beg your pardon. Herr Sievers informs you that his man has gone there and selected his people, and he asks you to see about . . .

EICHMANN: . . . having them sent to Natzweiler.

LESS: . . . about . . . about giving instructions.

EICHMANN: But, Herr Hauptmann, what sort of instructions was I expected to give?

LESS: I'm asking you. I'm very curious to know.

EICHMANN: Well . . . you see . . . I myself . . . I . . . I don't know . . . I . . . I . . . I . . . What instructions could I have given? To kill them? I wouldn't have had to give any instructions for that, Herr Hauptmann; Höss already had full powers to kill. I didn't have to give any instructions for a hundred and sixty people—I can only explain this by telling you something gruesome . . . hmm . . . very gruesome . . . It's the only way . . . Höss, you see . . . er . . . every week he'd get so and so many shipments, and the Führer had given orders to kill . . . so why would I have to give Höss, who killed thousands of people each week in line with the Führer's Order, why would I have to give him special instructions—which I couldn't have given in the first place, because it's a different outfit, he belonged to a different outfit—to kill a hundred and sixty people.

LESS: They weren't killed in Auschwitz; they were sent to Natzweiler.

EICHMANN: Or Natzweiler. People were killed . . . in every concentration camp if they were scheduled to be killed. The concentration-camp commanders . . . got those orders from the competent headquarters, from Administration and Supply. But I can't conceive of us, Bureau IV B 4, IV B 4, ever giving the Auschwitz concentration camp any orders. We probably passed the whole thing on to Administration and Supply for jurisdictional reasons. Basically, it comes to the same thing anyway, because the order came from the Reichsführer and chief of the German police. Whatever I may have done, I had no responsibility whatever, because the oath I had to take obligated me to loyalty and obedience. The order came from my highest hierarchical superior. That would have put me in a compulsive situation, I'd have had to obey. That's as plain as day.

LESS: But did this loyalty oath—which you had to take and did take—cover such actions?

EICHMANN: No exceptions were provided for.

LESS: Who was in charge of shipping, of shipping people?

EICHMANN: I was in charge of shipping. Of evacuations, you mean?

LESS: No, of shipping these hundred and sixty people, they, too, were ...

EICHMANN: Oh, *that* shipment, *that* shipment. I don't know if it was my men, Herr Hauptmann, but I won't say it wasn't, Herr Hauptmann, I won't disclaim it. Still, I imagine that this shipment from one concentration camp to another was carried out by members of the camp personnel.

LESS: There's one thing I don't quite understand. If Administration and Supply was in charge, why this correspondence with you, why a conversation with you?

EICHMANN: Well, I know it wasn't in our jurisdiction. Look at it this way, Herr Hauptmann: a hundred and sixty persons more or less won't affect the measure of my punishment. I'd be glad to admit it, I'd admit everything. But let me ask you just this: The whole correspondence for 1942, for November 1942, has been preserved. Wouldn't I have had to react to this in some way?

LESS: Yes, of course. But he refers to your letter, Sievers refers to your communication ...

EICHMANN: But the letter isn't there?

LESS: No, unfortunately.

EICHMANN: Strange. The whole question would be cleared up if you had that letter, at least. Strange that everything else should be here but not this one letter. —Strange.

LESS: The people who were given special treatment ... wasn't this special treatment decided by the Gestapo?

EICHMANN: No, by the Führer . . . er . . . by . . . by Hitler . . .

LESS: Wasn't the order to the camps given by the Gestapo?

EICHMANN: The order for gassing, for instance, to the concentration camps?

LESS: The order that Prisoner X or Prisoner Y . . .

EICHMANN: Oh, individual cases . . . individual cases . . . yes. Yes, yes.

LESS: So then, in this case, it was up to the Gestapo. These people were subjected to special treatment. Their skeletons were needed.

EICHMANN: That . . . that, Herr Hauptmann, is . . . there was no need to give this special order. The order of the supreme chief had already been given. All that remained was the organizational execution of this order, the purely administrative part of it, the transmission. So, if I could remember, I wouldn't hesitate to say so. Yes, I'd say, on the strength of the Reichsführer's order I passed the matter on to Auschwitz: Here, ship a hundred and sixty Jews previously selected by Hirt, or some such thing, to Natzweiler, etc. After all, I was covered. The Reichsführer had ordered it.

LESS: Were you, or your Bureau IV B 4, responsible for operating the Theresienstadt ghetto?

EICHMANN: IV B 4, no . . . IV B 4 was not responsible. The competent supervisory authority was the commander of the Security Police and the SD in Prague. We only had to go there [to Theresienstadt] when there were inspections. There were two inspections by the Red Cross, I believe, and then we had to go. As a rule, we went there in advance, because these inspections could not be authorized by the commander of the Security Police and the SD in the Protectorate; the Reichsführer reserved those things for himself. The first time it happened, Müller went there himself and took me with him.

LESS: But otherwise you were not in charge of the camp?

EICHMANN: When Baron von Neurath, the previous Reich Protector of Bohemia and Moravia, had to go, he was replaced as Deputy Protector by Obergruppenführer Heydrich, who, however, retained his position as chief of the Security Police and the SD. He had hardly been appointed when he gave a press conference. After that, he summoned me and Dr. Stahlecker, the commander of the Security Police in Prague. State Secretary K. H. Frank was also present. Two of Heydrich's sentences have stuck in my memory. One: that he was glad to have been transferred to a positive activity from the negative activity that all police work represents. Two: that he had let his tongue run away with him at his press conference, telling the press that the Protectorate would be free of Jews in eight weeks. And now we were paying for his foolishness. Now we had eight weeks in which to clear the territory of Bohemia and Moravia, with its roughly a hundred and twenty to a hundred and fifty thousand souls.

LESS: When you say souls, do you mean Jews?

EICHMANN: Yes, yes, Herr Hauptmann. So I said to the Deputy Reich Protector: There's only one possibility. Allot an area large enough to hold all the Jews now scattered around the Protectorate. Then various places were named between Heydrich and Frank, and finally Frank said: Theresienstadt. Heydrich agreed at once and gave the necessary instructions. I myself went to Theresienstadt and looked around. I saw that it was too small. I said: This won't work. But it didn't do any good. Karl Hermann Frank was not only a Czech-hater; Karl Hermann Frank was also a Jew-hater of the, let's say, of the Streicher type, the *Stürmer* type. Later on, new orders poured in every minute from the Reichsführer-SS, all to the effect that the Theresienstadt ghetto was to be made into an old people's ghetto.

LESS: When people were evacuated from Theresienstadt to Auschwitz or other camps, was it only the young and middle-aged, or was it old . . . older people as well?

EICHMANN: Whatever the orders were, Theresienstadt was subject to . . . direct, that's it . . . direct orders from Himmler. He reserved Theresienstadt . . . for himself, so to speak, and even the chief of the Security Police and the SD never—I believe—gave any orders in Theresienstadt on his own initiative, without securing the authorization of his superior.

LESS: Did your department issue guidelines with regard to . . . to deportation to Theresienstadt?

EICHMANN: Our department . . . guidelines . . . guidelines were issued on several occasions, I believe. When I was in Prague, only people from the Protectorate were sent there. Soon neighboring territories were added, wherever the Gauleiters or Kreisleiters could get the Reichsführer's approval. Then there were individual cases, where some Reich department or other had bent Himmler's ear. Then it so happened that I had a Jewish police force set up there—a hundred and fifty or two hundred men, I believe. And then somehow Himmler issued orders to turn Theresienstadt into a ghetto for old people, a purpose which none of us, which no one had originally thought of.

LESS: Were the guidelines for deportation to Theresienstadt issued by your department?

EICHMANN: Yes. Yes, after it . . . I can't remember now what the guidelines were . . . it was a ghetto for old people . . . the guidelines according to which the Reichsführer-SS and chief of the German police more or less specified what people should go there. They must have had to do with age and social position, because, according to an order of the Reichsführer, holders of decorations for bravery from the First World War were to be transferred to Theresienstadt; also persons wounded in the First World War, I remember that. And superior officers. Those are points I still remember.

LESS: Why was the deportation of Jews to Theresienstadt termed a change of residence [Wohnsitzverlegung]?

EICHMANN: Hmm, change of residence . . . I don't know either where that came from . . . It's true that the VIP's in Theresienstadt had residences [Wohnungen], in a manner of speaking; that is, places of their own to live in. I really can't remember. With Theresienstadt the term was always Wohnsitzverlegung, Wohnsitzverlegung to the ghetto for old people, and only very seldom, I believe . . . when someone was in a big hurry, he might put it down as "evacuation." The term in general use was "change of residence."*

LESS: But when you're talking about evacuation to the East, you don't call it change of residence.

EICHMANN: Maybe the higher-ups . . . I don't remember. Probably, I imagine, the term was coined to gild the old people's ghetto. Yes, that must be closer to the truth.

LESS: To make the pill easier to swallow?

EICHMANN: Something of the kind. To be perfectly frank, yes.

LESS: Now I'm going to show you the guidelines issued by your bureau on February 20, 1943, in connection with the removal [Wohnsitzverlegung] of the Jews to Theresienstadt. Do you wish to comment?

EICHMANN: Yes. They specify the competencies of the different bureaus, the groups of detainees affected, the transportation required, the escort personnel, the departure and arrival times. And then they deal with the costs and the

---

* The explanation of this rigmarole is that the root *Wohn*, meaning "dwelling," occurs both in the bureaucratic word *Wohnsitz*, or residence, and in *Wohnung*, which is the everyday word for a place to live, either a house or an apartment.—*Trans.*

handling of the evacuees' property and funds. In the specifications of the groups to be deported, I see points that must have originated with the Reichsführer-SS and chief of the German police himself, ideas of his: holders of the Medal for the Wounded, holders of high war distinctions, and so on. And all this here about the stipulations of the Judengesetz [Law Concerning the Jews], these are from the Minister of the Interior. And this, about totaling up the costs; what regulation that was, I don't know. *(Eichmann reads)* "With regard to handling of the property and funds of the Jews to be deported, special instructions will be issued on each occasion." I don't know myself what that is supposed to mean.

LESS: You said before that Himmler specified what groups were sent to Theresienstadt. Does that mean that it was obligatory to deport all other Jews, from fourteen to sixty-five years of age, to the East?

EICHMANN: According to this interpretation, I mean, what it . . . The ones that don't come under Paragraph 5 or Regulation 1 of the Reich Citizenship Law are subject to evacuation to the East. It couldn't mean anything else. The rest were borderline cases—so to speak—and they were transferred to Theresienstadt.

LESS: I still don't understand this distinction you make between transfer and evacuation. The Jews who were marked for Theresienstadt—everything, all funds and property, was taken away from them. They couldn't take anything with them. They had to part with everything. It says here what they were allowed to take with them: a suitcase or knapsack with articles of daily use—nothing cumbersome—a plate or bowl, spoons—not even a knife and fork—sheet, blanket, that was . . .

EICHMANN: True. But there's this to bear in mind, Herr Hauptmann. Life—not a normal life, of course—but if you compare life in a concentration camp with life in Theresienstadt, obviously they were as different as day and night. In Theresienstadt, for instance, it was the Jewish Council that planned the activities of the day. Whole categories were totally exempted from labor of any kind. When industry was moved to Theresienstadt, certain war-important industries . . . mica condensers, I believe, or something of the kind—the labor was paid. There . . . there really were differences. It wasn't like being sent to Auschwitz. And so the whole . . . Here's something that just occurred to me. In the summer of 1944, for instance, I took a whole group of engineers and architects and workers with me to Brandenburg, when it became necessary to build a fallback headquarters for Section IV, the Gestapo. Those men could have escaped at any time en route. They didn't. And the same in Theresienstadt. They'd be driven out to the country in trucks, to mow hay and that kind of thing.

LESS: What were home contracts?

EICHMANN: Home contracts?

LESS: Home contracts, which the Jews being deported to Theresienstadt were forced to sign.

EICHMANN: Never heard of them. Home contracts? First I've heard of them.

LESS: If I'm not mistaken, it was like this. The Jews who were being sent to Theresienstadt . . . were advised, more or less compelled, to sign over what money they had left, since they couldn't take it with them, to the Union of Jews in Germany, which you directed. In return, they were assured that they . . . that their stay in Theresienstadt would be paid for until the end of their lives. It would take care of their food, clothing, everything they . . .

EICHMANN: In any case, if such home contracts were made, Herr Hauptmann, nothing of the kind was . . . hmm, let's say entered in my time.

LESS: Were the guidelines for Theresienstadt issued before the people were shipped there or after?

EICHMANN: Several sets were issued. Basically, every time a shipment . . . And then everything was turned upside down by Himmler's order to turn Theresienstadt into a ghetto for old people.

LESS: Didn't the first guidelines date from 1942?

EICHMANN: I don't know. But in any case, whenever it was . . . these things were . . . the Czechs . . . were . . . When was Heydrich made Reich Protector? In 1939 . . . In '39, I believe . . . That was when the Czech population was moved out of Theresienstadt, but not by us, by the Czech Ministry of the Interior.

LESS: And when it says here: "Food is to be prepared in community kitchens. The financial support of the resettled Jews is to be drawn from the funds of the Jewish organizations in Berlin, Vienna, and Prague . . ."

EICHMANN: Yes, that's right . . . I . . . I have nothing to say about that . . . That's sure to be right.

LESS: Did you appoint the Jewish executives of the Jewish Council in Theresienstadt?

EICHMANN: Yes. At first . . . at the founding. Later . . . later I didn't . . . I had no influence later.

LESS: How often did you visit Theresienstadt?

EICHMANN: Oh, I was often there. We'd drive through. It was on the way to . . . Whether it was within my competence or not, I always . . . I always stopped there.

LESS: I would now like to show you a pamphlet dealing with the legal status of Jews in the Protectorate of Bohemia and Moravia, issued by Dr. Franz Friedemann on July 31, 1942. For the internal use of the Jewish community in Prague. Here, on page 26 . . . I'm quoting this because you say the Theresienstadt ghetto was established as early as 1939. Here it says: "Finally, it was decided to concentrate the Jews in a ghetto, to which end, by order of the Reich Protector of Bohemia and Moravia, an order was issued on February 16, 1942, dissolving the township of Theresienstadt. Paragraph 14 of this order empowered the commander of the Security Police in the office of the Reich Protector to take the required administrative measures for the construction of the Jewish settlement."

EICHMANN: Ah! Could I have got my dates so wrong?!

Eichmann wanted to be regarded as one of the founders of the Theresienstadt ghetto. This, he thought, would support his contention that he had never hated the Jews and would not have sent millions of Jews to their death if he had not been compelled to by his oath of loyalty to the SS and by Himmler's orders. On several occasions, he argues, he tried to procure a homeland for the Jews, but all his plans—Palestine, Nisko on the San in Poland, Madagascar—had proved impracticable. Theresienstadt, to be sure, had not turned out as he had wanted—it was too small, the installations had been too primitive. Still, it provided a refuge from the racist maniacs. But his claim to have helped found it would hold water only if the ghetto had been established in 1939, the year when he directed the Central Office for Jewish Emigration in Prague. That is his reason for moving the date of Heydrich's appointment as Protector from 1941 to 1939. It is true that the Theresienstadt ghetto was less inhuman than the other ghettos. Still, it was far from human. By National Socialist standards, it was not a concentration camp, there were no gas chambers, but the masses of people crowded into a very restricted area were no more free than the inmates of a prison; they were subject to arbitrary punishment and chicanery, and in constant danger of death. Many had given up everything they owned to buy their way into this old people's home, but that gave them no rights whatever. They lived and ate wretchedly, and often enough the masters of Theresienstadt would ship carloads of their boarders to the death camps to cut down on expenses. Even so, the Theresienstadt ghetto was never empty. Newcomers poured in to the very end, and even when the National Socialist regime was nearing collapse, the ghetto continued to serve as a showplace with which to fool foreign visitors and turn their minds away from the treatment meted out to millions of Jews.

LESS: Here I have a memorandum of December 6, 1941, from the commander of the Security Police in The Hague. It concerns Jewish emigration; specifically, a small group of Dutch Jews belonging to the NSB, the National Socialist Party of Holland. And another memorandum from the same commander. Do you wish to comment?

EICHMANN: Yes. The first memorandum states that five or six Jews, former members of the NSB, had now been excluded from the NSB and had thus ceased to be members of a National Socialist organization. The Reich commissar and commander of the SS and the police did not, however, think it fitting to lump these Jews with other Jews, in the event of an evacuation, for instance. He was therefore requesting authorization to let these so-called NSB Jews emigrate. What he had in mind was to attach five or six Jews to a party of V-man emigrants. These were parties of secret agents sent out of the country by Section VI, the Secret Service section of Reich Security Headquarters. In a postscript to this application, it is noted that on April 21, 1943, these Jews were removed to Theresienstadt. It is also noted that I had taken the position that in the present case an exceptional emigration could not be approved, but that shipment of the NSB Jews could be so long deferred that they would be the last to be deported.

LESS: Was this decision taken by you?

EICHMANN: Undoubtedly, because it was an easy one to take. Since December 20, 1941, we had the Reichsführer's general order prohibiting all emigration.

LESS: On this same subject, we have a memorandum from Bureau IV B 4, from the office of the commander of Security Police in The Hague, dated October 5, 1942, and signed by Zöpf, the Hague adviser on Jewish affairs.

EICHMANN: Yes, this is ... Here Zöpf writes that, according to information I had given him, there was a way out for Netherlands Jews, who on the one hand, for reasons of age or services rendered, could not be ranked with the other Auschwitz Jews, but need not simply be left in Holland, and that The Hague could at any time send a trainload of Jews from Westerbork concentration camp to the Theresienstadt propaganda camp. And I also see here a reference to guidelines according to which persons exceeding a certain age limit should not be sent to Auschwitz, but could be sent to Theresienstadt.

LESS: Should this be taken to mean that all Jews were to be deported, regardless of age or services to Germany?

EICHMANN: Yes, they could all go to Theresienstadt. All, that is, not all, only these exceptions.

LESS: When the Slovakian government wanted to see how the Jews deported from that country were living in Poland, you wrote in this document: "Careful! Instead of seeing a Jewish camp, let them visit Theresienstadt." Did you write that because Theresienstadt, in a manner of speaking...

EICHMANN: Naturally, of course. As I've already said, Herr Hauptmann, Himmler fixed up Theresienstadt as a showpiece for the outside world. As I see it, he wanted something he could show if some specialized foreign organizations came complaining about killing Jews and that kind of thing, and then he'd be able to say: "That's not true. Go to Theresienstadt." And then those people would say to themselves: "Oh well, it really doesn't seem as bad as the newspapers and propaganda say."

LESS: Weren't Jews deported to the death camps from Theresienstadt?

EICHMANN: Yes, by order of Himmler, "disencumberment measures" calling for the evacuation of so and so many Jews from Theresienstadt. As a rule, he decided where the shipments should go.

LESS: Whose job was it to organize the shipments?

EICHMANN: Mine. That is, my bureau arranged the scheduling conference—the usual thing—with the Ministry of Transportation. And then Administration and Supply would tell us what destination Himmler had decided on.

LESS: These shipments from the Theresienstadt ghetto—at first to the extermination camps of Riga and Minsk and the Government General and later exclusively to Auschwitz—did your department provide the supervisory personnel for them?

EICHMANN: Supervisory personnel? No, certainly not; Prague did all that.

LESS: Were you responsible for providing the rolling stock?

EICHMANN: That, yes, of course. Yes.

LESS: Did you accompany the Swiss Dunant of the International Red Cross on his visit to Theresienstadt on April 6, 1945?

EICHMANN: I don't know what his name was, Herr Hauptmann, but I accompanied him all right. Not just me, though. The most important member of the party was the commander of the Security Police and the SD in Prague. I went along, because I had orders from Berlin to go. And then, because K. H. Frank, the State Secretary, was too busy, the Swiss representative was invited to dinner at the Hradčany in his name.

LESS: Why did you attend?

EICHMANN: Because I had orders.

LESS: From whom?

EICHMANN: Probably from Kaltenbrunner, chief of Reich Security Headquarters and the SD. Or even from Himmler or somebody. In any case, the order came to me through Müller.

LESS: Here I have a booklet put out by the International Red Cross in Geneva in June 1946. The French title, translated, reads: "Documents concerning the Activity between 1939 and 1945 of the IRC Committee in Defense of the Civilian Inmates of the German Concentration Camps." On page 99 I read the following: "On April 5, 1945, I went to Prague with a view to inspecting the Theresienstadt ghetto. On April 6, we visited the ghetto and held lengthy conferences with Dr. Weinmann, head of the SD in the Protectorate of Bohemia and Moravia and with Oberführer Eichmann, the specialist for all Jewish questions. The last-named had come from Berlin to Prague to discuss various questions connected with the Jews with the representatives of the IRC. Oberführer Eichmann played a leading role in the concentration camps of Lublin and Auschwitz. As he informed me, he was the direct deputy of the Reichsführer-SS for all Jewish questions. During a reception held at the Hradčany, I had occasion to converse with these two men until late into the night. What especially interested the IRC was not so much the living conditions and installations in the ghetto, as knowing whether this ghetto served exclusively as a transit camp for the Jews and in what proportion deportations to the East (Auschwitz) had taken place. According to what I was able to learn in the Theresienstadt ghetto, Dr. Eppstein, head of the camp's Jewish Council, and many others had been deported to Auschwitz. On the basis of this fact, I demanded to know when these deportations had taken place and in what proportions. In the course of the evening, Eichmann developed his ideas about the Jewish problem. In his opinion, the Jews in Theresienstadt were much better off than many Germans, as far as food and medical care were concerned. He told us that Theresienstadt was the creation of Reichsführer-SS Himmler, who wished to give the Jews an opportunity to organize a community life under almost totally autonomous Jewish leadership and to give them a sense of racial solidarity. Later on, still according to Eichmann, the Jews of Theresienstadt were to be taken to a region where they would live entirely apart, segregated from the German population. As for the general problem of the Jews, Eichmann believed that Himmler was then thinking of adopting humane methods. Eichmann personally, so he said, did not entirely approve of Himmler's methods, but as a good soldier felt bound to obey the Reichsführer's orders blindly. In the course of the evening, I told Eichmann of my wish to visit the camp at Bergen-Belsen. Eichmann told me an epidemic of typhoid had broken out there, but promised to visit the camp with me in the next few days. This visit never materialized, for I was not able to reach Eichmann in Berlin."

EICHMANN: This report seems correct in the main. A few little inaccuracies. But it is absolutely untrue—I couldn't have told him that, because I'm not—that I was the Reichsführer's direct deputy for all Jewish questions. Maybe I said: I'm the Reichsführer's deputy here and now, in connection with this visit. I couldn't have played a leading role in the Lublin and Auschwitz concentration camps; there again, he's got his facts wrong. When the Theresienstadt ghetto was established, it was, basically, with the aim expressed here. But it couldn't be carried out, because every conceivable headquarters was exerting pressure, and they began shipping everybody to Theresienstadt.

LESS: How much do you know about what happened to the people of Lidice?

EICHMANN: Nothing at all. I had nothing whatever to do with it.

On May 27, 1942, SS-Obergruppenführer Reinhard Heydrich, Deputy Reich Protector and chief of Reich Security, was injured by a bomb and died a week later. The assassins were Czech émigrés, parachuted in by the British Secret Service. Under questioning by the Gestapo, they revealed that while in England they had received information from the mining town of Lidice, west of Prague. In retaliation, Hitler gave orders to shoot all the male inhabitants of Lidice, throw all the women into concentration camps, round up all the children and, insofar as they were "susceptible to Germanization, give them to SS families in the Reich. The others will be delivered to a different sort of upbringing." The village was burned to the ground. One hundred ninety-nine men were murdered by an action team. One hundred ninety-one women were taken to concentration camps. Eight children were found "susceptible to Germanization." Ninety children were taken to a camp in Warthegau, which the most radical of all the Gauleiters governed with despotic cruelty. Only sixteen children and one hundred forty-three women were alive at the end of the war.

LESS: Do you know what happened to most of the children?

EICHMANN: I do not know. I had nothing to do with Lidice, nothing whatever, nothing whatever . . . Not even any . . . I wasn't even informed.

LESS: Do you know anything about a shipment of children who were sent by the commander of the Security Police in Prague from Lidice to Litzmannstadt, formerly and now again the Polish city of Lodz?

EICHMANN: No, no. I don't know anything about it.

LESS: I'm going to show you some photostats of documents concerning the treatment of eighty-eight Czech children from Lidice, who arrived in Litzmannstadt on June 13, 1942. The first is a letter signed by Krumey, who worked with you for a time, and was then head of the Relocation Center in Litzmannstadt.

EICHMANN: Yes, that's Krumey's signature.

LESS: Dated Litzmannstadt, June 17, 1942. To the Commander of the Security Police and the SD in Prague. Re: The transfer of Czech children to Litzmannstadt. The second is a telegram of June 20, 1942, from Krumey in Litzmannstadt to Reich Security Headquarters, Bureau IV B 4. Attention: Obersturmbannführer Eichmann, Berlin. Re: Transfer of 88 Czech children from the town of Lidice to Litzmannstadt. Reference: Conference with Obersturmbannführer Eichmann. Do you wish to comment?

EICHMANN: Yes. In the first place, I must say that I absolutely don't remember any such thing. In the second place: If— I see that the matter was somehow handled by my bureau . . . it refers to a conference with me—I imagine that it must have been handled in a purely transportational sense and that . . . I see that the Race and Settlement Office passed on seven children as . . . as susceptible to re-Germanization.

LESS: What happened to the children who were not found susceptible to re-Germanization?

EICHMANN: I don't know that either. If they were shipped to Litzmannstadt . . . After all, these things weren't handled by me, by my bureau, I mean. This Lidice business was decided at the top. What they ordered, I don't know.

LESS: Were those children sent to Kulmhof concentration camp for special treatment?

EICHMANN: I don't know, Herr Hauptmann. I don't know. By that I mean that maybe they were and maybe they weren't. I don't know.

LESS: Were non-Jews as well as Jews liquidated in Kulmhof?

EICHMANN: I don't . . . Except for those first two times I've told . . . I never went to Kulmhof after that. I don't know. But this whole Lidice business must . . . must have been handled by some central headquarters. But I don't know which.

LESS: But why did Krumey write to you, rather than someone else, about those eighty-eight children?

EICHMANN: Maybe they got mixed up with us for transportational reasons. Maybe they were attached to a deportation train, a Jewish deportation train. Conceivably, I got orders to attach them to some deportation train. It's possible.

LESS: Was it up to you to—

EICHMANN: No, no, it was not up to me.

LESS: . . . decide what was to be done with them? To make arrangements?

EICHMANN: No, no. Certainly not.

LESS: In this telegram of June 22, 1942, Krumey writes to Reich Security Headquarters: "On June 13, 1942, 88 Czech children from the village of Lidice, orphaned by the action there, have arrived in Litzmannstadt. Since thus far no instructions concerning the disposition of these children have reached here, I request pertinent orders. I have notified IV B 4 of the transfer of these children on the assumption that they have been earmarked for special treatment. In the meantime, the Race and Settlement Office has removed seven children susceptible to re-Germanization."

EICHMANN: Hmm. Yes, that's another one of those . . . things. The whole business must have been ordered by a higher authority . . . Seeing it was a measure of retaliation for the assassination of Heydrich, I imagine the Reichsführer himself must have given the necessary orders.

LESS: In this letter to you, Krumey refers to a conversation with you. The second letter shows that he assumed these children were marked for special treatment, in other words, extermination. Doesn't it seem likely that this point came up in his conversation with you and that he wrote you this letter on the basis of said conversation?

EICHMANN: It is certainly possible that Krumey said that to himself and asked: How about it, should they be given special treatment or not? And I must have answered: It's not in my department. Jews are in my department, not Czech children. What orders were given after that, I don't know.

LESS: In this connection, I'm going to show you some more photostats. One is a letter of July 9, 1942, to Reich Security Headquarters IV B 4. Attention: Obersturmbann-führer Eichmann. "Re: Czech children. The SS Race and Settlement Office has sent us twelve un-Germanizable children, aged one to fifteen, from the districts of Lidice and Lesaki. Further instructions are requested."

The next is a telegram dated July 14, 1942, from Berlin. "To the Central Relocation Office, Litzmannstadt. Attention: Obersturmbannführer Krumey. Re: Czech children. Reference: Your telegram of July 9, 1942. Request you turn over the twelve un-Germanizable children immediately to Litzmannstadt Gestapo, which has received further instructions." Signed RSHA IV B 4. per proc. Günther. Do you wish to comment?

EICHMANN: I do. I've said I couldn't remember, and I must now repeat that none of this is known to me. As I told you, I did not handle the matter. My deputy signed.

LESS: Günther's telegram is signed IV B 4.

EICHMANN: Oh, well, telegrams . . . That is . . . anyway, the telegram is signed. That can't be denied. It makes no difference that it wasn't signed by me. Obviously, it was sent by the bureau . . . by my bureau. That's clear. But it was certainly signed and drafted by someone else, not by me. But . . . turn over Czech children immediately to the

Litzmannstadt Gestapo, which has received further instructions . . . ?

LESS: Can't we gather that the further instructions to the Litzmannstadt Gestapo were sent by your department?

EICHMANN: I could not, I mean Bureau IV B 4 could not have given instructions in this matter. At the most, it could have relayed them. The bureau had no authority to give orders in this matter. If it gave any definitive instructions, they must have come from higher up. Lidice was not handled by Bureau IV B 4. Lidice was handled from higher up, on the basis of a . . . of a general order.

LESS: Do these documents I have shown you indicate that you had something to do with the fate of these children?

EICHMANN: Something . . . that we shared the responsibility . . .

LESS: Yes.

EICHMANN: I'd put it this way. They definitely indicate . . . I won't say that I . . . but the bureau, yes, that's clear to me . . .

LESS: But in 1942 you were the bureau head!

EICHMANN: I was the bureau head, unquestionably. But Lidice was an affair which no bureau head, no department head or Gruppenleiter could decisively decide; it was handled higher . . . higher up . . . it . . .

LESS: Was the deportation of the gypsies to the death camps also handled by your Bureau IV B 4?

EICHMANN: Yes. But I don't know if all the gypsies, no, that I don't know. The gypsies from the West, from the West: No. To the camps? To . . . to a ghetto, not to the camps. To a ghetto in Litzmannstadt. That happened in the beginning, before the French war, the German-French war, broke out in the summer of 1940, I think. Or was it later? I don't know.

LESS: Weren't the gypsies taken to Auschwitz later and gassed?

EICHMANN: Herr Hauptmann, at this late date I don't know. All we had to do was make the rolling stock available and draw up the schedules.

LESS: You didn't supply guidelines—

EICHMANN: No guidelines, no guidelines.

LESS: . . . covering the gypsies?

EICHMANN: The Reichsführer himself made the decisions about the gypsies. That's it, and the . . . the guidelines for the gypsies were simple. I know all about them. I mean, there weren't any. The Reichsführer handled everything. Because, you see, with the other guidelines it was always necessary to consult other departments. You've seen how it was, Herr Hauptmann: the Foreign Office butts in, and then various specifications of nationality have to be considered, and so on . . . With the gypsies, as far as I remember . . . nobody worried in the least about any specification whatever.

LESS: Why really did they exterminate all the gypsies?

EICHMANN: Herr Hauptmann, that was one of those . . . one of those things, I think . . . Führer . . . Reichsführer . . . I don't know . . . there were . . . all of a sudden it happened . . . and the order went out . . . I don't know. And as far as I know, they were never seriously studied by any branch of Reich Security Headquarters. I mean: their origins, where they came from, manners, customs. Let me put it this way: In their case, you can't speak of organized communities . . . larger units and so on. Where the centers are and that kind of thing. I don't know if anyone worked on that . . . Certainly, no one did in Section IV. Nothing of the kind was planned with the gypsies.

LESS: Did you keep card files of individual cases?

EICHMANN: The order about the gypsies, if I remember right . . . I really don't remember these things. They weren't turned over to my bureau until much later. And when I did get them, there were none left. There hadn't been very many in the first place. There can't have been very many, because none of the countries in the West were out-and-out gypsy countries. Like Hungary or Rumania, for instance. They had appreciably more gypsies than . . . let's say, the Greater German Reich, as it was then called. I don't believe there were more than five or six thousand in the Reich. I don't believe there were any more.

LESS: Weren't there somewhere between seven hundred thousand and a million gypsies in Poland, Russia, Rumania, and Hungary?

EICHMANN: I don't know, Herr Hauptmann, I don't know.

LESS: You remember that you've spoken here several times about your deputy Günther . . . how he once told you about this prussic . . . about that gas business.

EICHMANN: Yes, I do. At the very beginning . . . right here I . . .

LESS: Didn't you say to Günther: "How could you? . . . How could you do such a thing? Why do you involve yourself in such things?"

EICHMANN: Yes, of course.

LESS: "How am I, Eichmann, to justify this to Müller?"

EICHMANN: I'm sure I never said that to him.

LESS: You didn't?

EICHMANN: No! I can imagine that he may have said: "Look here. I have orders to do this and that."

LESS: Now I'm going to show you four pages of documents. Do you wish to comment?

EICHMANN: These are letters of October 25, 1941, from the Reich Minister for Occupied Eastern Territories to the Reich Commissioner for Ostland. This one says that "Oberdienstleiter Brack of the Führer's Office has declared his willingness to cooperate in the production of the necessary housing and gassing apparatus. Such apparatus is not at present available in sufficient quantity. It has still to be produced. Since in Brack's opinion it would be far more difficult to produce this apparatus in the Reich than on the spot, Brack thinks it advisable to send his men, and in particular his chemist Dr. Kallmayer, to Riga immediately . . . etc., etc. Accordingly, you are requested to communicate with Oberdienstleiter Brack at the Führer's Office through your SS and police commander, and ask him to dispatch Dr. Kallmayer and the necessary assistants. Permit me to state that this procedure meets with the approval of Sturmbannführer Eichmann, the specialist for Jewish questions at Reich Security Headquarters. We are informed by Sturmbannführer Eichmann that camps for Jews are to be set up in Riga and Minsk, and that Jews from the Old Reich may possibly be sent to them."

I also have here a "Memorandum concerning consultations which our Amstsgerichtsrat collaborator"—name not given, probably Dr. Wetzel of the Reich Ministry for Occupied Eastern Territories—"has carried on with Oberdienstleiter Brack and the specialist Sturmbannführer Eichmann." I have no comment to make on that.

LESS: It's about the production of gas . . . of gassing apparatus, isn't it?

EICHMANN: Yes, but there's this to be said. I gather from this that the Führer's Office took charge of the procurement. Reich Security Headquarters was only asked for its consent, which consent was given through me. This convinces me that what I've just told you is just what I said to him. I wonder who instructed the Ministry for the East, or the people around Amtsgerichtsrat Dr. Wetzel, to do anything connected with gas machines. There must have been some prime mover. Maybe those Ministry of the East people said to themselves: "This has to be done more elegantly." They were no longer satisfied with shooting. Just now it occurred to me—because I didn't give Günther that order to buy a hundred kilos of prussic acid—it occurred to me that maybe my deputy Günther had a direct connection with Globocnik, so he supplied those people with the chemicals which . . . which maybe they themselves were originally supposed to procure.

LESS: But the crux of the matter is this: Could Günther have ordered that gas without your knowledge? You speak of a direct connection with Globocnik. But the first connection was made by you. You went to see Globocnik.

EICHMANN: Yes, that's a fact. That is a fact.

LESS: You went to see Globocnik. You went to Lemberg, you inspected Auschwitz. You went to all those extermination points, you saw the methods being used. In some places people were being gassed with motors, in others they were being shot. So your report to Müller or Heydrich or Himmler—wherever the report ended up—showed that these methods were, to put it crudely, inefficient. Consequently, some way had to be found to speed up the killing. It was also taken into consideration that such methods must have had a bad psychological effect on the men charged with carrying out the extermination measures. You had to consider that your own men might suffer from having to shoot hundreds and thousands of people. They weren't all natural-born murderers. Maybe their consciences would bother them later on. So better do it in a less visible form. Why not with gas? Maybe that was the train of thought. So Günther, probably with your knowledge, was told to take action, and the gas was supplied.

EICHMANN: I don't believe it happened that way, Herr Hauptmann. There'd be some trace of it in my memory. It wasn't the job of the Security Police to procure this gas. It simply was not our job.

LESS: How do you account for the fact that gassing was being done and that all the persons involved in this gassing point their finger at Eichmann and Bureau IV B 4?

EICHMANN: Well, that is a . . . that's just the funny part of it. Because we had nothing to do with it, nothing whatever . . . We had nothing to do with it. Nothing! Nothing! Nothing!

LESS: And all these statements are—

EICHMANN: Officially I . . . officially I had . . . Officially we had nothing to do with it, and unofficially I wasn't interested. I had . . . I had nothing to do with these things, I can tell you truthfully. And nobody here will ever prove the contrary.

LESS: But did you have official knowledge that gassing was going on?

EICHMANN: I knew it, of course I knew.

LESS: What was your attitude toward the total physical destruction of the Jewish people in the framework of the final solution of the Jewish question?

EICHMANN: I've already told you, Herr Hauptmann, that then . . . when I heard for the first time that . . . that . . . that . . . I felt as if someone had hit me over the head. And when I saw those first things, I've told you that too, I went weak in the knees. That's, that is a fact, and I was very glad in all those years that I had nothing to do with the killing. I had nothing to do with the killing.

LESS: But didn't deportation amount to killing?

EICHMANN: Herr Hauptmann, I've already told you . . . it wasn't my job to decide who was drawn into the work process and who was not. I had orders to deport. And when my colleague Wisliceny writes in his confessions that there were ways of circumventing Hitler's orders, I'd be glad to know what those ways were. I say: There was one way and only one way: to take a pistol and shoot yourself. That's obvious. I didn't.

(197)

LESS: In other words, you weren't opposed?

EICHMANN: I obeyed. Regardless of what I was ordered to do, I would have obeyed. Certainly, I would have obeyed. I obeyed, I obeyed. I can't shed my skin, Herr Hauptmann. I . . . that was my attitude at the time, and that's the way it was. When I received an order, I obeyed. An oath is an oath. In the observance of that oath, I was uncompromising. Today I'd never take an oath. No one could make me, no judge for instance, could make me take a witness's oath. I refuse; I refuse on moral grounds. Because I've learned by experience that if you let yourself be bound by an oath, you'll have to take the consequences someday. I see that today we have to pay for it because we never forgot our oath and that made us obey. If I hadn't obeyed then, I'd have been punished then. So which . . . whichever way things turn out, it's always bad to take an oath.

LESS: Your friend and colleague Dieter Wisliceny writes: "The men who worked with Eichmann were accustomed to carry out orders blindly. Apart from myself, the only one to attempt resistance in Hungary was Obersturmbann-führer Krumey. I often tried, by appealing to their reason, to get those men to engage in a little quiet sabotage or a slowdown. It was impossible. Most of those men were of a totally primitive type, and Eichmann's influence on them was too great."

EICHMANN: I never noticed any resistance, either on the part of Wisliceny or of Krumey. I noticed no resistance. None whatever.

Dieter Wisliceny joined the SS a little earlier than Eichmann, but advanced more quickly in the SD because of his superior education, especially in history, a subject much respected in the early days of National Socialist government. For a time, he was Eichmann's superior in Bureau IV B 4, though in Eich-

mann's opinion, Wisliceny was not exactly a hard worker. At that time, the two SS officers were such good friends that Wisliceny stood godfather to Eichmann's son Dieter. When Wisliceny, who at first outranked Eichmann, fell behind him in the competition for promotion, and when in the end Eichmann became head of the bureau, Wisliceny felt that he had been pushed aside. From then on, he bore Eichmann a secret grudge. Eichmann claims it was because Wisliceny was unmarried that Himmler refused to promote him. To avoid having to work directly under the bureau's new head, Wisliceny went into the "foreign service" and became adviser on Jewish affairs to the Slovakian government in Bratislava. The Jews deported from that satellite state were his responsibility. When for tactical reasons he was removed from Slovakia, he organized the shipment of Greek Jews to Auschwitz. After the war, Wisliceny was taken prisoner by the Western Allies and testified before the International Military Tribunal in Nuremberg. Extradited to Czechoslovakia, he was tried in Bratislava, sentenced to death, and executed.

EICHMANN: When Wisliceny writes in his confession: "On the strength of my personal experience, I once again state that Eichmann played a decisive part in the decimation of the European Jews and that, although he was covered by the orders of Hitler and Himmler, he must be held fully responsible, because there were ways of circumventing Hitler's orders"—I can only say that no man is justified in circumventing an order.

LESS: You have spoken of "responsibility for carrying out orders . . ."

EICHMANN: That's right. I am responsible for what I . . . for the things my orders obliged me to do. I told you at the start. Herr Hauptmann, I have no desire to evade that responsibility in any way whatsoever. Because I can't. On the other hand, I refuse to take responsibility for things I had no orders for and which were not in my department. I am not one of the people who said in 1945 and still say today: "I was always against it"—who try to save their necks with that sort of—let's say—sort of tawdry explanation. It wouldn't be true.

LESS: Can you tell me exactly from when to when you were in Hungary?

EICHMANN: Yes. Beginning on March 19, 1944. I remember the date because it was my birthday. I crossed the border on March 19. And at 3:30 p.m. on Christmas Eve, 1944, I left Budapest for the West.

LESS: Before your special team arrived, were any Jews deported from Hungary by the Hungarian government?

EICHMANN: I don't believe so; no, I'm sure they weren't.

LESS: You said something about building a camp near Berlin early in 1944. Was that at Wuhlheide?

EICHMANN: I don't remember the name. It was east of Berlin, about seventy or eighty kilometers. There had only been a railway station and maybe a few scattered houses. A real hole. So then, I think, ten, or let's say a dozen shacks were put up. The air raids were making it impossible to work seriously in Berlin. My boss finally realized that, and I suppose he said to himself: Why should the men sit around here, let them do something else.

So at the end of '43, or the beginning of '44, I was ordered to set up a village of shacks as a fallback headquarters for the Secret State Police. I brought in a contingent of technicians, architects, and workers from Theresienstadt. In March 1944, when we were almost finished, Gruppenführer Müller came on a tour of inspection. He looks the whole place over and then he tells me—by order of the Reichsführer, Himmler, that is—I'm to leave for Hungary to serve as adviser on Jewish affairs to the head of the Security Police there and take charge of shipping the Jews the Hungarian government had to evacuate, so as to get things moving in an orderly way. I went to the Mauthausen concentration camp, because that's where they were holding the meeting in connection with the Hungarian program, which had to be kept secret, because the whole action, like all such things, was treated as top secret at Reich Security Headquarters. At Mauthausen they took us to a separate part of the concentration camp. More and more people kept arriving: officials of the regular police, officials of the Security Police, lots of vehicles, maybe a hundred and sixty or a hundred and eighty vehicles. In a week or so, we were ready to move. Krumey and I were the highest-ranking officers; namely, Obersturmbannführer, which corresponds to Oberstleutnant. So this is what was decided: Krumey would start ahead as the advance party with some thirty vehicles, and twenty-five hours later I'd move off with about a hundred and forty vehicles. My column followed the First Armored Division. In Budapest the formation broke up. I was shown to a hotel room, where I lived for a few days.

What Eichmann describes almost casually was part of the German occupation of Hungary. In the spring of 1944, the whole of southeastern Europe was more or less in Hitler's power, apart from territories controlled by partisans. Up until then, Hungary, as an ally in the war against the Soviet Union, had managed to preserve a certain freedom from National Socialist doctrine. For over forty years, the seventy-five-year-old Nicholas von Horthy, formerly admiral of the Austro-Hungarian navy, had headed the state with the title of Regent. Even Hitler had to respect him, though Horthy refused for years to observe the radical anti-Semitism of the

National Socialists. At the beginning of 1944, there were some 800,000 Jews living in Hungary. Though harassed in many ways, they were not in danger of their lives. Eichmann and his associates in Bureau IV B 4 had already shipped the Jews from all other territories under German control to the concentration camps and gas chambers. When they seemed to be running out of work, Eichmann was assigned to the task of setting up a fallback headquarters for the Gestapo in the Brandenburg pine woods. But on March 12, 1944, Hitler, fearing that his military defeats would lead Hungary to secede from the German alliance, as the Badoglio government in Italy had done the year before, ordered Operation Margarete, the occupation of Hungary. Once again, Eichmann, the expert on Jewish affairs, was needed. The Russians were coming closer. Since a Jewish uprising would threaten the German armies from the rear, it was thought necessary to eliminate the Hungarian Jews in all haste. Eichmann spent only a few months in Hungary, but in that short time he sent more than 400,000 Hungarian Jews to their deaths; by his own estimate, 450,000.

EICHMANN: The Hungarian government fell when the Germans marched in. Wisliceny had made frequent visits to Hungary from Slovakia before that. In any case, he was acquainted with Laszlo Endre and Laszlo Baky, who both became undersecretaries at the Ministry of the Interior. At an informal meeting over a glass of Hungarian wine, I informed them that Himmler had issued an order to the German police and that he wanted the Hungarian Jews to be ghettoized, and then evacuated from East to West and shipped to Auschwitz. I said to them this is what the Reichsführer wants: age limit sixty, no one who isn't fit for labor, no children, no women unfit for labor, provisions for two days, avoidable cruelties to be avoided. Then the

Hungarian police carried out the anti-Jewish measures in Budapest. This ghettoization was not very severe. By that I mean, the Hungarians didn't do it the way it was done in the Government General—so cramped and over-crowded. And then boarded walls were seen again, windows boarded over and cemented. Dr. Endre came to terms with the Hungarian gendarmerie, because they didn't—that was a moot point—they didn't want any age limit, they wanted to evacuate everybody, lock, stock, and barrel. One of my men was always attached to the Hungarian police as German Security Police observer; his job was to see that the guidelines were adhered to.

LESS: Where did the shipments go?

EICHMANN: On Himmler's orders, they all went to Auschwitz, every last one of them. They weren't allowed to go anywhere else. A few times, the Hungarian gendarmes overloaded the cars without notifying anybody, and no observer could get there in time. They pummeled people into the cars. The guidelines provided for a maximum, the number of people allowed in the cars. Auschwitz would complain to Administration and Supply Headquarters. Administration and Supply forwarded the complaint to IV B 4, in the first place that the guidelines hadn't been observed, secondly that no food had been provided for the trip and the people had arrived half starved, and thirdly, they'd been beaten.

LESS: Did you also have guidelines for attaching the funds of the deported Jews?

EICHMANN: No, the German authorities weren't interested in that. The Hungarian authorities attended to it. We wouldn't have dared to interfere. I've been trying to remember about the escort troops. I'm pretty sure that on Hungarian territory the shipments were escorted by Hungarian gendarmes as far as the Austrian border and from there on by German regular police. In Hungary, my subordinates and I played a largely inactive role. There were observers in the field. I myself never went there. I never inspected a single shipment. I had no orders to do so, and in all these things, where I had no orders I didn't meddle.

LESS: I'm going to read you another quotation from Höss's book. What he writes about your activity outside of Germany.

"When a foreign government agreed to the deportation of its Jews, it set up an official agency to organize their arrest and delivery. Eichmann would arrange the details with this agency and give it the benefit of his experience in matters connected with the arrests. In Hungary, for example, the actions were carried out by the Ministry of the Interior and the police. Eichmann and his colleagues supervised their activities and interfered only if they were conducted too slowly or negligently. Eichmann's staff also had to provide the rolling stock and arrange the schedules with the Ministry of Transportation. On the orders of Pohl, chief of SS Administration and Supply Headquarters and hence also of the concentration camps, I went to Budapest three times, in order to form a rough estimate of the number of able-bodied Jews. This gave me an opportunity to observe Eichmann's methods of negotiating with the Hungarian government departments and military. His approach was exceedingly firm and efficient, yet friendly and polite. They all liked him, wherever he went, as is shown by the innumerable private invitations he received from the heads of these departments. Eichmann was convinced that if he succeeded in destroying the biological foundation of the Jews in the East, Jewry as a whole would never recover from the blow. He was obsessed by his mission and convinced that this extermination was necessary to preserve the German people from the destructive intentions of the Jews. He was also radically opposed to picking able-bodied Jews out of the shipments. He believed that this jeopardized the final solution, which should be carried out as quickly as possible, since it was impossible to foresee the outcome of the war. As early as 1943, he doubted the possibility of a complete German victory." Would you care to look at this and comment?

EICHMANN: If I had a red pencil, Herr Hauptmann, I would draw a red line through all the farfetched rubbish in what he says. It's such nonsense that I . . . it's so transparent that somebody must have worked on him. Trying to harm me by piling up all those lies . . . It doesn't even make me angry. I've seen so many of those reports that I'm pretty well hardened. If you wish, Herr Hauptmann, I'll comment point for point.

LESS: No, that won't be necessary.

EICHMANN: In principle, I reject the whole business as absolutely untrue. It's . . . I have no words for it, but it's typical.

LESS: Did you, shortly after your arrival, call a meeting of the Jewish functionaries in Budapest? And did you at that meeting tell them that there was no plan whatever to deport them?

EICHMANN: If I was sent to Hungary to deport people, Herr Hauptmann, I did not tell the Jewish functionaries that there would be no deporting. I never lied to Jewish functionaries. I dealt with Jewish functionaries for many years and I am sure there's not a single one who would accuse me of lying.

LESS: During what period of time, that is, during what months, were the approximately 450,000 Jews you have mentioned deported to Auschwitz and elsewhere?

EICHMANN: I believe, I believe that the deportations . . . my present guess . . . began at the earliest at the end of April 1944. It may even have been the beginning of May. For a while they proceeded according to timetable; then suddenly difficulties arose, and then it was smooth sailing again. It always went by fits and starts. But when it stopped, I don't remember. Maybe in . . . in October.

LESS: What do you know about Joel Brand's trip in connection with your offer to exchange a million Jews for ten thousand trucks?

EICHMANN: Herr Hauptmann, as far as I can remember, that business originated with . . . with Himmler. I can't quite visualize Joel Brand at the present time. Maybe our meetings were too short. He left immediately. The details were worked out by Krumey. All I remember is hearing that a million Jews were to be released somewhere in return for ten thousand all-weather trucks and the promise that these trucks would not under any circumstances be used on the Western front. That was the basis of the agreement, I think . . . I believe Himmler said at the time that he'd be glad to negotiate with Dr. Chaim Weizmann.

LESS: What did the Hungarian government say about this idea of exchanging a million Jews for ten thousand trucks?

EICHMANN: Well, actually, I don't think they knew anything about it. I don't know, maybe they got wind of it later on, because the Hungarian authorities watched us at every step.

LESS: When Joel Brand went abroad with your consent, to submit your proposal, did you promise him that no Jews would be deported in his absence?

EICHMANN: Some agreement was made, Herr Hauptmann. Some agreement. But today I don't even remember what he wrote about it in his book. Because at that time Dr. Kastner came running to us almost every day. I had to have some sort of decisions ready for the Hungarian authorities . . . so as . . . so I could somehow get this thing straightened out. I don't remember the details.

LESS: I would now like to read you a few passages from the report Dr. Kastner drew up for the Jewish Rescue Committee. Here he writes: "After Brand and Grosz left for Istanbul, I went to see Eichmann with Hansi Brand (Joel's wife). We knew we were face to face with the man who had done more than any other to organize the extermination of the Jews. But it was also in his power to help. The decision of life or death rested with him and him alone. We spoke to him frankly about the cruelties in the ghettoes and in the deportation trains. We asked him why the persons chosen for emigration had not been brought from the provinces to Budapest as Krumey had promised. We told him that under these conditions it would be difficult to conduct negotiations abroad with any hope of success. He talked about his trumped-up sympathy with the Zionists. In reply to concrete questions, he said: If it was true that in Carpathian Ruthenia ninety persons were penned into a single car, it was because the Jews in that region had so many children and children didn't take up much room. And moreover, he added, the Jews in that part of the country didn't expect much. That he should stop the deportations was out of the question. We shouldn't take him for a fool. Because, if he stopped the deportations, the Zionists would have no reason for negotiating with him. We should press the negotiations in Istanbul more energetically, because he was nobody's fool and there were limits to his patience."

EICHMANN: I don't remember these things. Undoubtedly there's a good part of truth in what he says, and undoubtedly his subjective attitude guided his thinking into channels favorable to his point of view. My refusing to stop the deportations—that's a concrete assertion and obviously untrue. What I probably said was: I can't stop them, because I didn't order them. I was only a . . . a receiver of orders.

LESS: But now we're on the subject of Joel Brand's trip. Continuing deportations at that time would obviously jeopardize Joel Brand's mission. Your answer to that, as Kastner says here, was that you wouldn't stop them.

EICHMANN: If that is true—assuming for the moment that I said that—the headquarters that approved this business must have given me such orders.

LESS: Let me read you what Dr. Kastner says elsewhere: "Eichmann returned to his office at eleven o'clock. I had myself announced immediately. Half an hour later, he called me in. His inner staff—Krumey, Wisliceny, Hunsche, and Nowack—were standing behind him. Eichmann begins to bellow. I keep quiet. You have to wait for his fits of rage to pass. It's obvious how much is at stake. It's not just a question of saving a few hundred Jews from the provinces. If Eichmann can't be forced to cooperate here and now, then the Vaadah, our Zionist secret organization, has been as naïve, as big a sucker as so many before us in occupied Europe who have put their money on the German number in this game of roulette for human lives. Then the millions paid out were a snare and a delusion. In this sort of game, a loser can just as well be called a traitor. Finally Eichmann starts the conversation: 'What do you actually want?'

"Kastner: "I must insist on your keeping our agreements. Will you bring the people proposed by us from the provinces to Budapest?'

"Eichmann: 'Once I've said no, it's no.'

"Kastner: 'In that case, it's pointless for us to negotiate any further.'

"I start getting up.

"Eichmann: 'Kastner, your nerves are shot. I'll send you to Theresienstadt to recover. Or would you prefer Auschwitz? Get me straight. I've got to clean this Jewish shit out of the provinces. No arguments or tears will help.'

"Kastner: 'If that's the case, our arguments won't help Joel Brand in his negotiations in Istanbul.'

"Eichmann: 'What good will those few Jews do you?'

"Kastner: 'It's not just them. The situation in Istanbul is bad, because you're speeding up the deportations. You've got to provide proof that your offers are meant seriously.'

"Eichmann: 'Get this through your head. The Hungarian government won't stand for it. I promised Laszlo Endre that not a single Jew would return alive.'"

EICHMANN: That's all very theatrical, all very theatrical. I . . . I have to say it again. There's a grain of truth in it, with a lot . . . a lot of decorative trimming. Those bad words, I certainly didn't use those words. About the substance, of course I can't say. Did I offer to send him to Theresienstadt or didn't I? I don't know.

LESS: I'm going to quote Dr. Kastner again. The time he's writing about must be close to June 1944.

"I pointed out to Eichmann that the killing of the deported Jews in Auschwitz put us, the Vaadah, in an impossible and untenable position vis-à-vis the foreign Jewish organizations and the Allies. 'Our moral credit is gone. No one abroad believes any longer that the Germans ever meant the rescue plan seriously.'

"Eichmann (bellowing): 'What do you think? Do you imagine that the Reich has enough food to feed a hundred thousand Hungarian Jews for months, or enough personnel or doctors to take care of their sick?'

"Kastner: 'What will happen if from one day to the next an agreement is concluded in Istanbul? If you have the Hungarian Jews gassed, where are you going to get the merchandise to exchange for your trucks?'

"Eichmann: 'Don't worry about that. There are children between twelve and fourteen. We're letting them live. In one or two years, they'll be old enough to work. But I can also deliver Polish Jews or [Czech] Jews from Theresienstadt. Don't worry, leave it to me.'

"Kastner: 'I'm convinced that you can't wring concessions from the Zionists with that. If you're really interested in this transaction, you'll have to demonstrate your good will. I'll make you a proposition. Guarantee the lives of a hundred thousand Hungarian Jews, inclusive of small children, old people, and the sick. As proof of our willingness to make sacrifices, we offer approximately five million Swiss francs in jewels, foreign currency, and pengö. We will deliver the money and valuables in installments in proportion as you deliver the counterpart.' "

Do you remember that?

EICHMANN: No. It's possible that he made me such a proposition. I don't deny it, because I'm not sure. But the truth of the matter is that I had orders, ten thousand trucks for a million Jews. And for me that was . . . those were my orders. That's all I can say about it.

LESS: Were there other business deals?

EICHMANN: Becher arranged with Dr. Kastner for delivery of some sort of goods, and in return Becher promised that some contingents of Jews would be allowed to emigrate to Palestine. Kastner was only interested in young Jews from eastern Hungary. The idea was to slip these groups across the Rumanian border secretly, without the knowledge of the Hungarian government. Once, I seem to remember, Dr. Kastner came to us with a suitcase full of foreign money. But then the Hungarian secret police got wind of it, especially the suitcase full of money. After that, it was extremely difficult working with the Hungarian police.

LESS: What was done with the money?

EICHMANN: I don't know, Herr Hauptmann. It went to the headquarters of the commander of the Security Police and the SD in Budapest.

*In Budapest, as in Vienna, Prague, and Berlin, Eichmann
convinced the functionaries of the Jewish Council that by
cooperating they could save the Jews from still greater
disasters. Dr. Rezsö Kastner, a lawyer and one of the leaders
of the Hungarian Jewish community, made a special effort to
win Eichmann's confidence as a shield for the rescue action
he was hoping to organize in collaboration with the knit-
goods dealer Joel Brand. It is still uncertain whether their
offer of ransom was meant seriously or was intended only to
stall the murder machine until the end of the war, which then
seemed imminent. At all events, Himmler, when informed of
the offer, instructed Eichmann to negotiate with Dr. Kastner
and Joel Brand. As they were both thought to be in close contact with the Center for World Jewry—an organization
existing only in the National Socialist imagination—and with
the head of the World Zionist Organization, Dr. Chaim
Weizmann in New York, Himmler wanted to make use of
them for a double game. He offered to put the brakes on the
murder machine if a certain number of trucks were provided
for use by the Waffen-SS. With this demand he was covering
himself vis-à-vis Hitler. But his secret hope was that once this
business deal put him in touch with Weizmann and the Western Allies he would be able to sell them his special plan for a
peace between the Allies and a new Germany with Himmler
at the helm. But the exchange did not take place; Joel Brand's
trip ended in a fiasco.*

LESS: Did you threaten the Jewish functionaries in Budapest
to set the "Auschwitz mill" in motion again if Joel Brand
returned empty-handed?

EICHMANN: I never threatened a Jewish functionary. Neither
in Hungary nor in any other country. And as for the
"Auschwitz mill," I heard that expression for the first time
in 19—1947, I believe—when a movie called *The Ausch-*

witz Mill was made in some village on the Lüneburger Heide. So if anyone says I threatened anybody with the "Auschwitz mill" . . . I know he's lying.

LESS: When you went to Hungary on March 19, 1944, with your special team, the Döme Sztojay government was in power. In July 1944, it was replaced by the government of General Geza Lakatos, which remained in power until the middle of October. Do you remember that?

EICHMANN: No, I don't, but, you see, I had nothing to do with the heads of the government. I dealt with only one person, and that was Undersecretary Endre.

LESS: Is it true that from July to October no Jews were deported, because the Lakatos government was opposed to it?

EICHMANN: You mean there were no shipments for all of three months? . . . That sounds like a long time to me, Herr Hauptmann. I do remember there were constant difficulties, and I know specifically that they came not so much from the Hungarian government as from the fact that the railway lines were always being cut by the constant bombings.

LESS: Do you remember that there was a putsch and that Horthy was dismissed?

EICHMANN: Yes, yes, I remember, that's right.

LESS: And that Szálasi took over?

EICHMANN: Yes, that's right—I remember now.

LESS: Were the deportations resumed?

EICHMANN: That must be it. That must be it.

Of course, the putsch of October 15, 1944, was engineered by the Germans. It was plain that Hungary had nothing to gain from the war, which was going badly, and Regent Horthy, through his son Nicholas, had started negotiations for an armistice. Hitler had them both arrested. The son was sent to

Mauthausen concentration camp, and the father was imprisoned in Hirschberg Schloss in Bavaria. In Hungary, the Fascist Arrow Cross movement took power and its leader Ferenc Szálasi became Prime Minister. Horthy, it is true, had done nothing to prevent the Jews in his own country from being pressed into labor gangs, but he had put a stop to Eichmann's deportations when he learned beyond any possible doubt that the deportees were being murdered. Now, under Szálasi, the murderers were given free rein.

LESS: Wasn't the whole deportation program a German Diktat, to which the Hungarian authorities were forced to submit?

EICHMANN: A Diktat, Herr Hauptmann, ha-ha-ha! . . . A Diktat? No, I never had that feeling. Up to the rank of undersecretary, at any rate, I never had that feeling. Just the opposite.

LESS: Now I'm going to show you an extract from the testimony given at the trial of Sztojay and associates before the People's Court in Budapest in April 1946. I quote: "In the course of the proceedings, Sztojay declared that Eichmann had made known to the Hungarian government the particulars of the solution of the Jewish question in Hungary." Do you wish to comment?

EICHMANN: Yes. From this document I infer that Szotjay, who was then Prime Minister, settled the whole matter on a high level with Kaltenbrunner and with SS-Gruppenführer Veesenmayer, the Reich Plenipotentiary for Hungary. Sztojay says that Eichmann had made known the particulars of the solution of the Jewish question in Hungary. Sztojay further states that Kaltenbrunner wanted the Hungarian Jewish question to be solved along German lines. Just as I said, Herr Hauptmann. Then I received orders to have Hungary combed through from east to west. I had no need to settle the other points, because the Hungarian gendarmerie had its orders from Endre. My activity in Hungary, as I've already said, was mostly of a moderating character, because SS Administration and Supply Headquarters was dissatisfied with the ... say ... the way they were handling the shipments, the speed and all.

LESS: In making known the particulars, did you mention the fact that the Jews would be sent to extermination camps? To Auschwitz?

EICHMANN: To Auschwitz? Of course. When it says I was instructing the Hungarian government, obviously the undersecretaries Laszlo Endre and Laszlo Baky are meant.

LESS: When the shipments arrived in Auschwitz, before the deportees entered the camp, wasn't there always a selection made, after which most were sent to the gas chambers?

EICHMANN: Yes, Herr Hauptmann, but they only asked for able-bodied persons, fit for labor. I originally believed that only able-bodied persons were being sent from Hungary. It's only here that I've learned that the shipments from Hungary included Jews who could only be classified as unfit for labor. That's why Höss ...

LESS: If they had all been fit for labor, no selection would have been made.

EICHMANN: Of course not. But it wasn't up to me to decide who was fit for labor and who was not. The age limit was up to me. I didn't draw up these guidelines on my own; they came to me from above, from the Reichsführer-SS and chief of the German police by way of the chief of the Reichs ... the chief of the Security Police and the SD, as I have several times had the honor of saying.

LESS: Weren't a lot of families with quantities of children evacuated to the death camps?

EICHMANN: I, I don't know, Herr Hauptmann. I don't know. I'm not trying to play stupid. From the documents I've seen here, from the fact that Höss complained, I infer what I must have thought at the time: Those fellows were obviously rounding everybody up helter-skelter.

LESS: Wasn't the term "labor service" a kind of camouflage altogether? To cover up the real purpose?

EICHMANN: No, no, no. At that time in Hungary . . . In Hungary, Herr Hauptmann, not at that time, no, no!

LESS: But earlier?

EICHMANN: If the word was . . . Earlier they didn't always say fit for labor—only in foreign countries. In the Government General and the occupied Eastern territories, I'm sure there wasn't that distinction.

LESS: I'm going to show you a document produced by the prosecution at the eleventh war crimes trial in Nuremberg. It's a telegram of June 17, 1944, from Budapest. Referring to Jews, it says: "Total number deported to the Reich, 326,009."

EICHMANN: If the figure was given by Veesenmayer, the Reich Plenipotentiary for Hungary, it's probably correct. He must have gotten it from me or one of my men.

LESS: Was there in Hungary a law legalizing the deportation of Jews to Germany and the German-occupied territories in the East?

EICHMANN: A Hungarian law, legaliz . . . Herr Hauptmann, I can't answer that question at this late date. Because the . . . my legalization, or rather the legalization for the German authorities in Hungary, was: first the orders given me, and secondly the fact that the . . . that all the operations connected with it were performed by the undersecretaries at the Hungarian Ministry of the Interior.

LESS: Was there in Germany, Austria, Bohemia–Moravia a deportation law on the basis of which masses of Jews, gypsies, or non-Jews could be sent to concentration camps?

EICHMANN: Yes, the Führer and Chancellor's Order. I did not personally re . . . receive the order from him, but from the chief of the Ger . . . from the Reichsführer-SS and chief of the German police, who then, insofar as it concerned the sector of the Security Police, passed it on to the chief of the Security Police and the SD, who in turn notified me through official channels insofar as my activities were concerned . . .

LESS: When I say law, I'm referring to the legal code, a formulation that appears in the Reich legal code.

EICHMANN: No, not that . . . It's not necessary. A codified law isn't necessary, Herr Hauptmann. Because there are also ordinances. And orders. And the story was—not just a story, a solid fact—that, I quote: "The Führer's orders have the force of law." The orders given by a commanding general aren't in the legal code either.

LESS: Then all that went under the heading "top secret"?

EICHMANN: Top secret. That's right.

LESS: Was there in Germany a law legalizing the mass gassing and mass shooting of Jews, gypsies, and non-Jews?

EICHMANN: There was an order from Hitler, which, for instance, the chief of the Security Police and the SD, Obergruppenführer Heydrich himself, once told me about, as I've already stated here. And I couldn't possibly have harbored any suspicion that the Führer and Chancellor of the German Reich hadn't actually issued such an order, because even an Obergruppenführer Heydrich would never have dared to make up such a thing.

The Hungarian gendarmes were hardly in love with the Jews, though their hatred was by no means as virulent as Eichmann wants us to think. At the start of his dealings with the Nazi regime, the chief of state, Admiral Horthy, had little objection to imposing economic restrictions on the Jewish citizens of his country. But it was only reluctantly and under pressure from Hitler that he allowed them to be used for forced labor in Germany. Then, on June 25, 1944, when he could not help realizing that most of the deportees were murdered soon after their arrival in the camps, he stopped the deportations and dismissed Undersecretaries Endre and Baky at the Ministry of the Interior, who had been supplying Eichmann with Auschwitz fodder. Moreover, he asked the Reich government to recall its Gestapo men, and especially Eichmann, to Germany. Without the help of the Hungarian gendarmerie, the German Jew-hunters were virtually helpless. Himmler pretended to give in. On August 25, he forbade further deportations from Hungary, and on September 28 he dissolved the "Eichmann team." Eichmann had no cause for dismay; he knew that he and his men would not be idle for long. At the moment Himmler had a different use for the Hungarian Jews, and to handle this new project he needed a man untainted with the smell of corpses. This was SS-Standartenführer Kurt Becher, who dealt with economic questions at the headquarters of the SS and police commander for Hungary, and whose master stroke had been the Aryanization of the Manfred Weiss Works in May 1944.

LESS: Was Standartenführer Kurt Becher empowered to block the deportation of Jews from Hungary?

EICHMANN: Herr Hauptmann, at first I didn't . . . I didn't know what was what with Becher. Becher . . . if you're interested, I'll tell you briefly about the business with Becher.

LESS: Of course. Go ahead.

EICHMANN: Becher came to see me—I hadn't known him before—during my first days in Budapest. I'm not sure if it was then that he told me he had a special mission from Himmler. He had to put through some economic deals for the Waffen-SS, and we were always having three-way conferences: Dr. Kastner, Becher, and myself. The purpose of these negotiations was always to obtain contingents of

Jews for Palestine, and for that Becher collected some sort of commission, which was part of his job. A few times Dr. Kastner managed to put through small shipments, and it seems to me that he even told me he had hidden Jews in various places, with the idea that the Germans would make the Hungarian gendarmerie or state police stay away from those places. One time, when I was back in Berlin, I reported on Becher to Gruppenführer Müller, because on several occasions Becher had . . . er . . . arrogated powers to himself that were not compatible with his belonging to the Waffen-SS. Because it's inconceivable that a member of the Waffen-SS should claim police powers. To me, Müller didn't say anything definite, he just said he wanted to speak to Becher. I told Becher that, but I don't think he reported to him. It was only when I was ordered to report to the Reichsführer along with Becher that it was made clear to me for the first time in black and white that he actually was acting on Himmler's orders in Hungary. As time went on, Becher's office in the center of Budapest got bigger and bigger.

LESS: But he didn't have the power to prevent deportations?

EICHMANN: No, he did not. He . . .

LESS: Did he ever make such a claim in speaking to you?

EICHMANN: He once said—that was when he made me so angry —he shouted at Dr. Kastner: "All right, if you don't do this or that, I'll tell the Obersturmbannführer to deport . . . I don't know, maybe ten thousand Jews." After that, I said to myself: that's pretty strong. In the first place, he, as a member of the Waffen-SS, can't make the police evacuate two Jews. In the second place, the way he said it made me extremely angry. So I told Gruppenführer Müller about it. Today I can only describe Becher as an out-and-out opportunist. He was always harping on some order from the Reichsführer, which he wouldn't be able to carry out unless evacuations were pushed ahead in a frenzy. He wanted the evacuations to be carried out on the double, and he said that was what the Reichsführer-SS wanted, too.

LESS: What were your personal relations with Becher?

EICHMANN: With Becher? Good—except for that time when he made me angry. His field of activity—I don't know if that's the right way to put it—in Hungary was liquidating the Manfred Weiss holdings. Manfred Weiss was the leading industrialist in Hungary, you might have called him the Hungarian Krupp, and Becher made himself a director or something of the sort. At least that's what he himself once told me. He sent the family of Manfred Weiss, the owner . . . they were flown out to Switzerland, I believe. Himmler himself took a hand in the whole Manfred Weiss business. Becher told me that.

Here Eichmann is mistaken on several points. Becher, the son of a Hamburg businessman, was first sent to Hungary to buy horses for the Waffen-SS. One of his Hungarian business connections asked him to help the Jewish members of the family of the late Manfred Weiss, the founder of the firm, who were in danger of being deported by Eichmann. Himmler wished to establish an industrial corporation, the profits from which would make the SS financially independent. By a contract concluded in mid-May, the Weiss heirs ceded more than half the share capital to the industrial enterprises of the SS. In return, forty-eight members of the family were flown to Portugal in two German planes. This was not Becher's only deal. He seems to have concealed a part of his undertakings from Eichmann. Eichmann looked upon Becher as his enemy, who abused the powers conferred on him by the Reichsführer to save the wealthiest, most prominent, and, from the standpoint of Nazi ideology, most dangerous Jews. The conflict between these two knights of the Black Order finally impelled Himmler to summon them together to his headquarters.

LESS: Here is a document presented by the prosecution at the eleventh war crimes trial in Nuremberg. It comes from the Foreign Office and concerns the shipment of 318 Hungarian Jews to Switzerland.

EICHMANN: Yes, it has to do with an illegal shipment, and in my opinion it's a mistake when it says here that this affair was arranged directly, and solely by word of mouth, between the Reichsführer-SS and Obersturmbannführer Eichmann. It would have been more correct to say Standartenführer Becher. He arranged those things with Dr. Kastner. Because that's the kind of thing it was. What the business deals were, I don't know. You'd have to ask Becher about that.

LESS: Why Becher? This is a communication from your bureau to Thadden of the Foreign Office. It refers to a conversation between you and Himmler. Becher isn't even mentioned.

EICHMANN: Well, it was . . . you see, both Becher and I were called to the Reichsführer. The two of us were in Himmler's office together; then he was ordered to report to Himmler by himself. What they decided, I don't know. But I did not put through this transaction to Switzerland. I only had to instruct the border posts not to make difficulties, and I had to cover the operation on the Hungarian side.

LESS: You didn't conduct the related negotiations with the Jewish functionaries . . .

EICHMANN: With Dr. Kastner, for instance, constantly.

LESS: What sums were paid in exchange?

EICHMANN: I don't know that, Herr Hauptmann. The amount, the economic end didn't . . . wasn't the concern of my department. Becher took care of the economic end. I was only interested in the police aspect. We made no deals, no deals of any kind with any Jewish functionaries; the bargaining was the business of Becher's team.

LESS: And you want me to believe that your department was ignorant enough to tell the Foreign Office that this shipment of Jews was the product of an oral agreement between Himmler and you?

EICHMANN: Well, it's . . . that information is half correct, Herr Hauptmann, because I reported to the Reichsführer with Becher. We both had orders to report. And you see, we had this division of labor; one had to take care of certain things, and one of certain other things. Becher, for instance, couldn't have gotten those Jews across the border safely. That was in my province.

LESS: When did this conference with Himmler take place?

EICHMANN: I think it was at the end of May or in June 1944. Himmler had his field headquarters somewhere in western Germany at the time. His train was outside a tunnel, and when there was an air-raid alarm the train was pulled into the tunnel. On the way there from Budapest, we traveled in two cars, Becher in his and I in mine. Becher was carrying—he showed it to me—a gold necklace, which he meant to give Himmler for the "liaison" that Himmler had a child with. That was the first I'd heard of it.

Here Eichmann makes several mistakes. First, as to the date. It was not until December 1944 that he went to Himmler's field headquarters. This was stated by Eichmann's companion, Kurt Becher, then an Obersturmbannführer, and is also confirmed by Eichmann's own account. It was not until shortly before the end of the year that Himmler took command of the German defense positions in the southwest, extending from the Swiss border through Alsace to the Palatinate. The Reichsführer-SS and his immediate staff were quartered—as they had been in the East—in a special train, which was stationed on the tracks of the Black Forest Railway near Triberg between the Rhine Valley and Donaueschingen. When enemy planes were reported, the train disappeared into one of the numerous tunnels in that mountainous region. Heinrich Himmler's mistress was Hedwig Potthast, his longtime secretary. She had two children by him, and lived near Berchtesgaden in a house he had built for her—largely with party funds loaned him by Martin Bormann.

EICHMANN: Himmler asked me for a report. Then, in Becher's presence, he said he was optimistic about the outcome of the war. He also said that if he had it to do all over again he wouldn't conduct the whole concentration-camp business in its present form, but along British lines. I can't remember exactly, but I believe he said at that conference that he had given, or would give, orders to stop the gassing.

LESS: Were you given the Iron Cross, First and Second Class? And do you remember when?

EICHMANN: I got it . . . yes, I got it for . . . I have to think back, Herr Hauptmann. I got the Iron Cross, Second Class, for the thing with the military hospital. And a little before that, I received the War Merit Cross, First Class with Swords, when Becher and I reported . . . reported to the Reichsführer.

LESS: Was that distinction awarded for your work in Hungary?

EICHMANN: That, Herr Hauptmann, that War Merit Cross, wasn't exactly a distinction, it was like this . . . so and so many . . . The Iron Cross, Second Class, was a distinction in the Security Police, but the War Merit Cross . . . A certain number of them were simply allotted to the Security Police from time to time, and then they were distributed, they came down from above.

LESS: Here I have some statements made by Kurt Becher at his hearing on July 10, 1947. I'll just read you a few passages in which he mentions you. "Now I would like to say a few things about the conference Eichmann and I had with Himmler at his headquarters in Triberg." Becher was then asked: "When?" His answer: "It must have been in the first half of December 1944. Herr Himmler received Eichmann for ten minutes in my presence. He bellowed at him: 'If up to now you've murdered Jews and I now command you to take care of Jews, tell me this: Will you or will you not carry out that order?' Herr Eichmann said: 'I will, Reichsführer!'—and froze at attention. After a further exchange, Himmler dismissed him, and I stayed. I begged him almost on my knees: 'For God's sake, straighten that out with Eichmann before he leaves your headquarters; the man will disobey your orders, he'll carry out more actions. I have an idea: Give him the War Merit Cross, First Class with Swords.' So Herr Eichmann was given the War Merit Cross, First Class with Swords. Herr Eichmann was pacified."

So much for Becher's statement.

EICHMANN: Here he takes the fact that the Reichsführer-SS and chief of the German police awarded me the War Merit Cross with Swords and builds up a story fit for . . . a movie scenario, but not for a witness who's supposed to tell the truth. It's a lie from A to Z.

The Reichsführer did not shout at me in front of Becher. His treatment of me was perfectly normal, reasonable, and correct. He did not shout at me, certainly not. And another thing. I'd like to see the Reichsführer-SS if he found out— and I was right there—that I disobeyed his orders. I'd never have left that command post; I'd have been arrested then and there, on the spot.

LESS: What was the substance of your conversation with Himmler?

EICHMANN: I received orders to go down there [to Hungary] with Becher, and I think he ordered me . . . ordered me to stop the shipments.

To wind up this Becher business, Herr Hauptmann, I want to say this: I'd read somewhere about Becher's statement. Or that he was set free or something; anyway, I read something or other over the years. But that he was such a liar and made such lying statements or gave such lying testimony, I wouldn't have thought it possible. He made that statement so he could wash his hands in innocence. He plays the role of a man who thinks he can somehow come out of the whole affair unscathed. I don't know what Becher had done before. I wouldn't want to say anything against the man. But judging by the proverb 'Those who lie have reasons why,' I can only assume that he had some reason for saying such a thing, because it's not true. But what could have led him to accuse me of acting contrary to the Reichsführer's orders, I simply can't understand . . . It's . . . I'm amazed that the man could have been a Standartenführer. Really amazed. And I'm also surprised that I got away from Himmler so easy and scot-free . . . when for lesser misdeeds men were heavily, heavily . . . let's say, punished.

LESS: Wilhelm Höttl, a former SS-Sturmbannführer, assigned to Reich Security Headquarters like yourself, said under questioning that you knew you were regarded at the United Nations as one of the leading war criminals.

EICHMANN: Well, that is untrue. Totally untrue. Some . . . some Polish newspaper once published a list of war criminals and I was, I think, number 7 or 17. A man who knew all about the press said: "That's journalism. Something they threw together." But I never heard anything about an international war criminal. On the contrary, in 1945, when the Nuremberg stories were coming out, I was very much surprised that such things could be made retroactive.

By insisting time and again that he only carried out orders and regulations and never harmed anyone on his own initia-

tive, Eichmann shows the line he intends to take with the defense: he is planning to plead Befehlsnotstand,* because in the Third Reich disobedience to orders was a capital offense. True, he repeats ad nauseam that he is prepared to answer for his crimes like a man and that he is fully expecting the death sentence, but he is looking for an escape hatch all the same. That is why he argues that, before the Nuremberg trials, genocide was not considered a crime and consequently that he cannot be punished on the basis of laws enacted after his alleged crimes were committed.

LESS: You have repeatedly stated that you acted only on orders. I will now show you some documents presented by the prosecution at the eleventh war crimes trial in Nuremberg. Do you wish to comment?

EICHMANN: This is a telegram to the Foreign Office, dated March 13, 1943, dealing with the anti-Jewish measures planned by the Italian Foreign Ministry. The second document is a note from the Reich Foreign Minister, asking us to determine, in consultation with the Reichsführer-SS, whether the anti-Jewish measures decided in the . . . in the Italian-occupied part of Greece were adequate, and if so, whether these measures were actually being carried out. Should this not be the case, steps would have to be taken by us. Thereupon, Legation Secretary Rademacher of the Foreign Office conferred with me, and it was established that in the opinion of the Reichsführung-SS—that's wrong, of course; it can't ever be called Reichsführung, it has to be called the Reichssicherheitshauptamt [Reich Security Headquarters]—in other words, of SS-Obersturmbannführer Eichmann, that these anti-Jewish measures were

---

* Literally, "command constraint," meaning the state of one who is not free because he is bound by his orders.—*Trans.*

inadequate, because, on the one hand, they were identical with the likewise inadequate anti-Jewish measures current in Italy, and on the other hand, experience gave ground for doubt that the measures were being honestly carried out.

This experience, this opinion, he writes, was shared by the Foreign Office in the light of similar experiences. —Well, of course I can't remember this particular case. Undoubtedly, as in all such matters, I must have entered it in my ledger and taken the case to Gruppenführer Müller. And then, apparently, I made this statement.

LESS: Can it be inferred from this document that the Reich Foreign Minister gave instructions to consult your bureau, so as to be sure of proceeding in accordance with your wishes and instructions? Am I to take it that in fundamental questions of this kind the Foreign Office couldn't make a decision without consulting your department?

EICHMANN: Well, yes . . . my department. I had to get instructions from my superior. Just as . . . as Rademacher had to get his from his superior, I had to get mine from my superior.

LESS: Now I'm going to show you a document submitted by the prosecution at the eleventh Nuremberg war crimes trial. It's a telegram, top secret, from Budapest, dated July 6, 1944. Do you wish to comment?

EICHMANN: It's a situation report, sent directly by Minister Veesenmayer to the Foreign Minister on the basis of . . . of an interview with Hungarian Prime Minister Sztojay. And it evidently deals with a crucial matter. It deals with a telegraph order issued by the Reich Foreign Minister. Sztojay was upset about this order, which must have been communicated to him, so he asked Veesenmayer for an interview. And in that interview Sztojay spoke of difficulties that the handling of the Jewish question was creating for Hungary. That's all I can say about it.

LESS: Does this report suggest that it was the Hungarian authorities who were demanding deportation? Or the opposite?

EICHMANN: The report suggests the opposite, but the fact is that I . . . insofar as my own practice, that is, my practical experience, is concerned—and I'm referring now to the lower echelons—I couldn't help observing the opposite, and I assure you, the whole course of events pointed in that direction. Because without the . . . without the help of the Hungarian gendarmerie it wouldn't have been possible. And another indication is that I made no attempt to influence the Hungarian government—as some people here, I believe, are trying to suggest. On the contrary, the document makes it clear that this thing originated with the highest Reich authority.

LESS: But it also shows clearly that the Hungarian civilian population wasn't exactly enthusiastic about your anti-Jewish policy.

EICHMANN: Yes, but the interests of the Hungarian civilian population weren't my primary concern. That wasn't my job. My job was to carry out . . . Herr Hauptmann, I had to carry out the orders that were given me. And these things were none of my business . . . You can see what it says here: these were things that concerned the highest spheres of leadership.

LESS: What did you do about Jews who fled across the Hungarian borders to escape deportation?

EICHMANN: As regards the question of . . . of flight . . . there must have been a lot of them . . . it depends, it depended on the nature of the case and the nature of the terrain . . . No German . . . no German headquarters was competent, because we had no personnel; the competent authority was the Hungarian gendarmerie, which among other things did the same work as our border police.

LESS: Weren't you interested in letting as few escape as

possible, since, after all, the aim was to deport as many as possible?

EICHMANN: According to my orders, yes . . . according to the orders I had, of course it was in my interest that the Jews resident in Hungary should be deported and that they shouldn't all escape. In a formal sense . . . so to speak . . . I opposed it, but in practice nothing was done, as you can see by . . . by the large number of those who actually did escape.

LESS: I'm going to show you a document presented by the prosecution at the eleventh Nuremberg war crimes trial. It's a telegram signed Veesenmayer, dated Budapest, June 14, 1944, and it concerns the flight of Jews to Slovakia. Would you care to read it through?

EICHMANN: Yes, it's a telegram from Veesenmayer to the Reich Foreign Minister. It deals with the information that more and more . . . Jews resident in Hungary are crossing over into Slovakia . . . and a suggestion that—if the Reich Foreign Minister is agreed—Veesenmayer, the German Minister in Budapest, should meet with Ludin, the German Minister in Slovakia, with a view to working out joint practical measures, since for political and military reasons these escapes were most undesirable. Well, you see, it's just as I said: the border zones naturally tempted people to escape . . . the woods, the mountains; and undoubtedly the initiator of this action was not so much the Eichmann team in Budapest as the regional commander of the German troops, or his intelligence officers, who called attention to this fact. And there seems to have actually been an uprising in eastern Slovakia. And the top brass in Germany seem to have taken that into account, because otherwise I wouldn't have been given orders to start in the east, even though the Hungarian authorities wanted to evacuate Budapest first.

LESS: You say that the military . . . the German military

authorities were the driving force in this matter. Doesn't it seem more likely that the special team charged with total evacuation called attention to the dangers?

EICHMANN: Obviously, I didn't say never mind, it's all right, just let them clear out.

LESS: After reading this document, can you still maintain that the Hungarians were the driving force behind the extermination of the Jews in Hungary?

EICHMANN: Herr Hauptmann, if in wartime people try to escape, regardless of whether they're Jews or Hungarians or Germans, even Germans, it stands to reason that steps must be taken to stop them during a war. That was my position then, and I can't deny it today.

LESS: When several Jewish functionaries fled to Rumania, did you get in touch with von Killinger, the German Minister in Bucharest, and demand that these escaped functionaries must be brought back to Hungary at all costs?

EICHMANN: At all costs? At all costs? In the first place, that is a . . . a . . . I couldn't have said those words. It's probable that my associate Krumey drafted a . . . a . . . let's say . . . a formal warrant, which, however, went right into the dead file. But at all costs . . . if those words are in it . . . certainly nobody said that . . . or anything like it.

LESS: Because of these Jewish functionaries escaping, did you have other Jewish functionaries in Budapest arrested in retaliation?

EICHMANN: No, no! On the other hand, it's obvious, Herr Hauptmann, that no Jew who emigrated from Germany, or left in some other way later on, would praise Germany to the skies. That's a foregone conclusion.

LESS: Is that why your guidelines for the shipments include the order: "In cases of attempted escape, firearms are to be used"?

EICHMANN: No, I never heard of that. In Hungary, that was definitely not the practice. In Hungary, I'm absolutely sure that weapons were not used in cases of attempted escape. I don't believe that, no, I don't believe it. In an isolated case or two, it may have somehow come to that, but I can't imagine any such thing. Thinking about it today, I don't see the need for it.

LESS: Had you informed Hungarian Undersecretary Endre that the half million Jews who were deported were sent to Auschwitz to be gassed?

EICHMANN: Yes. Endre knew. I personally believe, I still believe, that the majority of the 450,000 Hungarian Jews who were sent to Auschwitz survived. Because an order came . . . almost immediately, as a matter of fact . . . from Germany to stop the shipments.

LESS: From Himmler?

EICHMANN: Yes. The commander of the Security Police in Budapest received a suspension order. There were not to be any more deportations, because Auschwitz had no room anymore. That's why Himmler issued an order to stop the killing. Auschwitz was full up, there wasn't room for any more people. I believe there was a week's pause.

LESS: You mean it started up again?

EICHMANN: Started up again after that? Yes.

LESS: What is the meaning of "termination of the entire action, including deportation," as Legation Secretary von Thadden, your liaison in the Foreign Office, writes here?

EICHMANN: Obviously, that meant the total elimination of the Jews in Hungary.

LESS: Including babies, children, and old people?

EICHMANN: In this case, yes. In this case, yes. But they didn't even get started in Budapest.

LESS: This projected large-scale action in Budapest was planned by the German authorities, not by the Hungarians?

EICHMANN: The whole action was planned by both together, in close collaboration.

LESS: But we've seen from these documents that the Hungarian authorities resisted, with the possible exception of Undersecretary Endre. That's why you were there with your group, to exert sufficient pressure.

EICHMANN: Herr Hauptmann, resistance in Hungary was offered by Horthy and his closest associates. To break that resistance was not the work of a small team of Security Police and SD. It was the work of the combined top brass: the Reich Foreign Ministry, that is, the Foreign Office in Berlin, and the Reichsführer-SS and chief of the German police. All these heavyweights had to tackle the problem. And not the Eichmann special team, Herr Hauptmann.

LESS: Haven't we seen from the documents that the plan was to round up a million Jews within four months and deport them? In other words, that your action was carried out under extreme pressure to complete it as quickly as possible?

EICHMANN: That is true.

LESS: What Jews were left in Europe? Only Hungary was left.

EICHMANN: Herr Hauptmann, from the very start the orders were to evacuate as quickly as possible. Seeing I had been given orders to evacuate as quickly as possible from east to west, the German leadership must have had a pretty good idea of how the war situation would develop. But the pace, Herr Hauptmann, with the few men at my disposal I couldn't speed up the pace; only the Hungarian Ministry of the Interior could do that. If, for instance, the Hungarian gendarmerie had sab—to call a spade a spade, had sabotaged our action, nothing could have been done. Nothing.

LESS: Let me show you a telegram from Berlin to Budapest; von Thadden at the Foreign Office drafted this telegram, which concerns the anti-Jewish actions in Budapest. Would you care to read it through?

EICHMANN: Yes, Herr Hauptmann. This telegram expresses

the belief of the Foreign Office that a sudden large-scale action against the Budapest Jews would arouse violent reactions abroad. The press section is trying to persuade the Foreign Minister to arrange for pretexts, such as, for instance, explosives are discovered on the premises of Jewish organizations and synagogues, acts of sabotage, attacks on policemen, big foreign-currency swindles. —I don't know anything about that, I never heard of it. And, as far as I know, nothing of the kind was done.

LESS: Here I have a three-page telegram from Veesenmayer to the Foreign Office. Would you please read it?

EICHMANN: It's about sending some group of Jews to Palestine via Switzerland. Veesenmayer quotes me, for one, so evidently he asked me and I informed him that, as far as I knew, the Reichsführer-SS wouldn't consent to any emigration of Jews to Palestine under any circumstances. The Jews under consideration were without exception biologically valuable material, which made their emigration to Palestine most undesirable. Here I must say that that was the period when shipments to Palestine in return for industrial products were under way. In this connection, Becher had the Reichsführer's signature. I'm not up on these things, but as far as I know, Becher is at large in West Germany; I believe he was tried and acquitted after 1945, so I'm sure he could give you information about this business.

LESS: Veesenmayer writes here that he had arranged with you to speed up the deportations.

EICHMANN: He says it had been agreed with me that, insofar as further deportations of Jews from Budapest were authorized, they should take place as quickly as possible so that Jews eligible for emigration would be deported before they had time to complete the formalities. This shows again that not only the Security Police but other authorities as well were trying to get things over with as quickly as possible. But the fact is that these offices had no need to bring up, or let's say to mention, the question of pace, because Endre—and his gendarmerie—were moving so fast that Auschwitz was having the greatest difficulty in handling all those shipments.

LESS: Here is a report from von Thadden about his visit to Budapest. Dated May 26, 1944. He writes that a one-day large-scale action was planned in Budapest and that all Jews in the city were to be concentrated on an island in the Danube near Budapest and deported by the beginning of September at the latest, with the exception of eighty thousand. Was this the plan of your special team?

EICHMANN: Herr Hauptmann, he says there were 360,000 Jews in Budapest, and here he says they were planning to do it in one day. I didn't attach any importance to it, because it's practically impossible to move 350,000 or even 250,000 or 150,000 people in one day, even if the two places are only a few kilometers apart. Even Endre with his hard-hitting gendarmerie couldn't have done that.

LESS: Von Thadden writes: "For this purpose, an extensive one-day action is projected. A large force of Hungarian police from the provinces and all specialized units and police schools will be enlisted; all the postmen and chimney sweeps in Budapest will be used as guides. Bus and streetcar traffic will be suspended for this day, leaving all vehicles free for the transportation of the Jews." Is this the projected action?

EICHMANN: In the first place, it wasn't carried out. In the second place, I don't know who planned it, because it's . . . that sort of planning is sheer madness. Take this idea of bringing in chimney sweeps and postmen. That's the kind of thing that no specialized agency . . . that couldn't have been planned in any police headquarters.

LESS: Now I'm going to show you a note from the Foreign Office in Berlin to the German Ministry in Budapest, signed von Thadden. Among other things, it says: "In a conference held on May 23, 1944, between the undersigned and Obersturmbannführer Eichmann, the latter stated that he had ordered the arrest of Frau Glück, the Jewish sister of Mayor La Guardia of New York, provided it has not already been effected. In view of her brother's position, care should be taken that Frau Glück is not deported to the Eastern territories in a collective shipment but is kept within reach in one of the special camps in the Reich or Hungary for possible political purposes."

EICHMANN: Right, that was a very prominent Jewess. There must have been an order, unquestionably from no less a person than Himmler himself. She must have been sent somewhere, to some safe place, the same as Léon Blum, or Léon Blum's brother.

LESS: This arrest was ordered by you and not by the Hungarian police?

EICHMANN: Yes, it was ordered by me. Naturally, I had to . . . naturally, I couldn't have her arrested just like that, I had to ask the Hungarian police to do it.

LESS: When you ordered arrests of that kind, did the Hungarian police have to comply?

EICHMANN: In this case undoubtedly, because in this case I must have had an order from Himmler . . . from the Reichs-führer-SS and chief of the German police, and in this case he must have specified where she should be taken. I must have gone to Endre with that order.

LESS: Here's another letter from your department to the Foreign Office, Legation Secretary von Thadden, concerning the Jewess Gemma La Guardia, born in New York on April 24, 1887.

EICHMANN: Hmm . . . yes . . . The Foreign Office addressed an inquiry to Reich Security Headquarters concerning the whereabouts of the aforementioned, and here the Foreign Office is informed that the Glück woman, on orders from the Reichsführer-SS, is being held as a political hostage at Ravensbrück concentration camp. But I don't know this signature . . .

LESS: Panzinger. Doesn't it look like Panzinger?

EICHMANN: Ah yes, Panzinger. That was the man who replaced our section head, Gruppenführer Müller, when he was away from the office. Since this wasn't the usual sort of matter that . . . that, let's say, that's regulated by ordinances, regulations, etc., the letter could be drafted by a clerk but had to be signed by a higher authority.

LESS: Normally, shouldn't your deputy, Günther, have signed that?

EICHMANN: It's like this, Herr Hauptmann. It's a . . . the man was . . . It was the Mayor of New York's sister, and that kind of thing was ticklish, we always sent such things up through channels.

The less likely it seemed that Germany would win the war, the more intently Himmler collected hostages: members of ruling families, political figures, clergymen, prominent persons of every description, and, above all, Jews thought to be rich and influential. One of these was the former French Premier Léon Blum, founder of the Popular Front of Socialists and Communists. New York's Mayor Fiorello H. La Guardia was especially hated by the National Socialists, not only as a Jew, or at least a half Jew, but also as an active supporter of the detested President Franklin D. Roosevelt, and an outspoken enemy of Hitler and the Nazis. Apparently, Himmler hoped that hostages such as Gemma Glück would help him gain support in the United States.

LESS: Was the Hungarian government's refusal in August 1944 to send any more shipments of Jews to Auschwitz your reason for leaving Budapest that summer?

EICHMANN: No, that had nothing to do with it. Anyway, it took me as much by surprise as being sent to Hungary in the first place. I get a telephone call from Oberführer Dr. Geschke, the commander of the Security Police and the SD in Budapest, telling me to report with full field equipment and steel helmet. He tells me to drop everything, round up all the men I had available, and set out for Gross-Nikolsburg/Arad on the Hungarian–Rumanian border to evacuate ten thousand ethnic Germans, by force if necessary, to save them from the advancing Russian armies. It seemed the Reichsführer wanted those ten thousand ethnic Germans moved to German territory by fair means or foul.

LESS: When was this—approximately?

EICHMANN: Let me . . . Maybe the date will come back to me. Maybe August. Just a second, please . . .

LESS: August 1944?

EICHMANN: 1944 . . . that's right. For the first time I had a mission that took me near the front, and for the first time I made no attempt to be excused from it. On the contrary, I took all the men I had and all the vehicles I could get together. I went to see a division commander I knew, and he gave me a battery of heavy mortars and a whole truckload of ammunition. I was going to evacuate those ethnic Germans all right, but I was also determined to get myself surrounded if possible, so I wouldn't have to go back.

LESS: Here I have a document from August 1944. Would you care to read it?

EICHMANN: Yes. —Veesenmayer, the Reich Plenipotentiary for Hungary, reports here to the Foreign Office that the Hungarian Minister of the Interior had just informed SS-Obersturmbannführer Eichmann that contrary to his earlier

(237)

statements he had now been instructed, by order of the Regent, to begin on August 28 concentrating the Budapest Jews in five large camps still to be built outside the city, and that no provision was made for transportation from these camps to the Reich. "Eichmann will report this matter to Reich Security Headquarters and put in an application for the recall of himself and his team as superfluous." Yes, at the end of August the provinces had been—let's say—pretty well worked over, and the Hungarian Ministry of the Interior, that is, Undersecretary Endre, received instructions from above—hmm, here it says from the Regent, hmm . . . to leave the Budapest Jews alone. If Veesenmayer writes that I should report this to Reich Security Headquarters and apply for the recall of myself and my team as superfluous, it must be true.

LESS: There's also a . . .

EICHMANN: Yes . . . a memo from von Thadden. "Spoken with Sturmbannführer Günther. He tells me that in any case a partial team will stay down there for purposes of observation . . ."

LESS: Mightn't this relate to the . . . political change that had taken place in Hungary?

EICHMANN: Herr Hauptmann, I won't question that today, because I don't know anything about the political game in this connection. I presume that you have the data, Herr Hauptmann. So you must be right. I don't remember.

LESS: Wasn't Horthy arrested after that?

EICHMANN: Yes, yes. Of course, but by then I'd long been back in . . . In October, I wasn't down there on . . . on the Rumanian border. I was back again. So I don't know if it was a political game of the higher-ups, Herr Hauptmann. I'll just have to leave the whole business in the dark, because I don't know who and what agencies planned this thing and gave the orders for it. I was only a pawn on the chessboard. —One Sunday we were all set to march. In no time at all, we were near the front. Russian mortar shells were bursting all around us. The tires of the heavy truck that was carrying our mortars burst. I myself was standing with the drivers, who couldn't take cover because they had to change the tires. The road was littered with dead Hungarian soldiers.

LESS: Isn't it rather odd that suddenly, out of a clear sky, they should order you to Rumania?

EICHMANN: Herr Hauptmann, I had orders to evacuate ten thousand ethnic Germans, and a counterattack, a Hungarian counterattack, had been planned. So I had no reason to ask myself: What is this? What's going on here?

LESS: But they could certainly have taken more experienced soldiers?

EICHMANN: What do you mean, more experienced soldiers? It doesn't take experienced soldiers to evacuate ten thousand ethnic Germans.

LESS: From a place where military action was to be expected?

EICHMANN: What do you mean? I'd been trained as a soldier. I went to New Arad, on Rumanian territory. The enemy had just been thrown out, and all of a sudden my car was stormed by Red Cross nurses; I was driving in the lead. They recognized us as German soldiers and thought German troops were moving up. Some of the Red Cross nurses had been taken away by the Russians a few hours before; so had the slightly wounded. The heavily wounded and a few doctors were left behind. Then the top medic had everything packed up. I had procured a freight train somewhere, the hospital was put on board and that was the first thing to be evacuated. Then we split up into teams and combed the territory and tried with kindness and cajolery to get the people to leave. It was hard, because we absolutely couldn't say: "You've got to get out because the Russians will be here the day after tomorrow." If we said that, the Hungarian soldiers would have killed us. But, careful as we were, it wasn't long before the commander of this army, a Field Marshal Lieutenant So-and-So, sent his aide-de-camp to see me on the run, to tell me to report to him on the double. I kept away from him and had my teams act independently, without unified leadership. That way, they were able to work more easily, free from Hungarian interference. I drove straight back to Budapest, to report this disastrous situation. My secret wish to become involved in military action had been reduced ad absurdum. I believe I had to go back to Berlin about then.

LESS: I'm going to show you a document of September 29, 1944. It deals with the circumstances under which you were awarded the Iron Cross, Second Class.

EICHMANN: It's . . . I was awarded the Iron Cross, Second Class, by the Reichsführer, because I turned aside with my men and rescued the personnel of the military hospital. From my immediate superior, Gruppenführer Müller, I received an official reprimand for not carrying out my orders a hundred percent to the letter. In his opinion, I shouldn't have bothered about that hospital business, but should have headed, exactly as ordered, straight for the Gross-Nikolsburg area. It was not possible to fully carry out Himmler's order to evacuate the ethnic Germans. We couldn't use force; they'd have screamed and yelled, and the Hungarian police would have come running. On the contrary, we had to operate discreetly and politely—so, in the end, some tore themselves away more or less voluntarily from their possessions, but the rest stayed put.

LESS: Here your outfit is officially referred to as "Eichmann special team." Now I'll show you a document presented by the prosecution at the eleventh Nuremberg war crimes trial. It's dated Budapest, September 29, 1944.

EICHMANN: This is a memorandum submitted to Reich Plenipotentiary Veesenmayer by Lieutenant Colonel Ferenczy
of the Hungarian gendarmerie, who was in command of
their anti-Jewish actions. It says that my team was dissolved
on September 29, 1944, and indicates in detail where the
officers of said team were to go next. None of this is known
to me. Maybe the fact that the team moved to Rumania led
certain agencies to . . . Of course, a small detachment stayed
behind in Budapest under Krumey for internal work.
LESS: It says here that your special team was dis—
EICHMANN: That is simply not true! That is simply not true!
LESS: . . . but suggests waiting, because certain political
changes—
EICHMANN: That is simply not true. The team was never
dissolved, Herr Hauptmann! Never. Our move to the
Rumanian border may have led certain agencies to imagine
that the special team had gone out of existence. But it
functioned until . . . until December; I was the last man
to move out, and that was in December, in December, in
the afternoon.
LESS: It says here that the team was officially dissolved, but
was staying on for the present. Here it says: ". . . instructed
to remain in Budapest for another week, or so it is rumored,
in view of an expected change in the internal political
situation." Which did indeed occur with the arrest of
Horthy by the Germans on October 15, 1944.
EICHMANN: Oh, yes, it occurred all right, ha-ha! True
enough, but be that as it may, the team was never dissolved,
never dissolved. Only this much is true, that the team was
very much curtailed, because there was hardly any work
left. I myself had wanted to get out of there for a long
time, because, well . . . because there was practically
nothing left to do. I was bored a good deal of the time
because there was nothing to do. It was a mystery to me

why they kept me down there, especially with a war going on. I wasn't used to sitting around wasting my time.

Eichmann's insistence that his team was never dissolved can be explained in various ways. If Himmler relieved him of his mission in the last months of 1944—as seems likely—then his continued persecution of the Jews would disprove his contention throughout the present interrogation that he never did anything on his own initiative but merely carried out orders from above. But it is also conceivable that in this memorandum Ferenczy, the Hungarian gendarmerie commander, was in good faith passing on a bit of false information given him by some German agency, wishing with this report from a supposedly Hungarian source to convince Horthy, the Hungarian chief of state, that the dreaded exterminator of Jews had been dismissed and that, as Horthy had demanded, the killing had stopped. This latter hypothesis is supported by the fact that Eichmann's stay in Budapest was extended in anticipation of political changes and that two days after Horthy's dismissal Eichmann was back at work in the Hungarian capital.

LESS: Here I have a telegram signed Veesenmayer, Budapest, October 18, 1944. Now listen to this: "Obersturmbannführer Eichmann, who has returned to Budapest at the request of the local commander of the SS and the police, is engaged in consultations with the Hungarian authorities," etc. Do you wish to comment?

EICHMANN: The memorandum from Hungarian Lieutenant Colonel of Gendarmerie Ferenczy that we've just looked at says my team was dissolved on September 29. This document, dated October 18, makes it look as if I was out of Hungary during the whole intervening period. I was never out of Hungary, of Hungary, never out of Budapest for that long. Not even when I was called away to report.

Undoubtedly, I went to Berlin. Maybe they . . . maybe the higher-ups took some decision of which I had no knowledge—maybe they ordered me to report to Berlin, and Winkelmann, the commander of the SS and the police in Budapest, or Veesenmayer, the Reich Plenipotentiary in Hungary, somehow took advantage of my absence. Otherwise, I can't explain how the special team could have been dissolved, which isn't true, however, because there was no dissolution order. I was ordered to report to Müller in Berlin . . . two or three times, I think. And that must have taken, the trip there and back, about eight or ten days. Because on those occasions I'd take a day or two for private purposes, and that may . . . That may possibly . . . ? But it doesn't make sense, Herr Hauptmann, because in that case other parts of the team would have had to go, and not just me.

LESS: But didn't Wisliceny go, too, on that occasion? Because the others went, too, later on . . .

EICHMANN: The team was in Hungary the whole time, it was in Hungary the whole time.

LESS: Yes, but the one document says it had been officially dissolved. True, it says to wait, because . . .

EICHMANN: Yes, I saw that. Yes. But I beg your pardon, couldn't it be like this? Couldn't it have been, let's say . . . dissolved on paper . . . ? And now something else occurs to me: maybe it was dissolved on paper . . . by some higher authority . . . and this dissolution order was shown to the Hungarian authorities. But the dissolution never actually went into effect. That would be a third possibility.

LESS: Dr. Kastner, with whom you were negotiating in Budapest, writes the following about your return: "On October 17, 1944, two days after the putsch, when Horthy was forcibly removed, Eichmann arrived in Budapest after a hurried plane trip from Berlin. He summoned me to Becher's office, where he spoke as follows: 'Well, as you

(243)

see, I'm back again. I suppose you were thinking it would be the same here as in Rumania and Bulgaria. You seem to have forgotten that Hungary is still in the shadow of the Reich's ruins. Our arm is long enough to reach the Budapest Jews. Now pay close attention. This government of the Arrow Cross Party under Prime Minister Szálasi takes its orders from us. I'm going to contact Kovács, the minister in charge of the Jewish question, immediately. The Budapest Jews are going to be deported, this time on foot. Our transportation facilities are needed for other purposes now. But if you supply us with the corresponding number of trucks, these vehicles might be used for the deportation . . . Or doesn't that idea appeal to you? You're scared, *gell*?* But don't bother me anymore with your fairy tales about American dollars. Now we're going to get seriously to work. *Gell*?' In that moment he seemed the happiest man on earth. He was in his element again. Besides, as usual in that period, he was drunk."

EICHMANN: Ha! In the first place, I never flew. That's a first falsehood. I never flew to Hungary, I always drove in my car. In the second place . . . it's theatrical . . . his whole account is theatrical. And I wasn't drunk. I was never drunk on duty. Never!

LESS: But what about the content?

EICHMANN: In that form, absolutely impossible. It looks as if . . . That *gell* that he sprinkles around is obviously to make it sound like me. But in this form I . . . Why, the whole thing would have . . . if I had behaved the way he writes here, I'd be the biggest . . . how can I . . . words fail me. How can I give you a simple account of my dealings with Dr. Kastner? But it's perfectly obvious: In all these

* *Gell* is Bavarian dialect, meaning roughly "eh," or *n'est-ce pas*. ("You're scared, eh?")—*Trans.*

reports—I want to make this clear—whether they originate with Dr. Löwenherz in Vienna or with Dr. Kastner, or with Becher—it's obvious that when these people are asked to make statements, they all do their best to represent their dealings with me in a light favorable to themselves. They all know that the propaganda machine with its magazines and newspapers has made me its direct target. Seeing all my superior officers are either dead—about Müller, I'm not sure, anyway missing—they naturally try to contrast themselves with me, to make our whole relationship look different from what it originally was. Which is only natural, after all.

LESS: On page . . .

EICHMANN: I'm convinced—I beg your pardon—I'm convinced that if the Reichsführer-SS and chief of the German police were alive today, if Kaltenbrunner were alive, if Müller were alive, and if one of the four of us were, let's say, in court, all these things would take on a different complexion. On account of these facts, a lot of things have been completely transmogrified since 1945. If people took the objective view they did then, a lot of things would look different.

LESS: We were talking about these ten thousand Jews who were marched on foot from Hungary to Austria. Were there more such marches after that?

EICHMANN: I don't know anything about that. The whole western railway line from Budapest to Austria had been ripped up by bombs. The junction at Györ was completely out of commission. The replacement lines were also under constant attack by Allied planes. Endre was an amazingly energetic man, difficulties meant nothing to him. He said: If that's how it is, let them march to Vienna. From there on, they'll make connections.

LESS: Did that march pass through Strasshof?

EICHMANN: Strasshof? As far as I know, those Jews were taken over by the Austrian authorities in Burgenland and set to digging tank traps. As far as I know. I may be mistaken. But Strasshof? I don't even know where Strasshof is.

LESS: Did you have anything to do with the handling or planning of this march?

EICHMANN: Yes, of course, insofar as I told Endre the gendarmerie had to organize things in such a way that when this contingent reached . . . reached the Austrian border, the contingent would be intact. If it had been left to the Hungarians, they'd just have let the ten thousand march off, without planning for any stops. I said to myself, if they're going to march, I'd better watch out and not let myself in for any more accusations of not observing the guidelines. It seems to have gone all right for the first few kilometers, but the closer the column came to the Austrian border, the sadder it looked.

LESS: How big a column was it?

EICHMANN: There were ten sections of a thousand each.

LESS: Were there women and children?

EICHMANN: No children, no. Only younger women, capable of marching. As far as I remember. I can only remember the marching order. It was planned by Endre himself.

LESS: Does that mean that you gave your approval for this march? Did you send some of your men along as escorts?

EICHMANN: No, I had nothing to do with the march itself. As long as it was on the Hungarian side, it was no concern of mine.

LESS: About how many of those ten thousand reached the border?

EICHMANN: I don't think, Herr Hauptmann, I don't think many died, except that just normally some must have died.

LESS: Didn't you say it was sad?

EICHMANN: Yes, sad, to see civilians staggering along . . . the last kilometers. I didn't see it myself. On principle, I never went to look at anything unless I was expressly ordered to. And there was nothing I could do, I couldn't have done a thing. At the most I could have said: Kindly keep your Jews. We don't need them. They'd have gotten rid of them some other way, with the methods of the Hungarian gendarmerie.

LESS: Would you care to read this document and comment?

EICHMANN: It's a letter from Veesenmayer, classified secret, probably to the Foreign Office. It gives the result of my conversations with the new Hungarian Minister of the Interior. To wit: fifty thousand able-bodied Jews are to be marched on foot to Reich territory, for the Jäger program—probably something to do with airplanes*—and to relieve Russian prisoners of war who are needed elsewhere. On crossing the Reich border, a brief period of labor service on the Southeast Wall should be scheduled. The rest of the able-bodied Jews will be concentrated in Budapest, in four camps in the vicinity of the city, for labor service for Hungary. The Eichmann special team, aside from partially taking over the supervision of the above-mentioned foot march, will participate in the Budapest action only in an advisory capacity—the Hungarian gendarmerie will do the rest. On completion of said foot march, Eichmann intends to demand another fifty thousand Jews, with a view to achieving the ultimate aim—clearing Hungary of Jews. Here I must say that it's partly correct in substance, Herr Hauptmann. The figure of fifty thousand, I believe, was never mentioned; the figure of ten thousand was mentioned.

LESS: When . . . when is that dated?

* The German word *Jäger*, meaning "hunter" or "pursuit plane," can also be a proper name.—*Trans.*

EICHMANN: October 18, 1944. The height of the season, so to speak. Fifty thousand Jews were never sent out on foot. Never! But it's true that the foot march was handled by the Hungarian gendarmerie. Endre insisted on it, I can remember that. So I must have obtained authorization from the Reich to move those Jews on foot. And then I received instructions from higher-ups that these ten thousand must consist entirely of persons fit for labor . . .

LESS: Fifty thousand!

EICHMANN: All right, fifty thousand! I say that . . . fifty thousand can't be right. There was never any march of fifty thousand. I know about ten thousand. I believe that was all.

LESS: Did members of your special team escort this trek?

EICHMANN: Possibly. It takes strong men to march on foot. Because we were interested *(He takes a cigarette)*—thank you, gracias—interested in getting those Jews to the Austrian border in as good condition as possible.

LESS: When Veesenmayer speaks here of fifty thousand . . .

EICHMANN: Herr Hauptmann, I'm sure there was trouble enough with the ten thousand men marching in ten columns. I know what it's like marching smaller detachments . . . of uniformed troops . . . not two hundred kilometers, but only fifty. I myself have taken part in such marches with full field pack and I can imagine the incredible difficulty of organizing a march of fifty thousand. It could never have been completed by October 10, 1944. That's when the first tank shells fell on the outer districts of Budapest.

LESS: But what about the second trek that's mentioned here?

EICHMANN: People always exaggerate when it suits them. After these fifty thousand—I'll have to figure out sometime how long that would take—and then another fifty thousand? Those figures are pulled out of the air. You can't have another fifty thousand when the first fifty thousand haven't even started.

LESS: On the same subject, I have here a document submitted by the prosecution at the eleventh war crimes trial in Nuremberg. It's a telegram, dated Budapest, November 21, 1944, signed Veesenmayer, in which he reports on the foot marches and the further progress of the evacuation action in Budapest.

EICHMANN: Yes, it's another report by Veesenmayer, again to the Foreign Office, reporting that in the Lower Danube area, only extremely able-bodied men, if possible under forty years of age, can be used. They must have been digging the big tank trap. Then he speaks of some business with the Swiss and Swedish embassies—something I don't know anything about. Here he says: According to a new estimate, the Jews remaining in the general ghetto of Budapest do not seem to number more than eighty thousand, while there are probably about sixteen thousand in the special ghetto for holders of safe-conducts. "No more than 30,000 are now en route to Reich territory on foot for labor service. Hard to estimate the size of the contingent still to be expected. In the present situation, however, it seems unlikely that the number originally demanded . . ." I questioned that from the start. Fifty thousand!

LESS: So time and time again, in many different documents, we find this figure of fifty thousand who were dispatched on foot in October. And here in this letter of Veesenmayer's we see that the figure of thirty thousand had been attained.

EICHMANN: All right. I won't question the figure. But all I remember is that a march of ten thousand was put through once.

LESS: Now read what Wisliceny has to say about it.

EICHMANN: He says: "Even after Himmler's order of October

1944, Eichmann did not rest. The order prohibited only the destruction of the Jews, so he set to recruiting Jews from Budapest as laborers for the KZS"—I don't know what he's talking about . . . "KZS and building fortifications around Vienna." This looks again as if I'd suddenly thought up some way of activating the construction of fortifications and filling up the KZS. Ka-Zett-Es? What's that supposed to mean?

LESS: It should probably be Kazetts.*

EICHMANN: Kazetts, oh, Kazetts . . . I don't know. Maybe. He makes it look as if I'd thought that up all by myself. It's not true.

LESS: Listen to what SS-Standartenführer Kurt Becher had to say on this point when he was questioned on July 10, 1947. He maintained: "Herr Eichmann made a last attempt to circumvent Himmler's order to stop murdering. Through Herr Veesenmayer, and in close collaboration with the Arrow Cross people in the Hungarian government, an attempt was made to keep deporting Jews by way of Vienna. That this had nothing to do with labor service for the fortifications is evident from the fact that he took women and children—children of fifteen, actually of thirteen and over, and old men. I went to see Himmler three days later; I took Herr Winkelmann, the commander of the SS and the police in Budapest, with me. As we passed those pitiful marching columns, I said to Winkelmann: 'Do you think those children, that mother, and that old man will get to Vienna?' I got Himmler to stop the foot marches."

EICHMANN: Becher says that? He says that I evacuated in disobedience of the Reichsführer-SS's orders?

LESS: He says you went on with the foot marches.

* KZ, pronounced *Kazett*, the common colloquial term for "concentration camp."—*Trans.*

EICHMANN: That's insane!

LESS: He also says there were thirteen-year-old children in it.

EICHMANN: No . . . I wasn't there, Herr Hauptmann. The guidelines were given out and . . . Did he inspect them to see if they were thirteen? Just saying I acted contrary to an order of the Reichsführer is insane; it's a lie, it's typical of everything the man says.

LESS: Becher goes on: "Three days later I went to see Himmler, in East Prussia I think it was. There, in Winkelmann's presence, the order was issued prohibiting further deportation by foot march. That order went to Eichmann; Winkelmann transmitted it to Eichmann."

EICHMANN: That's . . . that's not true. If the Reichsführer's order came to stop, then we stopped, we stopped. If I received the order, that was the end of it. Then . . . then I'd have said to the Hungarian gendarmerie: Here's the Reichsführer's order! From now on, it's no go! Finished!

LESS: Then Becher said: "Herr Eichmann's intention was to go against Himmler's order, which I myself showed him."

EICHMANN: But that's a . . . that's . . . that's simply incredible. That tops all the incredibles I've ever encountered. It's simply inconceivable, inconceivable, that such a man could have been a Standartenführer.

LESS: Becher goes on to say: "Herr Eichmann then wanted to remove the last 150,000 Jews from Hungary. I also know that he said to me: 'I have the green light for fifty thousand; how I do it is my business.' "

EICHMANN: That's . . . all that is a mystery to me. That's all I can say.

LESS: Becher says: "I told Himmler that I couldn't help noticing time and time again that Eichmann sabotaged his orders. That foot march he organized was pure murder."

EICHMANN: I have the impression that Becher, who was in on the whole business, that he, either shortly before the end of the war, certainly after the end of the war, tried his level best, as he does here, to find a way of washing his hands in innocence. Here he stands things completely on their head. It's true that the deportations were stopped after our visit to the Reichsführer. But that Becher sparked off that decision . . . certainly not.

LESS: Under the heading "The Commandant of Auschwitz Opposes the Foot March," Dr. Kastner wrote the following in his book: "On November 16, 1944, a group of highly placed German guests arrived in Budapest. In response to Becher's invitation, Generaloberst Jüttner, the commanding general of the Waffen-SS, came to Budapest accompanied by Krumey and SS-Obersturmbannführer Höss, the commandant of Auschwitz. On the road between Vienna and Budapest, they were witnesses to the horrible foot march. The road heaped with corpses and the tortured marchers made a most unpleasant impression on the German gentlemen. Arrived in Budapest, they vented their indignation in Becher's presence over what they had seen. The commandant of Auschwitz was especially indignant. Besides, Höss had come from Himmler's headquarters, where he had been informed of the Reichsführer's new orientation. Jüttner ordered the Jewish-affairs team in Budapest to stop the foot march immediately. This was done on November 17. That day, some 7,500 Jews who had started on the march were brought back to Budapest. Eichmann was absent at the time. On November 13, he had modified the orders given him and decreed that all children over ten were to be deported. As soon as we learned of this, we alerted Becher. In my presence, he called Eichmann on the phone. At first Eichmann admitted nothing; he denied that such an order had been given and spoke of atrocity-mongering. Finally, Becher threatened to wire Himmler. The threat was effective. Eichmann withdrew the order."

EICHMANN: I assure you, I know nothing about those . . . those heaps of corpses on the road. And Becher telling me on the phone . . . threatening to go to the Reichsführer . . . That's not true, I did nothing but carry out the Reichsführer's orders . . . which didn't come to me directly from the Reichsführer, but through Veesenmayer and Winkelmann. If what Kastner says were true, if I disobeyed the Reichsführer's order, why didn't Veesenmayer expel me from Hungary, or why didn't Winkelmann have me arrested?

LESS: Were the guidelines concerning age limits changed at that time?

EICHMANN: Not that I know of, Herr Hauptmann.

LESS: Kastner goes on: "On November 21, Eichmann arrived back in Budapest and immediately gave orders to continue the foot march. It was typical of him that he had his defense against my protests ready. He sent for me and said he had no desire to interfere with Becher's negotiations, but that, immediately after his return, he had set further contingents on the march because he believed that the order to stop the foot marches had been issued on the strength of the mistaken impressions of 'a few' gentlemen, who had no way of judging whether people who had been on the march for seven or eight days could or could not be regarded as fit for labor. And he would have to reprimand those of his associates who had carried out the suspension order."

EICHMANN: According to this account, I was absent from Budapest on several occasions. Undoubtedly, I went to Berlin to . . . to report on events and obtain orders relating to my future conduct.

LESS: Furthermore, Kastner reports: "Eichmann went on: 'I absolutely need 65,000 to 75,000 Hungarian Jews. So far, only 38,000 have been received at the German border. I need at least another 20,000 pick-and-shovel Jews for the Southeast Wall in Ostmark. In the Reich, even German children and old men are building fortifications. The Reich has promised not to bump off any more Jews. I just want to tell you that Germany has passed the low point and is going to win the war. A new weapon is being produced, which the Allies will be powerless against.' "

EICHMANN: Here I have this to say: The expression "bump off." I never said that.

LESS: "Then he went on about the 'abuse' of the safe-conducts. He said he would hold the Swiss consul Lutz and Raoul Wallenberg, the representative of the Swedish Red Cross, responsible for this outrage. But he had one suggestion: he would close his eyes to the holders of these safe-conducts if we voluntarily provided him with 20,000 pick-and-shovel Jews. Otherwise, he would be obliged to set all Jews—without exception—on the march. Then I spoke of the Swiss negotiations. The Americans, I said, are well informed, they know about the foot march and have every reason to regard all concessions offered by the Germans in the Jewish question as a bluff."

EICHMANN: I don't remember anything about the particulars mentioned here.

LESS: Kastner reports that on November 26, 1944, Becher returned from Himmler's headquarters and informed him that Himmler had sent a telegram ordering the cessation of the foot march from Budapest. According to Dr. Kastner, you spoke as follows at a conference held on November 27. I quote: "Eichmann had recovered his old form. 'I saw it coming,' he said. 'I warned Becher time and time again not to let himself be hoodwinked. Now I have just this to say: Get a wire off to Switzerland, tell them to get this thing straightened out. Unless I have a positive answer from you in forty-eight hours, I'll give orders to bump off every stinking Jew in Budapest.' "

EICHMANN: That's very . . . very theatrical again. He says something about stinking Jews. I've never used such language in all these years, not once. That's a lie! It's all a lie.

What Eichmann wanted to "straighten out" was a deal which Becher, with Himmler's approval, had made with a Swiss representative of the American Joint Committee. Several hundred Hungarian Jews selected by Dr. Kastner had already arrived, via Bergen-Belsen, in Switzerland, from where they would continue on to Palestine. But the agreed payment in foreign currency had not arrived in Germany. This accounts for Eichmann's threat to "bump off" the remaining Hungarian Jews. If, after years of scrupulously maintained neutrality, the Swiss tolerated such arrangements in the last phase of the war, it was because, unlike Eichmann, they now expected Hitler to be defeated. For the same reason, the Swiss consul Charles Lutz and the Swedish banker Raoul Wallenberg were permitted to distribute safe-conducts among the wretched marchers between Budapest and Vienna. These documents, to be sure, were only occasionally respected by the Hungarian gendarmes and hardly ever by the Germans. Still, the holder of a safe-conduct had a chance of being separated from the other deportees and sent to a special camp. Raoul Wallenberg probably paid for his humanitarian activities with his life; he stayed in Hungary when the German troops moved out and the Red Army moved in. Then he disappeared. From time to time, someone claims to have seen him in a Soviet prison.

EICHMANN: Budapest was being turned into a front-line position. Work, at least evacuation work, was out of the question. Again I prepared for the military activity I had been
longing for all those years. The heavier the shelling grew
and the closer the front came, the happier and calmer and
more elated I became. I had sent my men away long ago. I
stayed there with only one driver. All I did was study the
situation at the front and wait impatiently to be appointed
military commander. But someone else got the appointment
and I was out of luck again. By the time I digested that,
it was December 24. That afternoon I had to leave Budapest in the last vehicle. Those were my orders.

LESS: What do you mean by that?

EICHMANN: If I'd been dead, it would have been all right. But
if I'd been alive or wounded, I'd have had to take the
consequences. By then, it was all the same to me. I had to
detour, because the road was already under Russian artillery
fire. I stopped somewhere for the night, because our progress was very slow, because the road was clogged with
burned vehicles, dead horses, and so on. On the first or
second day of Christmas, I reported in . . . in Ödenburg, I
think, that was the new headquarters of the commander of
the Security Police and the SD. They thought I'd been
killed. From there, I went on to Berlin.

LESS: To your old Gestapo office?

EICHMANN: I arrived in the first days of January 1945. There again, serious work was out of the question. Uninterrupted air raids were creating greater and greater devastation. Every day the communications network was repaired with the greatest difficulty, only to be disrupted again the following night. Without communications, normal work was inconceivable, evacuations were altogether inconceivable. I paid no more attention to State Police work, because no one paid any attention to me. I spent more time looking around in the ruins than at my desk; I was interested in only one thing . . . in building a defense line that would cost the enemy as much blood as possible. That was all I thought about. I had the field of rubble around my office in Kurfürstenstrasse transformed into a defense position, with streetcar tracks, tank traps, and nests of sharpshooters.

LESS: Who was supposed to defend it?

EICHMANN: The State Police Headquarters building in Berlin had also been destroyed. Some of the officers moved in with me. Prinz-Albrecht-Strasse, the main building of the Secret State Police, where Müller had his office, had also taken a direct hit. The department heads and Kaltenbrunner, the chief of the Security Police, took to eating lunch every day in our building. I was never invited. Then out of a clear sky the district military commander came to see me, an Oberstleutnant something or other, commander of the Landwehr Canal, that's what the district was called. He incorporated my defense system into his, he swallowed me up, so to speak. That was all right with me. About then, a conference of bureau heads was held in a room on Kurfürstenstrasse, and there I saw something I would never have thought possible. There was one of the bureau heads who did nothing but make out false papers, certificates, etc. He was working for members of the Security Police in Section IV, who wanted to change their names and prove they'd been insurance agents or something during the war.

Müller asked me if I was interested. I said I could do without. The only thing I cared about just then was my defense position, and for that I didn't need false papers. The order came to burn all our files, including the top-secret file. That took several days. At about that time, I said to the officers under me, who were sitting around dozing dejectedly, that in my opinion the war was definitely lost, and that I was looking forward to the battle for Berlin. If death didn't come to me, I'd go looking for it. That absurd business with the false papers sickened me. I'd rather have put a bullet through my brain than issue myself an official document.

LESS: What prevented you from taking part in the final battle for Berlin?

EICHMANN: I was suddenly ordered to report to Himmler. I think he had his field headquarters in a castle not far east of Berlin. Himmler told me he was planning to negotiate with Eisenhower, and he wanted me to bring a hundred, two hundred, anyway all the prominent Jews from Theresienstadt to a safe place in the Tyrol as quickly as possible, so he could use them as hostages for his negotiations. He wanted me to drive straight to Theresienstadt, get these VIP's ready to travel, and then go immediately to Hofer, that was the Gauleiter of the Tyrol, and arrange with him where they could be kept. I had to abandon my defense position that I'd built up so carefully, and I didn't know if I'd ever be able to use it, because the front was approaching Berlin with giant strides.

LESS: At least, that got you out of there.

EICHMANN: I hurried to get the Reichsführer's order out of the way and get back to Berlin as quickly as possible. I went to Prague, communicated the Reichsführer's order to the local Security Police and SD commander, and asked him —because I had no written orders; by then, we were always in such a hurry that we had stopped putting things in writing—to pass the instructions on to Theresienstadt. Then I went on to Austria by way of Kufstein. In Brixlegg I was right in the middle of the village when a squadron of enemy planes came over and the bombs started popping. I knew there was a heavy-water plant in Brixlegg, so when the first waves came over, I had an idea that this raid would last a long time. The explosions were so bad I stuck my nose in the ground and kept it there. My driver and I took advantage of a brief pause between two waves. It was a miracle. The car started right up, we didn't even have a flat tire. We had made it.

LESS: When Standartenführer Becher was interrogated in July 1947, he was asked: "When did you see Eichmann for the last time?" "On April 15," he said. He probably meant 1945.

EICHMANN: I'll only say this. That air raid in Brixlegg took place on the morning of April 17. Then I was in the Tyrol. At that time I drove from Berlin via Dresden and the Protectorate to Vienna, and from Vienna to Linz, that's right, Linz. Later, in Linz, a bomb fell across the street from State Police Headquarters and decimated the personnel of the State Police Headquarters, among them my former superior Dr. Pfiffrader. I don't know if I was even in Berlin on April 15, 1945.

LESS: Do you remember that Becher went to Bergen-Belsen about that time with Dr. Kastner to start a trainload of Jews off for Switzerland?

EICHMANN: No, I did not know that. May I . . . Did Dr. Kastner come to my office on Kurfürstenstrasse with Becher?

LESS: No, only Becher went to your office.

EICHMANN: Yes, but, but on April 15 that's . . . that's absolutely impossible.

LESS: Becher then said the following: "My relations with Eichmann were always difficult. I believe I have never in all my life met anyone who could lie so convincingly as Eichmann. He could tell you a story that sounded so realistic you couldn't believe it wasn't true. He was very fond of liquor. When he came to see me, I always had a bottle of cognac ready."

EICHMANN: To that, I have the following to say. When I went to see someone and he offered me a little drink, naturally I drank. Conversely, if someone came to see me, I, too, always served a drink first. But these difficult relations? That's beyond me, because we always got along fine. I fail to understand. That statement is a lie. The lying statement of a man trying to wriggle out of everything. That's as plain as day. It's his right. But there's no excuse for his way of doing it. And it's probably because he lies so outrageously that he ends by representing me as a master liar, to make his own lies seem more credible.

LESS: So you were in Brixlegg and then you went on to Innsbruck?

EICHMANN: In Innsbruck I wanted to speak to Gauleiter Hofer and give him Himmler's order. He sent word that he had other things on his mind than to bother about Jews. I could see that. Some department head at Gau headquarters was called in and he put two villages in the Brenner Pass, with hotels that were all empty at the time, at Himmler's disposal. Then I went to Linz and tried to call Prague, but it was impossible, I couldn't get through. Then I drove to Prague, and I couldn't find anybody, no commander of the Security Police, nobody, nobody at all. I go to the Hradčany and I say to myself, there must be some German authority around here. Well, State Secretary K. H. Frank, Gruppenführer Frank, was still there. He said he couldn't get through to Berlin. I said: I've got to report to Gruppenführer Müller. He said he didn't know if Müller was in Berlin, because Kaltenbrunner was in Altaussee. I had no choice. I had to go there to get rid of my report.

Himmler's SS and police bureaucrats had long since prepared their fallback headquarters in the mountainous region around the Austrian resort of Bad Aussee. Kaltenbrunner, the commander of Reich Security Headquarters, the Security Police and the SD, Obergruppenführer Karl Wolff, head of the SS and the police in Italy, and SS-Brigadeführer Walter Schellenberg, head of the German Secret Service, still paid lip service to the Führer but were all trying secretly to make connection with the Western Allies. Such contacts were most easily made from Austria, via Switzerland and Italy. Only Himmler remained in the north. He wanted to be on the spot if Hitler should abdicate voluntarily, and he was also trying to harness the Swedish Count Bernadotte and Norbert Masur, an emissary of the World Jewish Congress, to his cart by promising to depose the German dictator and take power himself. But no one wanted to have anything more to do with Eichmann.

EICHMANN: My life was hexed. Whatever I planned, whatever I did or tried to do, fate crossed me up. I had prepared everything in Berlin, but I had no chance to stay there and fight. And my private affairs prospered no better than my efforts all through the years to obtain land and soil for the Jews. In Altaussee I reported to Kaltenbrunner, but he had lost interest in the whole business. Then I received orders to prepare a line of resistance in the Totes Gebirge and convert to partisan activity. That was a worthwhile job and I went about it with my old enthusiasm.

LESS: All those other men who joined you in the mountains— how did they get to you?

EICHMANN: In Altaussee at that time . . . there was a whole

concentration of SD headquarters and State Police head-quarters, so in the end I had to take command of a company of a hundred or two hundred or maybe more than two hundred men. Some were half crippled and some were without military training, and with that bunch I was sup-posed to organize resistance in the mountains. Anybody else would have refused, but I had known those mountains well in my youth, and besides, I saw possibilities of survival, because it's a region with enormous amounts of game and lots of cattle in the summer. I thought I had time to give that scruffy outfit a little training.

In Altaussee they threw the Rumanian Horia-Sima gov-ernment in with me. They were living there in exile. I installed them in various chalets, and I myself, with the men I had left, moved into a place on one of the high pastures, Rettenbach Alm. I received a message from Kaltenbrunner by courier: "Reichsführer's orders: No one is to fire on Englishmen and Americans." That was the end. After that order, I dropped the weapons training and I said to myself: All I can do now is send the whole gang home, if that's where they want to go.

LESS: Your former associate Dieter Wisliceny was asked in one of his hearings: "When did you see Eichmann last?" His answer: "I saw Eichmann last in February 1945 in Berlin. He said that if the war was lost he would commit suicide."

EICHMANN: But Wisliceny also wrote in his report on me: "He himself and most of his associates disappeared at the time of the collapse, in May 1945." I underlined that, be-cause I wondered what motive he could have for . . . I never had any quarrel with Wisliceny except . . . except his not being promoted. There was nothing else. And it was a fact that he couldn't be promoted because he wasn't married. So I wondered what could have made the man bring in so many factual untruths, when actually I never did anything to him. And then this idea came to me. Maybe he said to himself: "All right, I'll show him. Here I am in the soup and . . . I'm . . . I'm all alone in the soup . . . I have to take my medicine, and he . . . the bureau head, has disappeared." But I didn't disappear.

LESS: But you did disappear until recently.

EICHMANN: I disappeared to the extent that I didn't tell everybody who I was. The Americans took me prisoner and there I stayed until January 1946. So it wasn't as if I—which is what he probably thought—as if I and most of my staff had prepared a nice little hiding place well in advance, while he'd had the bad luck to get into this nasty situation right away. I can see how he felt. I didn't prepare anything at all. I could have, but I rejected the idea.

Eichmann's supposition that his old friend Dieter Wisliceny had attacked his former comrades so violently because he felt they had abandoned him may be correct. The corpulent, comfort-loving Sturmbannführer was obliged to testify at the war crimes trials and was then turned over to the Czechoslovakians, who put him on trial for his activities as adviser on Jewish affairs in the satellite state of Slovakia. Since all his superiors had in one way or another escaped prosecution, the horror of world opinion, the hatred of the surviving victims, and the penal responsibility were for the present concentrated on him. This explains why in all his hearings he tried to claim extenuating circumstances by vilifying the Nazi system and his former comrades. In this, he did not succeed. At the scene of his activities, in Bratislava, which the Germans called Pressburg, he was condemned to death and hanged.

LESS: I have shown you a copy of a twenty-two-page report by your former associate Dieter Wisliceny, written in

Bratislava and dated November 18, 1946. Do you wish to comment?

EICHMANN: I do. It's a report on the whole Jewish business from 1936 to 1945. I must say that it's very hard for me to express an opinion. Because for the first time I would be obliged to . . . let's say, to apostrophize an SS officer, who was once my subordinate, as he deserves. Because after reading this report . . . written in his cell . . . I am almost surprised to remember that I was not the Reich commissar for the settlement of all Jewish affairs in Europe, with exclusive full powers. I am surprised to remember that I corresponded with other central authorities, etc., etc., and did not simply give orders on my own. And I am also surprised to learn—as I don't like to say but am obliged to say in this case—that Wisliceny was against it from the start. That is the position taken by a good many in 1945 after the collapse. I never took that position because I have no patience with . . . with silly subterfuges of that sort. Seeing I was in it and obeyed my orders, I refused to say that I had always been opposed. On the whole, this account is a mixture of truth and poetry, of private opinions, and of course an attempt—let's say—to prove that the writer was always opposed. I've also made a few marginal notes.

LESS: Go right ahead. I'm listening.

EICHMANN: He says among other things: Madagascar as a home for the Jews was not Eichmann's invention. I have never left room for doubt about where the Madagascar idea came from.

LESS: I beg your pardon, but what do you mean by that? Didn't you tell me that Madagascar was your plan?

EICHMANN: I mean . . . Here he says: But this was not Eichmann's invention. Madagascar had often been discussed as a country for immigration. Even the founder of Zionism, Theodor Herzl, etc., etc. . . . is cited. So in a certain sense he implies that . . . as if I . . . as if I'd ever . . . taken the attitude that suggesting the island of Madagascar as a possible refuge was a grandiose invention of mine. Obviously, I knew that others before me had toyed with the idea. And here he writes . . . true in part, but . . . Final solution! I remember, too, that the words "final solution" had been used a lot earlier. But when he says this final-solution formula was deliberately invented by me to deceive other agencies which had been told about the resettlement . . . resettlement plan . . . resettlement plans, that is untrue, insofar . . . Because I did not make up the phrase "final solution" meaning physical destruction, it was first used by higher authority and then handed down as a standard reference.

LESS: Here I'm showing you a memorandum concerning a conference of bureau heads and action-team commanders, held at Reich Security Headquarters on September 21, 1939; in other words, shortly before the end of the Polish campaign. Do you wish to comment?

EICHMANN: I do. It's about a report by Heydrich. This conference was attended by all the bureau heads and action-team commanders. I am mentioned among others: SS-Hauptsturmführer Eichmann, Center for Jewish Emigration. In the main, Heydrich gives a political and military survey of Poland, of the treatment of the Jews and other nationality questions. This was purely an SD affair. And the SD had no executive powers whatever.

LESS: But at that meeting the final goal was discussed with reference to a special-delivery letter from Heydrich.

EICHMANN: That is, I beg your pardon . . . I don't remember either the one or the other. But in any case I can infer this much: . . . that this was a report sent by the chief of the Security Police and the SD and that the man in charge of this business must have received the necessary instructions. So then he put the whole thing into the form of an ordinance.

LESS: Now here the first sentence says: "With reference to the conference held today in Berlin, I wish once again to point out that the projected measures, in other words, the final goal, are to be kept strictly secret." Which means that these projected measures, in other words, the final goal, were discussed at this conference, which you attended.

EICHMANN: Yes, yes, undoubtedly. It's perfectly possible. I mean, I've never denied that I was informed, but what I didn't . . . what I didn't realize was . . . that this happened so early. Because I remembered . . . the following . . . After the outbreak of the German–Russian war, I thought. But there's this to be said: Today it's easy to find out what was meant by "final solution." But at that time what was meant by "final solution," especially if you weren't active in the executive . . . wasn't at all the same as, for instance, the sentence that was flung in my face, so to speak, when I reported to Heydrich: The Führer has ordered the extermination of the Jews! Or when he sent me to the East to see how Globocnik was making out with his tank trap and report back to him.

LESS: But now let's get back to the report your subordinate Wisliceny wrote in his prison cell in Pressburg after the war.

EICHMANN: When he goes on to say that Himmler as well as Heydrich and his henchmen Müller and Eichmann were determined "to strike a blow at Jewry from which it would never recover, as Eichmann stated with cynical frankness in 1944," I have this to say: That sentence was spoken neither by Himmler nor by Heydrich nor by Müller nor by me. That . . . that sentence was used by Hitler in one of his speeches. Maybe I quoted that speech. That may be. But I heard it over the radio . . . in a speech of Hitler's that was broadcast over the radio. Also it's completely farfetched when he says I was inspired by the so-called Commissar Ordinances in which Hitler gave orders to shoot all

Red Army commissars that were taken prisoner and that this gave me the idea of exterminating all the rest of the Jews. The idea of exterminating didn't originate with me . . . and it didn't originate with Heydrich. It originated with . . . with Hitler himself, and it's fairly obvious that Eichmann of Bureau IV B 4—I don't remember what rank I held at that time—Sturmbannführer or something of the kind—that I could not have inspired Hitler.

LESS: On this point, I shall now give you a document from the eleventh war crimes trial in Nuremberg. It's a statutory declaration by former Gruppenleiter Waneck, dealing with your functions in Hungary. Do you wish to comment?

EICHMANN: Point 4 of the statutory declaration made by the former head of Reich Security Headquarters Section VI, Intelligence: "In conclusion, I declare that the former SS . . . the former Obersturmbannführer Eichmann with his agency in Hungary was answerable neither to the SS and police commander for Hungary nor to Dr. Veesenmayer, the German Minister, but was formally under the orders of Reich Security Headquarters. To my knowledge, he received his immediate instructions from Reich Security Headquarters and directly from Reichsführer-SS Himmler." So much for Waneck. To that I must say that of course it is partly true—to the extent that Müller informed me that Himmler had ordered me to Budapest. I received no running instructions directly from Himmler. The whole . . . the whole correspondence shows that. During my Hungarian period I . . . I reported once to the Reichsführer after he had sent for me. My immediate superior was Müller, head of Section IV.

LESS: But Wisliceny claims that in August 1942 you showed him a written murder order from Himmler.

EICHMANN: I believe I've said this once. I don't remember having had an order signed by Himmler calling for extermination, so to speak. It's possible, though, because

Wisliceny writes here: "Since the main content of Himmler's order was the exemption of able-bodied Jews . . ." It's possible that in this letter of Himmler's to the chief of the Security Police and the SD—that a thought occurred to him, as often happens—and he said: As regards the final solution, etc., I wish to point out that—let's say—able-bodied Jews are to be exempted for the time being—or something of the kind. It could . . . it could have been like that. It's possible that I had such a document. But I don't remember having a document signed by Himmler saying: I order . . . the destruction of the Jews, or anything like that. But indirectly . . . you could look at it that way . . . it's obviously possible, I won't deny it.

LESS: Wisliceny goes on to say that the Madagascar plan was dropped in the winter of 1941–42. Is that right?

EICHMANN: I thought it had been dropped before that. Then he writes: "He"—meaning me—"also wanted other work projects carried out by these slave laborers, such as planting a wooded belt in Eastern Europe to improve the climate." Oh, so Himmler wanted that . . . I had nothing to do with such . . . with such projects.

LESS: Did Himmler express himself to that effect?

EICHMANN: I don't know. I don't know if that's true. Planting a wooded belt in Eastern Europe . . . that seems very unlikely to me, because I'm sure there are plenty of forests in Eastern Europe, it's full of forests. Even virgin forests, actually.

Hitler, Himmler, and his "Ancestral Heritage" scientists actually did consider such projects in the hope of improving the climate of Central Europe.

EICHMANN: Wisliceny writes here: "By March–April 1942, Eichmann was in possession of orders to organize the deportation and extermination of the European Jews.

Auschwitz and some camps near Lublin were set up as extermination camps. Eichmann did not decide on any particular order for the different countries. He was in no hurry about this action, because he regarded the extermination of the Polish Jews and the deportations from Reich territory as more urgent." That's a . . . a ridiculous picture. It was not in my power to organize these actions as I pleased. I had to carry out the orders that were given me. Orders kept pouring in, and the mass of . . . of documents presented here show clearly how complicated all those actions were.

LESS: Now I'm going to show you a telegram dated April 4, 1944, from Veesenmayer, the German Minister in Budapest. Would you please read it?

EICHMANN: I will. Veesenmayer announces that the ghettoization projects in Carpathian Zone I and Transylvanian Zone I have been completed, that the deportation of 310,000 Jews is to begin in mid-May, that four daily shipments of three thousand Jews each are planned, and that a scheduling conference would be held on May 4 in Vienna. Since foreign Jews will presumably be included in this concentration, the German Ministry's liaison man with the Eichmann special team will visit eastern Hungary in the course of the week, and will screen out Jews of neutral and hostile countries and remove them to special camps.

LESS: I see here that Veesenmayer writes "Sondereinsatz-kommando Eichmann" [Eichmann Special Action Team]. Was that the official title?

EICHMANN: Actually, I was an adv . . . adviser to the commander of the Security Police and the SD in Hungary. But Standartenführer Becher appropriated, you might say, various buildings with this official title and secured them for himself. Becher simply wrote "Eichmann Action Team" on top of it and showed it to me, as a surprise, so to speak.

LESS: And after that, it was used in the official correspondence?

EICHMANN: It became official, it was taken over. Yes.

LESS: Where were these Jews concentrated after being evacuated from all those territories?

EICHMANN: Well, you see, Herr Hauptmann, I don't know. Were those assembly camps entirely liquidated or not? Too much . . . too much time has passed. But my information about these things doesn't matter so much, because there must be documentary evidence, either from the Hungarian gendarmerie or from the scheduling conference. I had a map and everything was entered on it with Roman numerals, just as the Hungarian gendarmerie planned it . . . operationally, so to speak. I had orders, and the orders said simply to comb the country from east to west in the quickest possible way and evacuate the Hungarian Jews to Theres . . . to Auschwitz.

LESS: But wasn't that rather summary planning?

EICHMANN: Yes, indeed. But there's this to consider: we had nothing to say about the implementation, the time element, call it—the purely operational aspect; that was the exclusive domain of the operations section of the Hungarian gendarmerie. The schedule was drawn up from their data, because we couldn't supply either the personnel or the cars. It's perfectly obvious that Budapest could also have been evacuated. Because the order doesn't say I was to leave Hungary out of it.

LESS (correcting him): Budapest.

EICHMANN: Leave Budapest out of it. In my opinion, the only reason Budapest was left out was that the bombing of the western railway made deportation impossible.

LESS: Do you know what German military law has to say about carrying out orders?

EICHMANN: Carrying out . . . I beg your pardon?

LESS: Orders, carrying out orders.

EICHMANN: You mean the Hague Land Warfare Convention? That sort of thing, Herr Hauptmann?

LESS: Yes, that sort of thing. But there must have been a German military penal code.

EICHMANN: We weren't subject to that. We were subject to SS and police jurisdiction.

LESS: The SS. Aha! And as a member of the Waffen-SS?

EICHMANN: SS and police jurisdiction. Our . . . our highest judicial . . . highest judicial authority was Himmler. Naturally, the highest was the Führer and Chancellor. Delegated to Himmler in matters concerning the SS and the police.

LESS: And do you know what the law said about carrying out orders? Was there a clause about illegal orders?

EICHMANN: Illegal orders. No. No.

LESS: Whether an illegal order should be carried out or rejected.

EICHMANN: No. Such . . . such, Herr Hauptmann, such . . . I mean to say, such . . . How shall I put it? . . . such distinctions were never even mentioned. Because it was taken for granted that a superior's order was an order and had to be carried out as specified in the oath.

LESS: Regardless of the nature of the order?

EICHMANN: During the war, in any case. You click your heels and say, "Yes, sir." That's all there was to it.

LESS: How about military law? Did it have a clause dealing with illegal orders?

EICHMANN: I don't believe so. We certainly had no such thing in the SS. A subordinate has no business interpreting a command. That, I believe, is fundamental. Because . . . I don't . . . it isn't . . . A subordinate doesn't interpret an order any more, as I've already said, than his superior officer justifies it. The commander has to take the responsibility. That's why the commander has the higher rank.

LESS: But according to the statutes, when a subordinate carries out a glaringly illegal order, doesn't he bear a share in the responsibility?

EICHMANN: A subordinate, Herr Hauptmann, can't carry out an illegal order, certainly not in wartime. He can do only one thing: obey his commander. If I don't obey, if a subordinate does not obey, he is court-martialed, brought before an SS or police tribunal, or in the army a court-martial. If he obeys and carries out a mistaken order, it's the commander who must take the responsibility. That's how it has always been.

LESS: Now I'm going to show you a telegram sent on June 14, 1944, from Berlin to Budapest and signed by von Thadden of the Foreign Office. It deals with offenses committed by the Germans . . . in three trains . . . against Jews being deported from Hungary. Would you please read it?

EICHMANN: I will. The gist of it is that Slovak military intelligence called the attention of certain German military intelligence officers to a report of the gendarmerie station in Kysak, Presov district, to the effect that the German troops escorting three deportation trains, carrying Jews from Hungary and evidently headed for Auschwitz, entered the cars and forced the Jews at gunpoint to hand over their jewelry and other valuables and that with the proceeds they went to the station restaurant and got drunk and sang . . . Yes, it's probable that when passing through Slovakian territory the Jews threw various articles of value out of the cars, which were picked up by children and railroad workers. The incident created a stir among the Slovak population that was bad for the German image. Political repercussions affecting the solution of the Jewish question by the Slovakian government are to be feared. I quote: "Request information and action to prevent a repetition of such incidents. Request immediate clarification with Eichmann office." I don't know anything about it, but if such a thing happened, appropriate measures must have been taken. Especially if the incident attracted notice. It must have been German deportation escorts, a squad of regular police, usually numbering fifteen men.

LESS: Now I'm going to show you a document in Bulgarian. I imagine you don't know Bulgarian. Here I have a translation. It's an agreement made in Sofia on February 22, 1943, concerning the deportation of twenty thousand Jews.

EICHMANN: It's an agreement between Belev, the Bulgarian commissioner for Jewish affairs, and SS-Hauptsturmführer Dannecker, who was active down there as an adviser on Jewish affairs. It states that Bulgaria, that is, the Bulgarian council of ministers, is to make twenty thousand Jews available for deportation and specifies from what places and in what places how many are to be loaded into how many trains. The rest deals with the guidelines governing this evacuation, that is, who is to be evacuated. On the remaining points, I have ... there is nothing I can say.

LESS: Were such agreements concerning the deportation of Jews also made in other countries between your representatives and the representatives of the respective countries?

EICHMANN: That's how it was, as a rule. And in this case the supreme German military or civilian authority gave its consent. Otherwise, Dannecker couldn't have made such arrangements . . . Yes, the Minister down there, that's obvious . . . Without the approval of the German Minister, who must have examined the broad outlines with the council of ministers, it couldn't have been done. Obviously, that's how it was done in France, and exactly the same in Pressburg, and in Rumania, too.

LESS: Were these agreements based on guidelines issued by you?

EICHMANN: No. These agreements . . . they were new, of

course, that is, this one . . . this one is new. Maybe that's because in Bulgaria a commissioner for Jewish affairs was especially appointed by the Bulgarian government. Who insisted on that, I don't know, because usually the whole thing was arranged in the form of letters going back and forth.

LESS: But what was the purpose of such an agreement? Was it a kind of commercial treaty, with the deported Jews figuring as merchandise?

EICHMANN: Yes, here Dannecker was covering himself, it seems to me. Because here it says that only Jews could be shipped. So he was making sure that nothing else would be shipped, say gypsies or some other persons the Bulgarians wanted to get rid of at the time—you know how it is. He also vetoes Jews living in mixed marriages, because that hadn't yet been . . . it hadn't yet been clarified.

LESS: Here at the top I read: "Jews regardless of age . . ."

EICHMANN: "Of age and sex." That means . . .

LESS: Babies and old people.

EICHMANN: Yes, that's a fact. Who gave this order, I don't know. Because . . . Naturally, that wasn't in the interest of the Reich. It was in the interest of the Reich to get workers, but not regardless of age. That runs through . . . through all the documents . . .

LESS: Wasn't it in the interest of the Reich to cleanse Europe of Jews by physical extermination?

EICHMANN: Herr Hauptmann, to cleanse Europe of Jews by physical extermination, that was a . . . the . . . er . . . it was a slogan . . . It could never have been carried out in practice. The main thing, I think, for Himmler was—how Hitler felt about it I don't know, I never discussed it with him—for Himmler, I'm pretty sure, the main thing was to get as much additional labor as possible.

LESS: Then why this "regardless of age"?

EICHMANN: I don't know. Maybe . . . Maybe the Bulgarian

commissioner for Jewish affairs set such a condition. Maybe the documents throw light . . . It . . . it makes no sense to me . . . But you see, among us bureau heads there were some who were rather . . . I won't say irresponsible . . . that's not the right word . . . rather superficial, I might say. That seems to fill the bill. These bureau heads often gave out some order and then they had problems and trouble. I hardly ever had any trouble because by nature I trained my subordinates to be punctilious. Nothing could be undertaken unless it could somehow be justified in black and white. I was known for that, and that is probably the only disagreeable point my subordinates can complain about. Because on that score I was absolutely intolerant.

LESS: Now I'm going to show you seven pages of a document from the eleventh Nuremberg war crimes trial. It is a statutory statement by Adolf Hetzinger of the German Ministry in Budapest. Do you wish to comment?

EICHMANN: I do. I personally don't remember Hetzinger, although . . . I don't even remember his name. Here he tells how, in spite of his strenuous efforts, etc., etc. . . . but finally succeeded in rescuing some Jews, so to speak . . . Obviously that's to make him look more deserving. He has every right. All these people use the same methods. On the one hand, he's trying to protect his own person, and on the other— which is just as understandable—he wants to clear his department. He writes: "On one occasion, an associate of Eichmann's told me Eichmann had served in an advisory capacity in drawing up the Hungarian anti-Jewish laws." I very much doubt that.

LESS: Did you serve in an advisory capacity in drawing up those laws?

EICHMANN: The anti-Jewish laws? Certainly not. As far as I know, the Hungarian government simply copied the German laws.

LESS: Did you at first refuse to let Hetzinger visit the camps where the Jews were concentrated for purposes of deportation?

EICHMANN: I don't know. I probably sent to Berlin for authorization.

LESS: Isn't that what he says here? That you probably obtained authorization in Berlin.

EICHMANN: That is possible. But it doesn't mean that I created difficulties for him or that my office created difficulties for him.

LESS: Did you tell Hetzinger that the Hungarian Jews were being sent to Auschwitz exclusively for labor service and that they were being sent with their families because, as it says here, separation might impair their willingness to work.

EICHMANN: I can't remember. At the end of April and May and June, at that time the language . . . at that time there was still talk of . . . I'm sure there was still no mention of Auschwitz. Perhaps . . . it seems possible . . . perhaps he . . . he attended one of the first scheduling conferences and heard the word Auschwitz for the first time.

LESS: Did you inform him of the fact that people were gassed in Auschwitz and that men and women were segregated?

EICHMANN: I don't know, Herr Hauptmann, because all I myself knew was that those who were fit for labor . . . all who were fit for labor, either manual or . . . or some other kind, were to be put to work.

LESS: And that no one was gassed there?

EICHMANN: Oh, of course I knew about that. Camp Commandant Höss told me that.

LESS: When you say whole families were deported, does that include these families' children? Young children, under fourteen?

EICHMANN: Herr Hauptmann, I don't know. I believe I've already told you that I don't know what the guidelines for Hungary were. The Reichsführer himself issued those guidelines. They varied so much that we had to look them up in each individual case.

LESS: If only parents and children over fourteen were deported to Auschwitz, what did you do with the younger children and babies? Did you look after them?

EICHMANN: Herr Hauptmann, I don't know. I've told you repeatedly, that wasn't in my jurisdiction. When they arrived and got out of the trains, my jurisdiction stopped.

LESS: Let me read you a few lines from the notes of Auschwitz Camp Commandant Höss. "On the occasion of a visit in the summer of 1942, the Reichsführer-SS inspected the whole extermination process from the unloading of the trains to the removal from Bunker 2. A short time after the Reichsführer's visit, Standartenführer Blobel came from Eichmann's bureau, bringing the Reichsführer's order that all mass graves should be emptied and the corpses burned. The ashes were also to be disposed of to make sure they wouldn't serve later on as an indication of the number of people burned. In Kulmhof, Blobel had already experimented with different methods of incineration. He had orders from Eichmann to show me these installations."

EICHMANN: I don't know what Höss has against me to keep bringing up these things. It sounds as if there'd been hostility between us, but there wasn't. Blobel wasn't under me. Neither was I under him, nor him under me.

LESS: And what does your subordinate Wisliceny say here in his confession?

EICHMANN: It's not true what he says: "Furthermore, there was a special team, formally under Eichmann's command, for eliminating the traces of the executions, Team 1005, set up by Standartenführer Blobel." SS-Standartenführer Blobel had previously commanded an action team in the East. He came to my bureau—as Müller said—"for economic housing purposes." He and his men had permission to spend the night in the rooms belonging to my bureau when they were in Berlin. Blobel's job was to find mass graves all over the East, have them opened and burned, and destroy the traces. For that purpose, he moved westward and did his work as the front came closer. For a long time, there was tension between me and Blobel. He was a crude man with a rough voice and he drank a lot. When he was drunk, he'd order my men around and behave like he was at home in my office. He had no right to do that. I gave him a piece of my mind. Naturally, he fought back, because he was a Standartenführer and I was an Obersturmbann-führer, one rank below him. Why I challenged him to a duel with pistols, I don't know. Müller stepped in and quashed the whole business. Later, when I was in Argentina, I heard the Americans had hanged him in Landsberg be-cause he'd belonged to a shooting team before. He never told me anything about that.

Team 1005 consisted of half a dozen SS officers, who merely supervised operations. The actual dirty work was done by concentration-camp inmates under the guard of auxiliary policemen, who had been recruited from POW camps in the East. When the work was done, the auxiliary policemen had to murder the camp inmates, and then an SS team murdered the auxiliary policemen.

LESS: Didn't Blobel's work suggest to you that Germany was losing the war?

EICHMANN: In 1941 I made statements for which Müller repri-manded me in the presence of other bureau heads. I often remarked to my men that if things went on as they were we would lose the war instead of winning it. Even before that, I had conversations with Wisliceny in which I said: "I don't believe in the Thousand-Year Reich. I believe that when Hitler dies, the Reich will disintegrate. Because

Alexander the Great's empire disintegrated. You just have to take a look at history. Whenever a large empire has been founded anywhere, it has usually disintegrated and been divided up at the death of the founder. Quarrels, struggles, general disintegration." I said that to Wisliceny, for instance. During the war years I once remarked to Günther that I had no faith in a victory. He still did. I must say, though, that when I heard about the rockets for the first time and then when I kept hearing about miracle weapons, I actually did believe we could win the war, and I was always one of the people who believed in miracle weapons. I have to add that.

LESS: You certainly weren't alone. But the hope was short-lived.

EICHMANN: At the time when faith in German miracle weapons, which I believe we had all set our hopes on, began to crumble, when hope dwindled and vanished—at about that time, men like Becher, Wisliceny, Krumey, and so on, got together and tried to work out a security formula that would put them in a halfway bearable position in case the war was lost. That accounts for their changed attitude toward me later on. It accounts for the relative uniformity of their respective statements. In modified form, this also applies to the members of Section IV of Reich Security Headquarters, to Höttl and Waneck of Foreign Intelligence. Also to von Thadden, Hetzinger, and Grell of the Foreign Office. Because the propaganda around my person, which kept rolling on in the newspapers and so on, was no secret to those men. Some of them larded their testimony with the crudest lies and slanders with respect to my person. They did that with the obvious intention of distancing themselves from my person—all this, of course, after 1945. Propaganda, you see, transformed me into a person I never was.

LESS: Aren't you, too, distancing yourself from those events?

(2 7 9)

EICHMANN: You see, Herr Hauptmann, the officers who planted the bomb in Hitler's headquarters on July 20, 1944 —well, in my eyes, and not only in mine, in everybody's eyes up to May 1945, those men were not guilty of high treason. They were common traitors, oath breakers and scoundrels. Today I divide them into men who committed high treason, who broke their oath out of idealistic motives, and into common traitors and oath breakers, because it is not permissible in wartime . . . regardless who the chief . . . the chief of state is . . . In many things—questions of philosophy or things that are of no interest to anyone but me, let's say ultimate things, or practical matters as well—in many such matters, I had an entirely different point of view up to May 8, 1945, than I do today. In those days, we had an entirely different . . . call it psychological attitude toward all these things, because in time of war the life and death of the nation was at stake. At that time, we thought of nothing else. Whether that resulted from propaganda or a sense of duty or something else is of secondary importance. Anyway, that was the situation. I wasn't the only one; there were millions; otherwise, the German nation wouldn't have held out for so many years against so many armies and so many powers. I'm not trying to put heroic ideas on record—I'm miles away from all that today, fifteen years later—but our attitude then was far different from what it is today.

LESS: But why do you think differently today?

EICHMANN: It was only afterwards, after 1945, that I saw I wasn't the only one who had revised his way of thinking and that many other people had revised their way of thinking. Some of them chucked the whole business overboard overnight. It seemed to me that such people had no better . . . er . . . no better moral values than the ones who made a show of loyalty during the war but actually thought

(2 8 0)

differently. But there were also people who thought the matter over and who struggled . . . yes, struggled, that's the word . . . with themselves. I, too, had an inner struggle. I have to confess it frankly: I wasn't able to chuck the whole thing overboard overnight. I shifted to a different stage only gradually and it took me a long, long time to arrive at my present attitude. Herr Hauptmann, to be perfectly frank again, it took me a very long time. To tell the truth, it took a rocket landing on the moon. From then on, a radical change went on inside me . . . I didn't bring it about, it happened automatically as I thought the whole thing over, this whole complex, the whole war complex, the whole nation complex, nationalism and all that. Up to May 8, 1945, I rejected and despised it, because I couldn't break my oath and my only alternative would have been to shoot myself.

Eichmann went to great lengths to survive the Third Reich. Allegedly, he despised those of his colleagues who at the collapse went underground with forged papers. But he himself went underground in Germany, with forged papers and an assumed name, and remained there until the spring of 1950. In the spring of 1945, he made his way from Aussee to Ulm under the identity of Adolf Barth, a corporal in the Luftwaffe. He was captured by the Americans, but when U.S. Army Intelligence began to question him, he managed to escape. He did not go far. As SS-Oberscharführer Adolf Barth, he landed in another American POW camp at Weiden in the Palatinate. There he transformed himself into SS-Untersturmführer Eckmann, who again escaped and under the name of Otto Heninger took refuge with a peasant in Prien on the Chiemsee in Bavaria. In March 1946, this Otto Heninger, born in Breslau (where the records had presumably been destroyed), registered as a forestry worker with the police in the Lower Saxon town of Eversen, and soon found work. His employer was bankrupted by the currency reform, but Eichmann stayed in the region. In Altensalzkoth, near Celle, he leased a piece of land, on which he raised chickens. By the spring of 1950, he had saved enough for his long-planned ocean voyage. He slipped across the border from Austria to Italy and there obtained a passport in the name of Ricardo Klement. After obtaining a visa from the Argentine consul in Genoa, he set sail for Buenos Aires on July 14, 1950.

LESS: Would you please take a look at this photograph? Is it your picture?

EICHMANN: Yes. It was taken in Argentina.

LESS: In what year?

EICHMANN: Hmm, that must have been . . . in Tucumán, I think . . . Yes, I can tell by the suit, in Tucumán. That would make it about . . . 1951 or 1952. No, not 1952. Yes, '51, I think. '50 or '51.

LESS: And you wrote this? The handwriting is yours? "Adolf Eichmann, SS-Obersturmbannführer, Ret."

EICHMANN: Oh, yes. I can't remember who I wrote it for. Maybe for Geller. Maybe he wanted it.

LESS: Who was Geller?

EICHMANN: Geller—I went over with him—was another SS man, a Standartenführer. But now it occurs to me, it wasn't necessarily Geller. It may have been someone else. A close friend. Not a female, no, it was a . . . male, and I remember vaguely, he absolutely wanted me to—thank you *(He takes a cigarette)* . . . to write my rank underneath.

LESS *(ironically)*: I see.

EICHMANN: I can't remember auto . . . autographing this picture like a movie star. No, I can sooner see myself writing my name on the back. This is a picture I had to have taken, I think, for the Capri Company personnel records; the original wasn't so big. Those pictures were smaller and

I wouldn't have . . . Maybe in making copies they photographed the signature on the back and transferred it like this to the front.

LESS: But the picture does date approximately from '50 or '51?

EICHMANN: From '50 or '51, when I was working for Capri. When I was living in Tucumán and working there.

The tribunal is in possession of a second photograph of Eichmann. It shows him and two other men in civilian clothing leaning against the railing of the ship that is taking them to South America. The Capri Company worked for the Argentine government, prospecting for water-power sites and planning hydroelectric plants. Most of its employees were Germans who had left Germany after the war. Now provided with an Argentine passport, the experienced organizer Ricardo Klement supervised a crew of native workers and was soon making enough money to send for his family. At the end of June 1952, Vera Eichmann, née Liebl, resident in Aussee, and her sons, Klaus, Dieter, and Horst, set out for Genoa, Buenos Aires, and Tucumán. At first, Eichmann's sons knew him as Uncle Ricardo. They kept their family name, and their mother used her maiden name. When the Capri Company failed for want of government commissions, Ricardo Klement moved with his family to a suburb of Buenos Aires—and took up lodgings in a house owned by Francisco Schmidt, a Jew. When questioned later, Schmidt had only good things to say about his tenant. Successively, Eichmann operated a small laundry, worked in an office, and managed a rabbit farm. Finally, he was employed by Daimler-Benz, where he rose in a few months to department head. He was soon in a position to buy a piece of land and build a house.

LESS: Did your last rank in the SS correspond to your powers and functions?

EICHMANN: A Referent [bureau head] at Secret State Police

Headquarters, in other words a Regierungsrat,* held the rank of Sturmbannführer or Oberregierungsrat,* that is, Obersturmbannführer. If you got to be a Referent at SD headquarters, that would also have rated an SS-Oberführer, given the requisite years of service. I think that I was as high as you could go. I believe, for instance, that I held my rank of Obersturmbannführer for four years. Normally, I should have gone up at least one notch. Gruppenführer Müller once asked me: "Well, Eichmann, what would you say to a civil-service position?" And I said: "If it's not a must, I'd rather not be classified as a civil servant, I'd rather keep my straight military rank." Because I wanted to get back into the army. Or, if I couldn't do that, march back to some city as police president.

LESS: Your work was top secret?

EICHMANN: Since I haven't been a bearer of secrets for a long time, neither secrets nor top secrets, I am in no way bound by the oath I took long ago and observed to the letter until May 8, 1945. From that time on, I have felt inwardly free, regardless of what happens to my person. I no longer feel bound by any moral constraint. So I see no reason whatever for refusing to testify.

LESS: So you're concealing nothing?

EICHMANN: One might be tempted to say that I admit everything, as long as—let's say—as long as it's not too damaging, but that in certain points—let's say—where the crux as such is concerned, I take refuge in lapses of memory. I must reject this supposition for conscientious reasons, because in my opinion that would be tantamount to a cowardly evasion.

LESS: So you haven't glossed anything over?

EICHMANN: About a year and a half ago, a friend who had

* The corresponding civil-service title.—*Trans.*

come back from a trip to Germany told me that in certain segments of the German youth a certain sense of guilt was making itself felt, certain guilt complexes about all those events. To me, this fact was a milestone, so to speak, the same as when I heard about the first human rocket landing on the moon. It became a cardinal point in my inner life, with many thoughts circling around it. It was this realization that made me refuse to escape prosecution by flight when I couldn't help seeing that I was surrounded by spies, so to speak, and that the noose around me was drawing tighter and tighter. First, I read in the paper how Israeli Prime Minister Ben-Gurion had issued the order to look for me. Second, I heard about a commando making inquiries in my neighborhood about putting up a sewing-machine factory. They wanted to buy land. But in that particular area there was neither electric current nor fresh water, and then I found out that—to judge by their language, at least—they were probably North American Jews. I'd have had a marvelous way of going underground again. I didn't do it, I just went on with my work and let my fate overtake me. For instance, with the certificates and papers I had, I could easily have found employment in some Argentine government institution, in Patagonia, for instance. I rejected that idea, because I said to myself that I no longer had the right to disappear, especially after being so impressed by what I'd heard about the guilt feelings of German youth.

By the end of 1959, agents of the Israeli Secret Service had begun to shadow Ricardo Klement in Olivos, a suburb of Buenos Aires. It was Fritz Bauer, the late Frankfurt prosecuting attorney, who first called the attention of his Israeli colleagues to Argentina. But it was not until March 1960 that they had proof that this man was really Adolf Eichmann. Preparations had already been made for the kidnapping when the family moved into their newly built house in the outskirts. There, between his house and the nearest bus stop, Klement was dragged into a car, taken to a hiding place, and asked: "What is your name?" He replied: "I am Adolf Eichmann. And you are Israelis?" That was on May 11, 1960. For the next few days he was held prisoner, most of the time under heavy sedation. On the evening of May 20, he was driven to the airport, placed in a wheelchair, represented as a wealthy invalid who wished to die in the Promised Land, and rolled aboard an Israeli commercial aircraft which had flown to Buenos Aires expressly to take delivery of Adolf Eichmann. On May 23, 1961, an Israeli magistrate read him the indictment, accusing him "of having in the years from 1938 to 1945 caused the deaths of millions of Jews in the occupied territories." He was asked: "Do you plead guilty?" He replied: "I have nothing to say except that I am not responsible for the events of which I am accused. I shall prove it in due time."

LESS: I would now like to read you a few passages from the German periodical *Stern*. The issue of July 9, 1960, contains an article about you. I'll only read you a few bits. Here it says: "And so he writes"—meaning you—"on the title page of Dr. Fritz Kahn's book *The Atom*: 'I mentally digested this book and found it a magnificent confirmation of the National Socialist religion and theism; and because this faith is remotely related to the Communist doctrine of matter, that is, to Leninist materialism, I warn my children not to lump them all together. Leninist-Marxist doctrine teaches materialism. It is cold and lifeless. Theism, on the other hand, is loving, natural, and always alive. But unfortunately I fear that, considering the ignorance of my three sons, all this will be no more than empty talk to them.'" Do you remember anything like that?

EICHMANN: My house must have been searched after I was dragged off. That's what I infer. I know I wrote that thing. Because my sons were so absolutely disinterested in their . . . their . . . let's say faculties for spiritual development, I wrote that as a warning to them.

LESS: The article goes on to say: "He told them the excuse or justification he had prepared for himself. He said their father was wanted, that he was accused of hideous crimes, but it was not true. He had only been a conscientious official who had done what he was ordered to do but never killed anyone."

EICHMANN: And that is the truth!

LESS: It continues: "With friends he admits who he is, engages in endless conversations, reads everything that has been published since the war about his field of activity, the 'Jewish question.' He clings desperately to the one remaining justification for his actions: his oath to the flag, his sense of duty and obedience. And everyone who in the last hours of the Thousand-Year Reich put human feeling above unconditional obedience is the object of Eichmann's irreconcilable hatred. He has read Gerhard Boldt's book *The Last Days of the Reich Chancellery* and discovered that Boldt, the author, was not obedient to his Führer down to the last comma. The description on the dust jacket begins with the words: 'In January 1945, a young front-line officer . . .' Eichmann crosses out 'front-line officer' and writes in 'scoundrel,' 'traitor,' 'skunk.' Wherever Boldt's name appears in the book, he adds 'scoundrel,' 'traitor,' or 'skunk.' Where Boldt says that in the last days of the National Socialist Reich high SS leaders, who had been haughty and arrogant up until then, suddenly shriveled and appealed for sympathy to anyone who would listen,

Eichmann makes the marginal note: 'The author is a stupid asshole. The swine's name is Boldt.'

"In another passage, Eichmann writes: 'The author should be skinned alive for his treachery. With scoundrels of his ilk, the war was bound to be lost.' And finally, on the last pages of the book, Eichmann's resumé:

1. Every man is entitled to live as he pleases.

2. But then he has no right to call himself an officer, because

3. Officer = fulfillment of duty as specified in the soldier's oath.

"There we have it again, 'fulfillment of duty,' that straw he clings to, and in defense of which he develops a passion and a vocabulary he was not yet familiar with in the days when he was coldly and with murderous precision helping to solve the 'Jewish question.' "

Did you make such marginal notes?

EICHMANN: I did. But it's disgusting of the man to speak of a . . . straw, which was not yet familiar to me at that time. It has always been familiar to me. In fact, it's my norm. I have taken Kant's categorical imperative as my norm, I did long ago. I have ordered my life by that imperative, and continued to do so in my sermons to my sons when I realized that they were letting themselves go. In view of their laziness, their *désintéressement* about going on with their education, I tried to make them see reason with strong words . . . Sometimes when reading a book . . . I was seized with righteous indignation, and in that mood I reached for a pencil and wrote what seemed significant to me at the moment.

LESS: The *Stern* article goes on: "Friends and acquaintances who spoke with him in Argentina at that time describe him as a man who had gone to pieces, who recognized his unspeakable guilt but who, instead of confessing it to himself, cast about with an obstinate rage for formal justifications, to avoid having to condemn himself."

EICHMANN: That's not true. That's . . . that's . . . journalistic rubbish.

LESS: And now this: "Eichmann's conscience . . . 'I'm getting sick and tired,' he writes, 'of living the life of an anonymous wanderer between two worlds. The voice of my heart, which no man can escape, has always whispered to me to look for peace. I would also like to be at peace with my former enemies. Maybe that is a part of the German character. I would be only too glad to surrender to the German authorities, if I were not obliged to consider that people may still be too much interested in the political aspect of the matter to permit of a clear, objective outcome. Far be it from me to doubt that a German court would arrive at a just verdict, but I am not at all clear about the juridical status that would be accorded today to a former receiver of orders, whose duty it was to be loyal to his oath and to carry out the orders and instructions given him. I was no more than a faithful, decent, correct, conscientious, and enthusiastic member of the SS and of Reich Security Headquarters, inspired solely by idealistic feelings toward the fatherland to which I have the honor of belonging. Despite conscientious self-examination, I must find in my favor that I was neither a murderer nor a mass murderer. But to be absolutely truthful, I must accuse myself of complicity in killing, because I passed on the deportation orders I received and because at least a fraction of the deportees were killed, though by an entirely different unit. I have said that I would have to accuse myself of complicity in killing, if I were to judge myself with merciless severity. But I do not yet see clearly whether I have the right to do this vis-à-vis my immediate subordinates. Therefore, I am still engaged in an inner struggle. My subjective attitude toward the things that happened was my belief in the necessity of a total war, because I could not help believing in the constant proclamations issued by the leaders of the then German Reich, such as: Victory in this total war or the German nation will perish. On the strength of that attitude, I did my commanded duty with a clear conscience and a faithful heart.' "

EICHMANN: Exactly!

LESS: Did you write those things or . . .

EICHMANN: I can't remember where I wrote them, but the words are mine. I recognize the words . . . Where they come from . . . I can't explain.

LESS: And *Stern* goes on to say: "This Eichmann was neither depraved nor unfeeling. According to his own credible testimony, he was rather sensitive. And yet, consciously and with open eyes, this man signed the deportation orders which for many hundreds of thousands meant death. He was a bureaucrat of murder and he knew it. At that time he had neither inhibitions nor any desire to plead Befehls-notstand. He must bear full responsibility."

EICHMANN: That last is journalistic rubbish. My attitude was that I should loyally obey my oath . . . That can't be changed and it can't be interpreted. Journalists, yes, journalists can do it. And novelists, they can do it, too.

LESS: Do you subscribe to the notations in your books?

EICHMANN: With regard to the quotations I wrote in my books, I take the point of view that no one has a right to take an interest in what I write in my private books unless I lend him the books. And I never lent anyone those books.

Herr Hauptmann, may I, in conclusion, make some personal remarks and announce a personal decision I have made. I have stated here as much as I could recall to mind in spite of the fifteen years that have meanwhile elapsed. Fundamentally—or so at least I believe—nothing worth mentioning remains to be said. But there must be, of that I am sure, any number of details which, if released by some stimulus, will rise up in images before my eyes. I wish to say that I am prepared to divulge everything, absolutely everything known to me concerning the events in question. I have long been inwardly prepared to make a general statement of this sort, but I did not know where fate would call on me to make it. As early as January of this year, someone told me that I would appear in court before the year was out. I was also told that I would not survive my fifty-sixth year. One of these prophecies has already come true, and the other—I believe—is inexorable. This alone gives me an unstinting inner readiness to tell everything I know of my own free will, spontaneously, without regard for my own person, which no longer matters to me. All my life I have been accustomed to obedience, from early childhood to May 8, 1945—an obedience which in my years of membership in the SS became blind and unconditional. What would I have gained by disobedience? And whom would it have served? I never at any time played an essential, decisive role in the events from 1935 to 1945; for that, my rank and functions placed me in far too low a position. Nevertheless, I realize of course that I cannot wash my hands in innocence, because the fact that I was an absolute receiver of orders has undoubtedly ceased to mean anything. Though there is no blood on my hands, I shall certainly be convicted of complicity in murder. But, be that as it may, I am inwardly prepared to atone for the terrible events. I know the death penalty awaits me. I am not asking you for mercy, because I am not entitled to it. In fact, if it seems to be a greater act of atonement, I am prepared, as an example and deterrent to all the anti-Semites of the earth, to hang myself in public. But let me first write a book about these horrible events as a warning and example for the young people of the present and future, and then let my life on earth end. May I, Herr Hauptmann, give you this statement for your records?

Eichmann shared the wish to write his memoirs with Rudolf Höss, the commandant of the Auschwitz death camp, and Dr. Hans Frank, Governor General of occupied Poland. Those two got their wish. Eichmann, it is true, left written confessions of sorts, but they are sparse and fragmentary, avoid concrete details, and were obviously intended to justify him to his family. Thus, the record of his interrogation in Israel becomes the most important and complete documentation of the character and acts of a man whose name, throughout the world, is mentioned immediately after Hitler's when the destruction of the Jews by the Nazis is discussed.

The man chosen to interrogate Eichmann was Police Captain Avner Less, a onetime Berliner, who was familiar with conditions in Germany before 1933 and could speak to Eichmann in his mother tongue. To throw the accused off balance, Less resorts in his questioning to the criminal investigator's old trick of jumping from one set of crimes to another and back again. This makes the 3,564 pages of the transcript difficult reading. Jochen von Lang and Claus Sibyll have therefore collated the dispersed discussions of the various subjects, so as to present the record in logical and chronological order.

It has been necessary to make a selection. The editors have attached prime importance to those of Eichmann's statements which throw light on the magnitude and methods of the Nazi crimes or which show how historical circumstances, the public glorification of violence, and the fascination of a leader figure, a "Führer," could turn an average man of middle-class origins and normal middle-class upbringing, a man without identifiable criminal tendencies, into a monster.

The series of interrogations began on May 29, 1960, nine days after Eichmann's arrival in Israel. From then until February 2, 1961, Less spent a total of 275 hours with the prisoner. Questions and answers were taped and transcribed. Eichmann was given the transcripts of each tape, seventy-seven in all. In his spidery hand, he made a few changes, and in every case certified "that I have compared this transcript with the tape recording and corrected it with my own hand. I certify the accuracy and correctness of the reproduction with my signature."

Two months after the last hearing, on April 11, 1961, the trial opened in Jerusalem. The court for this special case was established by a new law. A number of Jews who had played leading roles in the Jewish communities of Berlin, Vienna, Prague, and Budapest appeared as witnesses for the prosecution. Eichmann confessed to a considerable extent, but tried to justify himself on the strength of orders from above. If he secretly hoped to be convicted only of complicity in murder and so escape with his life, the scope of his activities, if nothing else, made this impossible. It was a fair trial as far as the feelings of the judges toward the defendant permitted. The trial went on for seven months, and in every session the sufferings and deaths of Jews were reenacted. On December 11, the presiding judge handed down the death sentence. Six months later, on May 31, 1962, Adolf Eichmann was hanged. His body was cremated and the ashes strewn into the sea.